STUDIES IN THE HISTORY OF CHRISTIAN MISSIONS

R. E. Frykenberg
Brian Stanley
General Editors

STUDIES IN THE HISTORY OF CHRISTIAN MISSIONS

Judith M. Brown and Robert Eric Frykenberg, *Editors*

Christians, Cultural Interactions, and India's Religious Traditions

Robert Eric Frykenberg

Christians and Missionaries in India: Cross-Cultural Communication since 1500

Susan Billington Harper

In the Shadow of the Mahatma: Bishop V. S. Azariah and the Travails of Christianity in British India

D. Dennis Hudson

Protestant Origins in India: Tamil Evangelical Christians, 1706-1835

Andrew Porter, *Editor*

The Imperial Horizons of British Protestant Missions, 1880-1914

Brian Stanley, *Editor*

Christian Missions and the Enlightenment

Kevin Ward and Brian Stanley, *Editors*

The Church Mission Society and World Christianity, 1799-1999

The Imperial Horizons of British Protestant Missions, 1880-1914

Edited by

Andrew Porter

William B. Eerdmans Publishing Company
Grand Rapids, Michigan / Cambridge, U.K.

Wm. B. Eerdmans Publishing Co.
255 Jefferson Ave. S.E., Grand Rapids, Michigan 49503 /
P.O. Box 163, Cambridge CB3 9PU U.K.

Printed in the United States of America

08 07 06 05 04 03 7 6 5 4 3 2 1

Library of Congress Cataloging-in-Publication Data

The imperial horizons of British Protestant missions, 1880-1914 /
edited by Andrew Porter.
p. cm. — (Studies in the history of Christian missions)
Includes bibliographical references and index.
ISBN 0-8028-6087-7 (pbk.: alk. paper)
1. Missions, British — History —19th century — Congresses.
2. Protestant churches — Missions — History — 19th century — Congresses.
3. Missions, British — History — 20th century — Congresses.
4. Protestant churches — Missions — History — 20th century — Congresses.
I. Porter, A. N. (Andrew N.) II. Series.
BV2420.I47 2003
266′.02341 — dc21

2003052857

www.eerdmans.com

Contents

General Editors' Foreword

The Imperial Horizons of British Protestant Missions, 1880-1914 is one of the fruits of the North Atlantic Missiology Project (latterly the Currents in World Christianity Project). The Project was established by the Pew Charitable Trusts of Philadelphia in 1996 as an international scholarly enterprise based in the Centre for Advanced Religious and Theological Studies in the Faculty of Divinity in the University of Cambridge. The primary concern of the North Atlantic Missiology Project was to elucidate the connections between theory and experience in Protestant overseas missions in the period from 1740 to 1968. The first volume of papers produced by the Project, *Christian Missions and the Enlightenment,* edited by Dr. Brian Stanley, was published in this series in the spring of 2001. This volume publishes revised versions of papers delivered at a consultation held at Westminster College, Cambridge, in April 1998. We are most grateful to Professor Andrew Porter for the time and effort he has devoted to bringing this collection to publication. We also gratefully acknowledge the generous support of the Pew Charitable Trusts, without whom this book would not have been possible. The opinions expressed in the chapters that follow are, of course, solely those of the authors, and do not necessarily represent the views of the Pew Charitable Trusts. We should also like to thank William B. Eerdmans, Jr., and his staff, of Wm. B. Eerdmans Publishing Company, and Malcolm Campbell and Jonathan Price of Curzon Press for their unfailing support of this series.

Robert E. Frykenberg
University of Wisconsin–Madison

Brian Stanley
University of Cambridge

List of Contributors

DAVID BEBBINGTON is a professor of history at the University of Stirling. His books include *The Nonconformist Conscience* (1982); *Evangelicalism in Modern Britain* (1989); *Evangelicalism: Comparative Studies in Popular Protestantism* (coeditor, 1994); and *William Ewart Gladstone: Faith and Politics in Modern Britain* (1994). He is at present writing a study of the mind of Gladstone.

DEBORAH GAITSKELL has lectured in history at the School of Oriental and African Studies, and is a senior research fellow at the Institute of Commonwealth Studies, London, where she organizes the Seminar on Gender in Empire and Commonwealth. She is writing a book on women missionaries in twentieth-century South Africa, and has published on topics such as women and nationalism, domesticity and mission education, and the spirituality of churchwomen's groups.

JOHN W. DE GRUCHY is director of the Graduate School in Humanities at the University of Cape Town and Robert Selby Taylor Professor of Christian Studies. He is the author of various books, including *The Church Struggle in South Africa; Liberating Reformed Theology* and *Christianity and Democracy;* and is editor of *The Cambridge Companion to Dietrich Bonhoeffer.* He is also editor of the *Journal of Theology for Southern Africa.*

JOHN M. MACKENZIE is an honorary research professor at the Research Institute of Irish and Scottish Studies at the University of Aberdeen, working on the Scottish diaspora project. He is cocurator of an exhibition on the Victorians at the Victoria and Albert Museum, and has edited the accompanying book, *Victorian Visions.* He has published a number of articles on David Livingstone and was editor of *David Livingstone and the Victorian Encounter with Africa* (1996).

CHANDRA MALLAMPALLI is assistant professor of history at Westmont College, Santa Barbara, California. His research deals with issues of religious nationalism, the secular state, and the formation of religious identity in colonial South India.

STEVEN S. MAUGHAN is associate professor of history at Albertson College, in Caldwell, Idaho. He has written on the metropolitan culture and institutions of British foreign missions, and is completing a book on Anglican missions and imperial culture in late Victorian and Edwardian Britain.

LAUREN F. PFISTER is associate professor in the Religion and Philosophy Department of Hong Kong Baptist University. An associate editor of the *Journal of Chinese Philosophy,* he is also an elected deacon of the University Baptist Church. He works on comparative philosophical and religious issues in modern China, and has major publications on both the Scottish missionary-scholar James Legge (1815-97) and the contemporary Chinese philosopher Feng Youlan (1895-1990).

ANDREW PORTER is Rhodes Professor of Imperial History in the University of London, and teaches at King's College. His books include *The Origins of the South African War* (1980); *Victorian Shipping, Business, and Imperial Policy* (1986); *European Imperialism, 1860-1914* (1994); and, as editor and contributor, *The Oxford History of the British Empire,* vol. 3, *The Nineteenth Century* (1999). He has published extensively on missions and has just finished a book on British Protestant missions and imperial expansion, 1700-1914.

ANDREW C. ROSS is an honorary fellow of the University of Edinburgh. He served as a minister of the Church of Central Africa Presbyterian (Malawi) from 1958 to 1965, and taught "History of Christian Mission" at Edinburgh from 1966 until 1998. Visiting professor at the Federal Theological Seminary, Dartmouth College, and the universities of Witwatersrand and Malawi, his books include *John Philip (1775-1851): Missions, Race, and Politics in South Africa* (1986) and *Blantyre Mission and the Making of Modern Malawi* (1996).

BRIAN STANLEY was director of the Currents in World Christianity Project and is a fellow of St. Edmund's College, University of Cambridge. His writings include *The Bible and the Flag: Protestant Missions and British Imperialism in the Nineteenth and Twentieth Centuries* (1990) and *The History of the Baptist Missionary Society, 1792-1992* (1992). He has edited for this series *The Church Mission Society and World Christianity, 1799-1999* (with Kevin Ward, 2000), and *Christian Missions and the Enlightenment* (2001).

List of Abbreviations

ABCFM American Board of Commissioners for Foreign Missions
AZM American Zulu Mission [of the ABCFM]
BMS Baptist Missionary Society
BR *Bankim Rachanavali*, ed. Shri Jogesh Chandra Bagal (Calcutta, 1969)
CCAP Church of Central Africa Presbyterian
CIM China Inland Mission
CMS Church Missionary Society
CR Community of the Resurrection
CWC Currents in World Christianity
CR *Chinese Recorder*
CWW Committee of Women's Work [of the SPG]
FMC Foreign Missions Committee [of the Church of Scotland]
GMS Glasgow Missionary Society
HTCOC *Hudson Taylor and China's Open Century*, by A. J. Broomhall, 7 vols. (London, 1981-89)
HTS Hindu Tract Society
INC Indian National Congress
JCMA Junior Clergy Missionary Association
LMS London Missionary Society
MG *Report of Commission VII: Missions and Governments* (from World Missionary Conference, Edinburgh 1910)
SDCGK Society for the Diffusion of Christian and General Knowledge among the Chinese
SPFEE Society for the Promotion of Female Education in the East

SPG	Society for the Propagation of the Gospel in Foreign Parts
SSJE	Society for Saint John the Evangelist
SVMU	Student Volunteer Missionary Union
UMCA	Universities' Mission to Central Africa
USPG	United Society for the Propagation of the Gospel
UTS	Union Theological Seminary (New York)
WA	Women's Auxiliary [of the WMMS and Methodist Conference of South Africa]
WMA	Women's Missionary Association [of the SPG]
WMMS	Wesleyan Methodist Missionary Society

List of Illustrations

Introduction

ANDREW PORTER

Christian missions have long been associated both with the growth of empire and with colonial rule. For just as long, the nature and consequences of that association have provoked animated debate, and in recent years the increased interest of historians in questions of "culture" and "identity" has stimulated rather than stilled argument. Unsurprisingly, therefore, it was decided to organize as part of the North Atlantic Missiology Project a consultation around the theme of missions and empire, providing an opportunity to discuss at length some of the recent work in the field. In April 1998 an international group of scholars met by invitation at Westminster College, Cambridge, to consider "The Imperial Horizons of British Protestant Missions, 1880-1914: The Interplay of Representation and Experience." The essays that follow represent a substantial and revised selection of the papers originally offered for consideration and discussed at that gathering.

The consultation's focus on the period 1880-1914 needs little justification. Even those who question whether this period really witnessed a "new imperialism" can accept that these were years of hectic European territorial expansion. This was especially so in Africa, but these years also witnessed the intensification of Britain's impact in countries such as China. Colonial expansion and national assertiveness were the consequences not only of British pride and confidence, but also of heightened international competition, fear, and insecurity. Nevertheless, Britain's position in many parts of her empire, for example in India, was almost certainly more firmly established, secure, and less disputed than at any other time. The extent and prosperity of the colonies of white settlement were particularly striking, prompting many to imagine that they would provide the foundation for Britain's continuing position as a great power in the twentieth century. Most contemporaries also had no difficulty in agreeing that imperial preeminence reflected Britain's racial and cultural superiority. Many felt that preeminence and singular privilege in turn carried with them obligations to weaker and less favored societies, not least the duty to civilize and convert to Christianity. Some — among them rapidly growing numbers of missionaries, mission society organizers, and their supporters — tried to give effect to those obligations.

How did the missions define or redefine their tasks in these years? How did they see themselves, and how do we now see them, fitting into the imperial world circa 1900? The various imperial contexts of their work certainly raised a host of questions about both their past attainments and their future plans. In numerous places such as Bengal, south India, Sierra Leone, and southern Africa, a long-established missionary presence periodically and necessarily prompted consideration of progress made. For example, what had been achieved in numbers of conversions; in the successful formation of Christian communities; in establishing indigenous Christian teachers, catechists, and ministers; and in combating the challenges offered either by Roman Catholicism or by other religions such as Islam? Although plenty of evidence points to the continuing optimism of a movement always inclined to assess its prospects of global success as guaranteed in terms of a divine plan, the period was also one in which criticism of the movement's past looms large. Together with the geographical extension of their own activities, the expansion of British imperial control either into new territory or into further areas of everyday life also posed new questions about the future for missions. For instance, a marked increase in interdenominational competition in the mission field was not always managed easily by the missions themselves; like missionary conflict with those of other religious persuasions, this competition frequently became a concern for both colonial and indigenous authorities anxious to preserve their own prestige or official control. The consequences of mission education and their need for funds, and government controls over land or labor, brought missions and political authorities (indigenous as well as British) together in new and more complex ways.

Missionary assessments, diagnoses, and practical responses to these questions raised by the fin de siècle world were no less complicated. Who actually spoke for "the missionary"? Individuals either direct from the field, home on leave, or retired; the secretaries for local corresponding committees, missionary conferences, or society headquarters in Britain; lay or clerical supporters engaged in fund-raising; or the editors of mission periodicals? All at different times claimed to do so, and were inclined to alter their messages according to the audiences they addressed. Scholars today are well aware that these contemporary comments and action, the manner in which missionaries both experienced empire and interpreted that experience for others at home and overseas, varied under the shifting influences of racial perceptions, denominational politics, gender, class, and theological fashion. From various directions the papers in this volume both demonstrate and attempt to unravel some of these complexities.

Historians of empire are currently engrossed in examining the impact which the acquisition and possession of empire may have had on Britain itself, especially those areas of life in which expansion overseas may have shaped metropolitan British culture. Many of them have concluded that the reflex influence of empire was far-reaching.[1] So also to many contemporary supporters of missions, the answer to such a question was never in doubt. At many points in the history of the modern missionary movement they have argued as a prime justification for missions the importance they would have as agents not only for conversion but for the revival and support of the church at home.[2] Effort and progress abroad stimulated religious vigor and commitment at home.

Steven Maughan's essay, which focuses on one such missionary activist, H. H. Montgomery, bishop of Tasmania, makes an important contribution both to this historiographical debate and to the history of such missionary ambitions. The linking of the national Anglican Church and imperial expansion was widely seen at this time as a matter of concern.[3] Following Barry, and other bishops such as Knight-Bruce and Gaul in central Africa, Montgomery's career at the head of a colonial diocese had made him sensitive to the lack of material support, especially for the white settler colonies, from the central seats of the Church of England. His missionary enthusiasm brought home to him the divisions within Anglicanism, as he saw High Church, Anglo-Catholic volunteers making their way into missions such as the Universities' Mission to Central Africa or the Cambridge Mission to Delhi, and

1. For an introduction, see John M. MacKenzie, "Empire and Metropolitan Cultures," in *The Oxford History of the British Empire*, vol. 3, *The Nineteenth Century*, ed. Andrew Porter (Oxford, 1999), pp. 270-93.

2. Roger H. Martin, *Evangelicals United: Ecumenical Stirrings in Pre-Victorian Britain, 1795-1830* (Metuchen, N.J., and London, 1983).

3. Alfred Barry, *The Ecclesiastical Expansion of England in the Growth of the Anglican Communion: The Hulsean Lectures for 1894-95* (London, 1895); Henry W. Tucker, *The English Church in Other Lands; or the Spiritual Expansion of England* (London, 1886 and 1901); and the Bampton Lectures for 1909, by Walter Hobhouse, *The Church and the World in Idea and History* (London, 1910), pp. 312-27. Barry was formerly bishop of Sydney and primate of Australia and Tasmania.

low evangelicals swelling the ranks of the Church Missionary Society (CMS). He therefore returned to Britain in 1901 as secretary to the Society for the Propagation of the Gospel (SPG), full of hopes for the Society as the means to renew metropolitan Anglicanism via its increased missionary engagement with empire. His energy was boundless, hampered only by an element of egotism, and some of his achievements were notable, such as the introduction of women into the SPG. But in his main object he failed. The dominant domestic preoccupations of the Church of England remained in place; Montgomery's strategy was unpopular with the rank and file of the church where the money had to be raised; and the Pan-Anglican Congress of 1908 refused to focus its attention on overseas missions. Perhaps an explanation for this lay in the comparatively moderate and nonpartisan character of the SPG, at a time when both high and above all low partisanship were buoying up other Anglican missions; perhaps too little attention was paid to those areas in which the SPG might have developed its cooperation with the CMS. What does seem clear, however, is that when it was most felt to be needed, the prospect of activity on the imperial stage did not provide a significant stimulus to ecclesiastical unity and cooperation at home. Contrary to the expectations of mission enthusiasts, such as members of the Junior Clergy Missionary Association, and to the conclusions of recent historians, metropolitan audiences in this case remained unmoved and the imperial backwash failed to materialize.

Unlike many to whom he made his appeal, Montgomery was an ecclesiastical imperialist, an Anglican convinced that nation, church, mission, and empire should be closely linked. As a missionary organizer, he naturally attempted to plan, to shape opinion, and to mobilize support around these pillars. His campaign and its lack of success are not only revealing of much in the church politics of the day, but serve to highlight the relative vigor of other currents of missionary enterprise. Most missionaries were not conscious imperialists in either a political or denominational sense. The dominant strands of evangelical enthusiasm were those associated with the Keswick Conventions, the North American Student Volunteer Movement, its British arm — the Student Volunteer Missionary Union — and the Young Men's Christian Association; they fed directly into bodies as diverse as the CMS, China Inland Mission (CIM), and the Salvation Army. For the most part their members' horizons were far less directly shaped by either thoughts of empire or even particular ecclesiastical models. Instead they were characterized by a growing impatience of denominational restraints and a mounting sense of global, international involvement. Montgomery's ambitions were ultimately brought to an end by developments in each of these areas. Serious party divisions, especially among Anglicans, followed from the various reactions to the theological compromises or confusion associated with the Kikuyu Conference (1913). In a rather different fashion, the enthusiasm generated by the proceedings of the World Missionary Conference at Edinburgh in 1910 similarly threatened to push aside both particularity and the signposts of authority. Two papers in this collection bear on these issues.

David Bebbington directly addresses a question barely considered by historians of empire, that of thc manner in which theological sanction was provided by the churches for the empire building and colonial rule of the period. Drawing on two outstanding evangelical periodicals, the *Record* and the *Christian World,* he shows how especially among Nonconformists "the advance of British rule as the remedy" for the wrongs of the world steadily came to assume much greater prominence in metropolitan evangelical thought.[4] Attention increasingly spread beyond the confines of Britain's existing overseas territories. "Inhibitions about imperial expansion weakened among Nonconformists, and a sense of the value of British authority as a force for righteousness grew."[5] In theological terms, the exercise of imperial power offered a providential force for the eradication of the sins of others, the exercise of imperial authority a vehicle for atonement and reparation for sins of one's own.

These were not new categories in evangelical discourse linking fundamental beliefs with evangelical action. William Wilberforce, for example, suggested in 1789 that Britain should "make amends as we can for the mischiefs we have done to that unhappy continent. . . . Let us make reparation to Africa, so far as we can."[6] The utterances quoted by Bebbington are largely the reinvigorated preoccupations of the late nineteenth-century evangelical leaders in the British press and pulpit. Inevitably the extent to which they, any more than Montgomery, spoke for the missionary overseas remains an important and open question. That they nevertheless both represented and helped shape the views of a large domestic audience, ultimately responsible both for the financial support of those missionaries and for nurturing new volunteers to increase their numbers, can hardly be in doubt.

Such conditioning and pressure from "the home base" toward missionary conformity nevertheless had their limits. Missionaries departed for their fields with a good deal of metropolitan baggage, intellectual as well as material. How far its theological components withstood the tests of incomprehen-

4. See below, p. 26.

5. See below, p. 28.

6. Quoted in Klaus E. Knorr, *British Colonial Theories, 1570-1850* (1944; reprint, London, 1963), p. 378.

sion, counterargument, and time-consuming application to local problems varied greatly. For most missionaries, representations of the mission field solemnly pieced together at home from various sources — private and official letters, lantern slides, drawings, committee reports, and pulpit descriptions — were ill matched with their personal experience of its conditions. Divergence in outlook or sentiment between those serving and those back in Britain was therefore commonplace, and missionaries themselves were often ill equipped to bridge the gap. Lack of imagination, verbal or literary ineptitude, shortages of time and energy, the self-effacement demanded by social convention of men as well as women — all were obstacles to effective communication. So too were the tendencies at mission headquarters where busy secretaries might miss significant allusions and read only what they wished or expected to hear. Even deputations were likely to visit the fields with their own preestablished agendas, paying scant attention to local worries.[7]

Brian Stanley's essay, which examines the construction of the report by Commission VII on missions and governments to the Edinburgh conference in 1910, is especially revealing of these tensions. Care was taken in compiling such reports for conference discussion both to send out substantial questionnaires to mission societies and working missionaries, and to include a few such figures as members on the commissions responsible for drawing them up. In the end, however, the report from Commission VII failed quite seriously to represent current missionary experience, not least because panels were largely composed of busy metropolitan public figures. Many of them had their own well-developed worldviews, and were either remote from missionary affairs or inclined perhaps to regard all missionaries as narrow and insular.[8] The commission's failure is clear in three main areas. Missionary relations with imperial powers were discussed within the restrictive setting of a hierarchy of civilizations, an approach that revealed missionaries as both much more open than panel members to the importance of understanding local cultures and far more sensitive in particular to the values of African cultures. On questions of obedience to governments and the avoidance of politics, the report was oblivious to many practical issues and overlooked the

7. For a recent, albeit somewhat flawed, introduction to one such deputation by Daniel Tyerman and George Bennet of the LMS, see Tom Hiney, *On the Missionary Trail: The Classic Georgian Adventure of Two Englishmen, Sent on a Journey around the World, 1821-29* (London, 2000); also Andrew Porter, "Language, 'Native Agency' and Missionary Control: Rufus Anderson's Journey to India 1854-55," in *Missions and Missionaries: Studies in Church History: Subsidia 13*, ed. Pieter N. Holtrop and Hugh McLeod (Woodbridge, Suffolk, 2000).

8. See below, pp. 59, 80.

subtlety of missionary responses, not least some evident sympathy with local nationalist movements. Finally, the extent of missionary criticism of Western — especially British — government policies was greatly underplayed.

The value of the report lay in its later influence on missionary concerns especially after 1918, and in what it reveals of the contemporary high politics of the missionary movement. Only in tangential ways did it represent the serving missionary's viewpoint, and it illustrates forcefully the contrasts that existed between formal or official publications and local realities. Analysis of most other commissions has yet to be undertaken, and will need to follow Stanley's path in examining the rich background papers to "Edinburgh 1910" preserved in the archives in Geneva and New York. If the experience of Commission VII is representative, it seems probable that historians will need to moderate the emphasis placed by earlier studies on the unity and ecumenical character of the conference's proceedings.

In searching for those categories of representation and experience which go furthest in drawing the disparate elements of the missionary movement together, that of the missionary as "civilizer" and "hero," and the influence exerted by concepts of "race," are of particular importance. The former is discussed in the essay by John MacKenzie included here, and the latter by Andrew Ross.

Taking up the missionary slogan of "Christianity and Civilization," MacKenzie argues that a vital part of that civilization was provided by Western science. "Missionaries . . . invariably viewed themselves as scientists. Modern, empirical, experimental science was what distinguished their society from that of Africans."[9] As agents of enlightenment, missionaries saw themselves as entering worlds without science, achieving heroic status in significant measure by their efforts to introduce new knowledge and technology. To an undreamed-of degree, these made control over harsh environments possible. By satisfying existing needs or by creating new ones, they provided means for the cultural incorporation of indigenous societies into Western ways, and perhaps paved the way for imperial political authority and control to follow.[10]

The argument is telling, and scholars are only beginning to test its comprehensiveness, for example, in the work now being done on medical missionaries. In pursuing these investigations they will certainly ask how far this representation held good for missionaries operating not only in African but

9. See below, p. 130.

10. For the development of this theme, see J. V. Thomas, "The Role of the Medical Missionary in British East Africa, 1874-1904" (D.Phil. thesis, University of Oxford, 1982).

in Asian societies as well.[11] There were, nevertheless, competing missionary identities or images. Equally widespread in this period as in others was the image of the missionary as weak and vulnerable, someone whose heroism was derived from the willingness to risk everything and to place an unquestioning trust in God to provide. The missionary strategy of "identification" with local people in every way possible, found frequently not only in "faith missions" such as the CIM but also in the London Missionary Society and High Church bodies such as the Universities' Mission to Central Africa, positively encouraged a simplicity and asceticism at odds with images of the missionary as environmental controller or scientific ambassador.[12] Equally influential in this period was that critical strand in missionary thought, based on both representation and experience of Britain itself as well as Britons abroad, that sought to escape all Western cultural influence. Christianity both could and should be separated from "civilization." Missionaries should travel light and operate outside or, if possible, even beyond the networks of trade, labor recruitment, and imperial bureaucracy. These were the convictions that led Graham Wilmot Brooke into the western Sudan and to the upper Niger, where he died of blackwater fever in 1892.[13]

Logic might suggest that those who embraced the exclusive or separatist notions of biological "race" were potentially far more likely to adopt the image or ideal of the missionary hero as purveyor of a superior, essentially technocratic "civilization." The starting point for Andrew Ross's essay is the early nineteenth-century "belief in the essential equality of all human beings irrespective of race," the prevailing "sense of [the] oneness of humanity."[14] He agrees with those scholars — Philip Curtin, Christine Bolt, Douglas Lorimer, T. F. Gossett, and others — who have detected in the 1850s a decisive turn toward racial classifications of the world's peoples and an acceptance of the axiom that cultural and racial superiority necessarily went hand in hand. Ross argues that the consequences of this intellectual shift for the missionary movement were dire. To illustrate them, he examines the careers of Bishop

11. For example, David Arnold, ed., *Imperial Medicine and Indigenous Societies* (Manchester, 1988); Mark Harrison, *Public Health in British India: Anglo-Indian Preventive Medicine, 1859-1914* (Cambridge, 1994); Rosemary Fitzgerald, "Piety and Physic: Women Medical Missionaries in India, 1860-1914," CWC Position Paper (unpublished).

12. Jonathan J. Bonk, *The Theory and Practice of Missionary Identification, 1860-1920* (Lewiston, 1989).

13. Andrew Porter, "Evangelical Enthusiasm, Missionary Motivation, and West Africa in the Late Nineteenth Century: The Career of G. W. Brooke," *Journal of Imperial and Commonwealth History* 6, no. 1 (1977): 23-46.

14. See below, pp. 86, 87.

Samuel Crowther on the Niger, David Clement Scott in Nyasaland, and Bishop Alfred Tucker in Uganda. Each of these men tried to keep alive the universalism of the earlier period, and each also saw his work and achievements wrecked in the process. In a powerful illustration of the adage that history is written by the victors, Ross comments suggestively on the bias in the writing of missionary biography, which until recently ignored David Livingstone's respect for traditional African medicine and healers, and denied Scott a biography of any kind.

Ross shows that those like Tucker and Scott, who fought hardest in defense of a traditional egalitarianism, were also those who insisted to the end on both the capacity of Africans to match the attainments of whites in any field and the desirability of their doing so. African leadership in church and state was ultimately their goal. While prepared to impart scientific knowledge and technology, Crowther, Scott, and Tucker brought with them a Christianity that required them to eschew the heroic image. They cast themselves in the role of the servant, not of paternal benefactor.

Were, then, those who retained the notion of missionary heroism those who also insisted on its racial underpinning? The question is perhaps not well directed. The image of the missionary hero was far more often a metropolitan creation for a metropolitan readership attracted to missionary biographies or periodicals than it was the stock-in-trade of missionaries themselves. Perhaps those missionaries who came to view the world through the prism of race had little need of an additional appeal to heroism.

The essays collected here clearly demonstrate that analyzing the complex blend of ingredients in the makeup of missionary culture is more than enough to test the most discerning of historians. If John MacKenzie and Andrew Ross quite explicitly bridge the gap between metropolitan center and the locality, the remaining papers in the collection address the situation of missionaries and missionized in the mission field itself.

Taking southern Africa as her case study, Deborah Gaitskell assesses how far missionary activity was transformed by the enormous late nineteenth-century increase in female recruitment, above all of single women. Although India and China continued to profit most from the influx of women following the midcentury "discovery of the zenana," concerns about female seclusion or exclusion, and a strategic concentration on "women's work for women," South Africa nevertheless took an increasing share of female volunteers. In particular, the influence of the High Anglican tradition of celibate priests, the opening of the SPG to women from 1902, and the presence of new sisterhoods together transformed the Anglican presence. For all denominations, however, South Africa's rapid industrialization and urban growth, especially on the Rand, seems to have accentuated general changes that in various degrees were affecting missionary work elsewhere overseas.

The early nineteenth-century prominence given to missionary wives was increasingly overshadowed. Although a traditional insistence on "domesticity" and its significance for converts' lives remained important to many, simultaneously the larger numbers of single women, often with professional qualifications and more directly involved in evangelization, steadily carried the dominant sphere for women's work away from the home. These were gains of a sort, especially perhaps for African women, but notwithstanding the triumphalism they encouraged in the minds of women's committees in the home country, on the spot they were often insecurely grounded and ambiguous. For all the representation of women as independent and speaking for themselves, in the mission field no less than at home they continued in practice to operate largely in a man's world. In South Africa this meant not least a settler and colonial society where, for example, Anglicans and Methodists were equally concerned with "sustaining a British colonial church as well as reaching the 'heathen.'"[15] Ecclesiastical norms reinforced gender stereotypes with the result that compromises were legion. At least until the 1920s, women missionaries' role remained theologically and institutionally less influential than their numbers alone might either suggest or have warranted.

A very different colonial world is explored by Chandra Mallampalli in addressing the complex responses both of different Indian nationalists to missionary Christianity and of different Christian missionaries to the nationalist movement. On every side there was substantial movement and change. In the north, Mallampalli traces the development of mutually antagonistic strands of Hindu nationalism in Calcutta. He explores on one side a moderate Hindu nationalism, grounded in a self-confident acceptance and adaptation of local society and its customs in the face of Western rule. Increasingly at odds with it was the nationalism of those, for instance, in the Swadeshi movement of 1904-8, who reacted to missionary and other Western criticisms with a conservative, often extreme reassertion of popular Hindu beliefs and practice. Different again was the line taken by many nationalists in Madras who, in still more reactionary vein, appropriated the modern techniques of Western missionaries for the propagation of a traditional Hinduism.

While nationalists were thus divided over what had become less a calculated campaign for political rights than an emotional defense of differing conceptions of Hindu society, missionaries too were no less divided in their strategic responses to India. An expanding nationalist movement and an absence of con-

15. See below, p. 147.

versions inevitably prompted missionaries to search their own souls. Those such as the Scottish minister William Hastie held firmly to a long tradition of evangelical polemic against the "irrationality" and "corruption" of Indian society, and advocated the continuing importance of Alexander Duff's educational methods. However, by the 1880s there were vocal missionary critics to whom this seemed a bankrupt strategy. They argued that far from succeeding, it was likely to encourage the nationalist movement as the vehicle of an anti-Christian renaissance, and therefore ought to be replaced with an emphasis on fundamental evangelical preaching. Yet others, devotees of the novel "fulfillment" theology, such as William Miller and W. H. Findlay, argued that the reforming Hinduism widely represented among nationalists was in fact a Christianized Hinduism. It reflected a significant success for Christian missions in the form of a broad cultural rather than narrowly religious conversion.

This subtle treatment of the question of who influenced whom draws attention to a range of crosscurrents not only barely perceived by missionaries and nationalists engaged in India, but wholly unappreciated by their respective sympathizers in Britain. The "imperial horizons" and the influence of British Protestant missions as illustrated in the detail of Mallampalli's study were often invisible to missionaries and went undetected by nationalists. All were confined to representing each other not only on the basis of restricted personal experience but within the frameworks of wholly distinct and often divided goals. A measure of conditioning arising from the shared circumstances of imperial rule and their common struggle to win over mass support was inescapable, and influence was exerted unconsciously by all parties on each other.

Christian missionary activity in China provides many examples of the same divided but essentially complementary strategies that existed in India and elsewhere. There were those who saw in evangelistic preaching, peripatetic activity, and the use of vernacular language or literature the best and most direct means to secure mass support. Others favored the cultivation of social and political elites and the imparting of Western culture along with the Christian religion — sometimes in the vernacular — as the most likely way to convert a people. These different emphases, however, often meant more to armchair strategists at home than they did in the field. Thus J. Hudson Taylor, founder of the CIM, and the influential Welsh Baptist Timothy Richard have often been seen by Western scholars as competitors pursuing contradictory policies, when to the Chinese their Western origins and complementary approaches to evangelism have seemed to place them in a single category.[16]

16. For a recent account of Richard's work, see Brian Stanley, *The History of the Baptist Missionary Society, 1792-1992* (Edinburgh, 1992), pp. 180-206, 303-7.

Lauren Pfister has examined the work of the two men from this "Chinese" perspective. He argues that their evangelistic strategies each addressed different aspects of Chinese society, aspects frequently neglected by existing practices, and thus provided a "corrective" to what were then standard missionary and Western approaches to China. Taylor adopted an expansive itinerant strategy, intended to reach the mass of the Chinese people and designed to counteract the official Chinese wish to restrict, and if possible even exclude, missionary activity. Richard steadily targeted those elite elements in Chinese society who were willing to consider Western ideas; he rejected the commonly held Western view that they were universally antiforeign in their outlook, and attached great importance to their wider influence within China. Both men also took careful account of the ethnic diversity of the Qing empire.

At the same time Pfister emphasizes how both Taylor and Richard constantly surprise scholars by departing from their own standard self-images. Both men's messages were directed at Westerners as well as the Chinese. The CIM's periodical, *China's Millions,* Pfister suggests, was of critical importance in breaking down stereotypes — graphic as well as intellectual — and in conveying to English-speaking audiences a much more humane, realistic, and nuanced picture of Chinese life. Richard, although concentrating on Chinese-language materials of different kinds, including translations of Western publications, used the influential *Chinese Recorder* to reach a Western audience, thereby establishing for himself a role similar to Taylor's as an image-maker for the English-speaking public. Their impact seems to have gained much from the care each took to avoid that inevitable loss of dimension which occurred when representation was tied to the preoccupations of missionary fund-raising. As a result, missionary understanding of China's different ethnic groups rapidly outstripped that of the anthropologists in its precision and detail, and contributed much to breaking down the oversimplified racial categories of the theorists at home.

The frequent depiction of Taylor as "conservative" and Richard as "liberal" was at the time and still is a preeminently metropolitan, British-centered representation. While they represented important and potentially divergent trends that resurface at intervals in the history of the missionary movement, such polarization not only does little justice to the versatility and variety of their activities, but does much to disguise the extent of their shared outlooks. Vigorous pursuit of evangelical goals went together with a degree of open-mindedness and flexibility as to method that greatly enhanced their influence and ability to permeate Chinese society. Both avoided disparagement of the Chinese state, recognized the problems for missions caused by the "unequal" treaties of 1842 and 1860, which had allowed them into the country, and preferred the mandarins to any reliance on their national authorities. Like others in this volume, Pfister's essay brings home yet again the fact that missionaries often moved well beyond any specifically "imperial" horizons, in the territories where they worked, in their regard for political authority, and in their understanding of indigenous cultures and religion so very different from their own.

It is notable that of the individuals considered in these essays, arguably the one whose hopes and expectations were completely dashed was Montgomery. The ecclesiastical administrator entirely lacking direct missionary experience outside the empire's English-speaking communities was also the man who, while at the SPG, most seriously misjudged his audiences both in Britain and overseas. Few missionaries could escape being influenced by the conventional wisdom of their time, and missionary experience at first hand might reinforce both homebred and local colonial assumptions of racial and cultural superiority. However, it could also force missionaries to rethink such categories, to modify their representations of the extra-European world, and to change their understanding of evangelism. The individual determinants of theology, culture, gender, race, and varied personal experience never tied missionaries to one dominant imperial framework or narrowly defined missionary strategy. As knowledge and understanding accumulated within the movement as a whole, the pressures toward flexibility, cooperation, and experimentation tended to grow, even while each new generation of volunteers was at first inclined to be as single-minded as its predecessor. This may mean, paradoxically, that the missionary encounter in the "high imperial age," 1880-1914, was increasingly likely not to create or reinforce imperial structures but to subvert them.[17]

17. For further discussion, see Andrew Porter, "Religion, Missionary Enthusiasm, and Empire," in *The Oxford History of the British Empire,* 3:222-46; and Norman Etherington, "Missions and Empire," in *The Oxford History of the British Empire,* vol. 5, *Historiography,* ed. Robin Winks (Oxford, 1999), pp. 303-14.

Atonement, Sin, and Empire, 1880-1914

D. W. BEBBINGTON

The standard literature on the history of the British Empire tends to relegate religion to the margins of the analysis. Missions are usually thought to deserve a mention, but the churches rarely put in an appearance because politics and economics fill the picture. Thus in volume 1 of Cain and Hopkins's *British Imperialism*, the single-minded case in favor of "gentlemanly capitalism" as the dynamic of empire is supported by only one sentence referring to religion: the contention that in the late nineteenth century the Church Missionary Society (CMS) became more assertive, confident that "the service class of the Home Counties was destined to dominate the world."[1] Ronald Hyam's *Britain's Imperial Century, 1815-1914*, after suggesting that the Evangelical Revival produced "a whole crop of fanatics determined to impose the Christian religion on Buddhists and Hindus," goes on to argue that such missionaries were not significant agents of imperial expansion and that, except in New Zealand, the Pacific, and parts of central Africa, their role may be discounted. The churches, as such, are passed over.[2] Bernard Porter, while describing missionaries more fully, proposes that a number of British institutions came to depend on empire: the public schools, the monarchy, the sense of nationality — and, he adds, "the Christian churches, of course, were deeply involved," but we hear no more of them.[3] These three texts, extremely valuable surveys of the themes they cover, show little or no interest in the attitude

1. P. J. Cain and A. G. Hopkins, *British Imperialism: Innovation and Expansion, 1688-1914* (London, 1993), p. 358.

2. Ronald Hyam, *Britain's Imperial Century, 1815-1914*, 2nd ed. (London, 1993), pp. 75, 96, 286.

3. Bernard Porter, *The Lion's Share*, 3rd ed. (London, 1996), p. 205.

of the churches to empire. Even the body of publications inspired by John MacKenzie's work on the culture of popular imperialism allocates little space to religion. MacKenzie's seminal *Propaganda and Empire* includes some coverage of religious literature, but only in the context of reading for children.[4] So the question of the relationship between the churches and imperialism is not significantly illuminated in the most influential secondary writing in the field.

A number of more specialist works have examined the attitude of missionaries to the empire. A pioneer exploration of this area was Roland Oliver's book *The Missionary Factor in East Africa* (1952), which pointed to the late 1880s as the juncture when, in response to the German initiative in Africa, missionaries began to seek shelter under the British imperial umbrella.[5] The same period was picked out in H. A. C. Cairns's *Prelude to Imperialism* (1965) as the time by which missionaries were consistently favorable to the expansion of British control in central Africa.[6] Neither book, however, carried the analysis beyond the missionaries to the churches they represented. That verdict is less true of certain careful case studies of particular territories, such as A. J. Dachs's scrutiny of John Mackenzie's pressure for the creation of a protectorate over Bechuanaland (Botswana) or John McCracken's examination of Presbyterian demands for the establishment of indirect rule in what became Malawi, but even they concentrate primarily, and very reasonably, on the missions rather than their home constituencies.[7] Botswana and Malawi, together with Fiji and Uganda, are taken as the basis for Brian Stanley's sensitive evaluation of the ambiguities in the interaction of missions and imperialism in the later nineteenth century, but the stance of the churches at home to empire on a broader front is not within his brief.[8] Likewise Andrew Porter, in his stimulating inaugural lecture on religion and empire, focuses his concern on the missionary movement.[9] Perhaps Stephen Koss's article "Wesleyanism and Empire" is the most explicit consideration of the attitude of a religious

4. J. M. MacKenzie, *Propaganda and Empire: The Manipulation of British Public Opinion, 1880-1960* (Manchester, 1984), chap. 8.

5. Roland Oliver, *The Missionary Factor in East Africa* (London, 1952).

6. H. A. C. Cairns, *Prelude to Imperialism: British Reactions to Central African Society, 1840-1890* (London, 1965), p. 240.

7. A. J. Dachs, "Missionary Imperialism: The Case of Bechuanaland," *Journal of African History* 13 (1972): 647-58; K. J. McCracken, *Politics and Christianity in Malawi, 1875-1940* (Cambridge, 1977).

8. Brian Stanley, *The Bible and the Flag: Protestant Missions and British Imperialism in the Nineteenth and Twentieth Centuries* (Leicester, 1990).

9. Andrew Porter, "Religion and Empire: British Expansion in the Long Nineteenth Century, 1780-1914," *Journal of Imperial and Commonwealth History* 20 (1992): 370-90.

body to imperialism, and that is now a quarter-century old.[10] There is ample scope for exploration of the ecclesiastical attitudes to British rule abroad that undergirded, conditioned, and were in turn conditioned by missionary strategies. That is what, in outline, is attempted here. Did the theological preoccupations of the British churches have a discernible relationship with the new imperialism?

The inquiry, it needs to be said at the outset, is confined to the evangelical sections of the religious world. From the point of view of missions, that is not a major limitation: in 1870 only about 10 percent of financial support to missionary bodies went to the rival High Church organizations.[11] From a broader ecclesiastical point of view, however, it is a more serious restriction because within the Church of England in the later nineteenth century the evangelicals formed a receding party that lacked weight in the high counsels of church or state. Nevertheless, evangelicalism was a major force in British society because it embraced almost all the Protestant Nonconformists of England, who constituted not far short of half the religious nation; their counterparts in Wales, who represented fully four-fifths of the churchgoers there; and the Presbyterians of Scotland, who formed roughly the same proportion of worshipers north of the border. All upheld a form of popular Protestantism that was Bible centered, energetic, and eager for conversions. Above all, for the purposes of this study, they made the doctrine of the atonement the fulcrum of their theological system. Boyd Hilton has argued persuasively that themes associated with the cross of Christ were so pervasive in society at large in the earlier nineteenth century that the period down to the 1860s can be called "The Age of Atonement." The influence of evangelicals was then sufficiently powerful to make themes of redemption, sacrifice, and the like salient in matters of social policy, economic strategy, and political style. Afterward, as the evangelical party fell from prominence in the Church of England, social thought became less tinctured by motifs associated with atonement and more affected by ideas connected with the doctrine of the incarnation.[12] The central question to be addressed is therefore how the churches that still upheld the evangelical priorities in the later nineteenth and early twentieth centuries engaged with imperial questions. To what ex-

10. Stephen Koss, "Wesleyanism and Empire," *Historical Journal* 18 (1975): 105-18. There is also chap. 6 in my book *The Nonconformist Conscience: Chapel and Politics, 1870-1914* (London, 1982).

11. W. A. Scott Robertson, *British Contributions to Foreign Missions* (London, 1872), p. 1.

12. Boyd Hilton, *The Age of Atonement: The Influence of Evangelicalism on Social and Economic Thought, 1785-1865* (Oxford, 1988).

tent did they promote popular imperialism? What was the relationship between atonement and empire?

It has to be insisted that a cross-centered evangelicalism was still a vibrant force around the beginning of the twentieth century. The trend in the Church of England was toward a higher churchmanship, and many evangelical clergy trod the same path. They wore the surplice to preach, organized church choirs, and allowed flower displays in the sanctuary — all once seen as sinister ritualist innovations. Some evangelicals were also swayed by Broad Church currents of opinion, but broadening was less marked than heightening. When, in 1904, there was comment on the emergence of "liberal Evangelicalism," it meant such practices as adopting a Roman altar, covering it with a colored frontal varied according to season, and placing on it a tall brass cross and candlesticks.[13] Liturgical development of this kind was often combined with what evangelicals called "sound teaching," the preaching of a gospel that magnified the significance of the crucifixion. In the same way, Nonconformity had by no means abandoned evangelicalism for the sake of theological liberalism. It has been argued by R. J. Helmstadter that biblical criticism and Darwinism had joined forces to sap the vitality of the chapels by the last years of the nineteenth century.[14] The so-called higher criticism of the Bible, however, was accepted with remarkable ease by Nonconformist theologians and provoked no concerted opposition in a denomination until 1913.[15] Although a few individuals expressed strong reservations, in general Darwinian evolution had also been assimilated by the turn of the century: John Clifford, a leading Baptist, even published a book entitled *Typical Christian Leaders* (1898), in which the subject of one chapter was Charles Darwin.[16] Pulpit instruction, it is true, was becoming less legalistic, perhaps less definite, but in general it was not ceasing to be evangelical. When a leading Congregational minister, R. J. Campbell, adopted a form of spiritualized pantheism in 1907, the denomination rallied against him in defense of received evangelical

13. G. Wigram Neatby, to the editor of the *Record*, 26 August 1904, p. 858.

14. R. J. Helmstadter, "The Nonconformist Conscience," in *The Conscience of the Victorian State*, ed. Peter Marsh (Hassocks, Sussex, 1979), reprinted in Gerald Parsons, ed., *Religion in Victorian Britain*, vol. 4, *Interpretations* (Manchester, 1988), pp. 61-95.

15. W. B. Glover, *Evangelical Nonconformists and Higher Criticism in the Nineteenth Century* (London, 1954). D. W. Bebbington, "The Persecution of George Jackson: A British Fundamentalist Controversy," in *Persecution and Toleration*, ed. W. J. Sheils, Studies in Church History 21 (Oxford, 1984), pp. 421-33.

16. David N. Livingstone, *Darwin's Forgotten Defenders: The Encounter between Evangelical Theology and Evolutionary Thought* (Grand Rapids, 1987); John Clifford, "Charles Darwin, or evolution and Christianity," in his *Typical Christian Leaders* (London, 1898).

views.[17] The few prominent thinkers such as James Baldwin Brown and John Scott Lidgett who, swayed by F. D. Maurice, moved toward an incarnational theology, were not yet followed by the rank and file. And the Presbyterians of Scotland, even when broad-minded, were distinctly cruci-centric in their emphases.[18] Carnegie Simpson, for instance, explicitly repudiated the incarnationalism of Bishop Westcott.[19] Attention still concentrated on what the Evangelical Anglican newspaper the *Record* called "that theme of all themes, the death of our Lord Jesus Christ."[20]

Particular attention to the atonement does not mean other theological topics were ignored. On the contrary, various inherited themes continued to receive special emphasis. Hilton, like Roger Anstey before him, points out the importance in the evangelical worldview of the doctrine of providence.[21] Although the idea of an active divine government of the world was by no means confined to the evangelicals in the earlier nineteenth century, it was a subject on which they dwelt with particular satisfaction. Because it dealt with events in the public arena, it was a doctrine that readily meshed with attitudes to empire. In 1856, for example, the editor of the *General Baptist Repository* noted that, although Lord Dalhousie had gone to India pledged not to extend British territory, there had in fact been vast additions, the last being Oudh. "The Providence of God," he went on, "puts these nations under British rule for their emancipation, enlightenment, and salvation."[22] Annexation was surprising but not accidental, for in the divine plan the event had a definite purpose. The belief that providence rather than British arms was ultimately responsible for the growth of empire mollified anxieties that might otherwise have arisen over the legitimacy of the process. There was the risk, as a friendly French critic put it in 1899, that they might "put a bullet through a black man, pick him up and dress his wound, and affectionately exclaim, 'This is a providential opening for the Gospel!'"[23] Because the contention was offensive to other nations, a future archbishop of Canterbury warned in 1905 against identifying the advance of empire with the provi-

17. Keith Robbins, "The Spiritual Pilgrimage of the Rev. R. J. Campbell," *Journal of Ecclesiastical History* 30 (1979): 261-76.

18. Alan P. F. Sell, *Defending and Declaring the Faith: Some Scottish Examples, 1860-1920* (Exeter, 1987).

19. P. Carnegie Simpson, *Christus Crucifixus* (London, 1909), p. 66.

20. *Record,* 7 January 1910, p. 17.

21. Hilton, *The Age of Atonement;* Roger Anstey, *The Atlantic Slave Trade and British Abolition, 1760-1810* (London, 1975), chap. 5.

22. *General Baptist Repository,* April 1856, p. 157.

23. Théodore Monod, *Record,* 21 April 1899, p. 406.

dence of God.[24] But evangelicals, especially those in the Church of England, were still strongly attached to the theme around the turn of the century. England, they claimed, had been blessed with empire as a reward for staunchness in Reformation principles; parallels were drawn with the Roman Empire in that both institutions permitted the easier preaching of the gospel; and on one occasion Dean Lefroy declared that because only eight of the sixty-three colonies had come by conquest, their population had clearly been "committed to us by the Providence of God."[25] The manifest destiny of Britain, it seemed, was to engage in global expansion.

It was harder to relate the doctrine of the cross directly to empire. There was a strong sense that Britain needed to make atonement for the evils of the slave trade, but expiation was to be achieved not by imperial rule but by Christian missions.[26] Prebendary H. W. Webb-Peploe took up a similar theme in 1885. "If we look over the globe," he declared, "we may ask ourselves whether we are not indebted to every race for some tremendous injuries inflicted in days gone by." The remedy, however, was not British authority — that was part of the problem — but lay in "self-sacrifice" through missionary work.[27] A close approximation to seeing the white man's burden as expiatory came when Sir John Kennaway, the president of the CMS, remarked during the Boer War that the establishment of "freedom and justice and equality between races black and white" would bring greater blessings to Britain "than we could have enjoyed if we had not suffered and sorrowed."[28] Kennaway stopped short, however, of connecting the suffering with the crucifixion, perhaps because like others, he fought shy of compromising the uniqueness of the redemptive work of Christ on the cross. Although on one occasion an exuberant clerical speaker pointed out that "the flag which is always unfurled over every land and every sea" consisted of nothing but "the Cross three times,"[29] empire was not theologized in terms of the atonement in a more elaborate way.

Nevertheless, the idea of redemption was central in forming the evangelical worldview in a very specific manner. What, asked the *Evangelical Free*

24. Cosmo Gordon Lang, "The Empire and the Church," in *The Empire and the Century,* ed. Charles Sydney Goldman (London, 1905), pp. 166-67.

25. Noel Stanton (bishop of Sodor and Man), *Record,* 22 February 1895, p. 184; E. G. Ingham (former bishop of Sierra Leone), *From Japan to Jerusalem* (London, 1911), p. 138; Dean Lefroy of Norwich, *Record,* 4 May 1900, p. 404.

26. Cairns, p. 151.

27. H. W. Webb-Peploe, *Record,* 8 May 1885, pp. 460-61.

28. *Record,* 4 May 1900, p. 421.

29. E. Grose Hodge, *Record,* 6 May 1910, p. 441.

Church Catechism issued in 1899, did Christ accomplish for us by his death on the cross? "By offering Himself a sacrifice without blemish unto God," ran the answer, "He fulfilled the requirements of Divine Holiness, atoned for all our sins, and broke the power of Sin." The atonement, that is to say, was the panacea for the wrong in the world, whether considered as particular wicked acts or as the dominant principle of evil. What, asked an earlier question, is sin? "Sin," according to the reply, "is any thought or feeling, word or act, which either is contrary to God's holy law, or falls short of what it requires."[30] The rest of the catechism, which was composed by a representative committee of evangelical Free Churchmen and so contains a consensus of the popular theology of the time, goes on to stress the Ten Commandments and their meaning, so explaining the law whose infringement was the content of sin. Law and sin, in fact, occupy a disproportionate amount of space in the catechism, far greater, for instance, than what is allocated to the doctrine of God. So in understanding the problems of the world, at home and abroad, evangelicals interpreted them in terms of broken divine laws. Evangelicals might differ over details of theology, over points of church polity and supremely in the late nineteenth century over the legitimacy of an established church, but all their ecclesiastical differences — and all their individual differences too — were overlaid by a common understanding of the world as impregnated with wickedness. "At the back of all the world's trouble and social and economic distress," the Congregational leader J. D. Jones was reported saying in 1908, "there lay the fact of sin."[31] The redemption that was the constant concern of evangelical religion was salvation from sin. It is not surprising that its adherents saw examples of the phenomenon all about them.

This preoccupation molded the attitude of evangelicalism to public affairs. Adherents of the movement had consistently been stirred into action by calls to deal with sin. The best means of rousing evangelical audiences against colonial slavery, the chief agitator on the subject had discovered in the early 1830s, was to condemn it as "criminal before God."[32] Subsequent campaigns habitually targeted what was identified as outright wrong. Hence these crusades were characteristically "anti": antislavery, anti–corn laws (among the Dissenters), antiritualism (among Evangelical Anglicans), anti–Contagious Diseases Acts, and so on. It was still so at the end of the century. The Wesleyan Conference of 1891 urged members, in the centenary year of Wesley's death, to exert a distinctive

30. *An Evangelical Free Church Catechism* (London, [1899]), pp. 10, 8.

31. *Christian World*, 7 May 1908, p. 22.

32. George Stephen, *Anti-slavery Recollections in a Series of Letters Addressed to Mrs Beecher Stowe* [1854] (London, 1971), p. 248.

influence on society. They could promote temperance, philanthropy, and orphanages, but they also had other priorities as citizens. "Let us protest against evils," ran the address, "against impurity, in speech as well as in act; against gambling; against cruelty to little children; against aggressive war; against trade oppression, by master or man; against the blasphemies that stain English conversation."[33] The program was typically negative. Evangelicals en masse could not be expected to grasp detailed policy proposals, but they could recognize what was condemned by the ethics of the gospel and call for its elimination. A feature of the campaigns that has been specially analyzed in the case of the temperance movement was therefore an unquestioning moral absolutism. There could be no question of compromise with sin, and so, temperance reformers insisted, their demands must be met in full.[34] Evangelicalism generated a powerful series of movements protesting against wickedness.[35]

This populist style was not the only evangelical approach to public affairs. The tradition of Wilberforce operated by quiet influence over individual politicians, and Shaftesbury was often able to exert a comparable leverage on political decisions. Such methods, however, were open only to those with an entrée to the heart of the political system. Most evangelicals, and particularly Nonconformists, were outsiders. They might have the vote, especially in the wake of the parliamentary reforms of 1867 and 1884, but they did not have a grasp on power. Accordingly their campaigning was typically designed to draw attention to the strength of the cause in numbers and depth of feeling. Monster meetings featured fiery oratory up and down the country, with, for instance, a Nonconformist demonstration on the education question in 1896 displaying "the highest order of eloquence — that which springs from passion at glowing heat and inspires answering passion."[36] This technique was typical of the Nonconformist conscience that flourished in the period, but it was equally the method favored by the militant antiritualists who roused Evangelical Anglicans, especially around the 1900 general election.[37] Often leaders of the evangelical community, both ordained and lay, sympathized wholeheartedly with the causes embraced by popular enthusiasm and were

33. *Minutes of Several Conversations of the People called Methodists* (London, 1891), p. 378.

34. D. A. Hamer, *The Politics of Electoral Pressure: A Study in the History of Victorian Reform Agitations* (Hassocks, Sussex, 1977), chaps. 9–13.

35. This popular evangelical activism is discussed in David Bebbington, "Evangelicals and Reform," *Third Way* (May 1983): 10-13.

36. *Christian World,* 4 June 1896, p. 443.

37. I. T. Foster, "Anglican Evangelicalism and Politics, 1895-1906" (Ph.D. diss., University of Cambridge, 1994), chap. 4.

happy to help whip them up. That, however, was not always the case. Repeatedly mass movements had taken agitation further than responsible leaders thought prudent: opponents of slavery had begun to call not for gradual but for immediate emancipation in the 1820s; root-and-branch Dissenters had gone beyond calls for the redress of their grievances to demands for disestablishment in the 1830s; critics of ritualism had wanted to press ahead with prosecutions when there was no prospect of success in the later nineteenth century.[38] In each case the moderate leadership was unable to contain the pressure for decisive action coming from below. The conviction that sin had to be put down at whatever cost swept aside the inhibitions of the more timid. The mass evangelical political style was impatient of restraint.

Over the long term, evangelicals had commonly associated three categories of sin with empire: wrongs within the British Empire, evils bound up with its extension, and forms of wickedness practiced beyond its bounds. Typical of the first class were the features of India to which early Baptist Missionary Society agents drew attention. On one hand were the cruel traditional practices of which widow burning was the most offensive, and on the other was the British sponsorship of Hindu idolatry such as the temple of Juggernaut.[39] In the second class was the propensity for waging war, annexing territory, and disregarding indigenous rights on the fringe of empire. Although even the Quaker reforming politician John Bright valued the empire, Nonconformists frequently deplored efforts to extend it. Thus James Guinness Rogers, a leading Congregational minister, denounced the forward policy in Afghanistan in 1879 as a breach of Christian ethics.[40] The third class included the continuing slave trade and barbarities of many kinds, but the phenomenon that most provoked evangelical wrath was Roman Catholicism. Far from being seen as a slightly mistaken variant of the Christian faith, the Roman Church was abominated as a cunning imposture that carried souls to destruction. Evangelistic rivalry between evangelicals and Catholics was overlaid with a host of anxieties inherited from previous generations.[41] The gospel and popery seemed locked in

38. D. B. Davis, "The Emergence of Immediatism in British and American Antislavery Thought," *Mississippi Valley Historical Review* 48 (1962): 209-30; G. I. T. Machin, *Politics and the Churches in Great Britain, 1832 to 1868* (Oxford, 1977), pp. 45-47; James Bentley, *Ritualism and Politics in Victorian Britain: The Attempt to Legislate for Belief* (Oxford, 1978), pp. 114-20.

39. E. D. Potts, *British Baptist Missionaries in India, 1793-1837: The History of Serampore and Its Missions* (Cambridge, 1967), chap. 7.

40. *Congregationalist,* May 1879, p. 256.

41. G. F. A. Best, "Popular Protestantism in Victorian Britain," in *Ideas and Institutions of Victorian Britain,* ed. Robert Robson (London, 1967), pp. 115-42.

mortal combat on a global scale. Catholicism appeared sufficiently sinister to fall into the class of evils to be resisted.

Each of the three categories of institutionalized wickedness had different effects on evangelical attitudes to empire. The first cast the British authorities in the role of potential benefactors who might eliminate evil practices, and yet at the same time those officials committed wrongs such as promoting false religion themselves. Evangelicals were simultaneously attracted and repelled, so that the consequences for their view of empire were ambiguous. In the second category the colonial rulers seemed the agents of international brigandage, and so, especially in Nonconformist circles, there was strong suspicion of imperial expansion. The third category, however, had the opposite effect: Britain possessed the power to put down evils on the borders of her territory and, by annexation, to deliver whole regions from the risk of domination by another power with Catholic sympathies. British authorities were not expected to exclude Catholic missionaries, let alone to propagate Protestantism, but it was assumed that they would give no favor to Rome and hoped that they would erect no obstacles to the gospel. This third factor tended to turn evangelicals into friends of the growth of empire. So their overall stance on the question of imperialism was determined in large measure by how far British power abroad was seen as a harbinger of righteousness. For much of the nineteenth century, the three factors were in rough equilibrium. Apart from internal evils, which pulled the evangelical constituency in opposite directions at once, there were the iniquities of expansion to balance against the advantages of combating wrongs such as slavery and offering protection against the Roman menace. Although Anglicans might normally have fewer inhibitions about military adventures than Nonconformists, evangelicals in general saw no reason to lean strongly toward territorial advance. The empire was almost as likely to do harm as to put down wrong. In the age of high imperialism, however, in many respects that judgment was to change. Before the nineteenth century was over, the balance sheet of global sin was to be read in a different way.

There was, however, a high degree of continuity between the earlier and later periods in the assessment of wrongs within the empire. When Victor Buxton, an Evangelical Anglican layman, returned from a visit to East Africa in 1905, he reported that, although British administration had established peace and security, it had also brought "the breaking down of old restraints" and the result was "liberty to do evil as well as good."[42] There was a corrupting power in European contact with indigenous peoples. Even more serious, the imperial authorities did not always hold the ring for competing religious influences. As

42. *Record*, 5 May 1905, p. 430.

once in India under company rule, so in the years around the opening of the twentieth century, the authorities in the Sudan and northern Nigeria refused permission for evangelistic work for fear of stirring up disturbances in Muslim areas.[43] British power was committing one of the worst of crimes, obstructing the spread of the gospel. Furthermore, in India it protected the opium trade to China and established the state regulation of prostitution; in the Pacific and southern Africa it tolerated the virtual slave traffic of indentured laborers.[44] Wrongs aplenty were tolerated within the empire. On the other hand, the colonial power sometimes acted in the interests of righteousness. Bishop Tugwell, who had waged a long war against the import of spirits into West Africa, opened a speech in 1905 by referring to his satisfaction at the response of the authorities: "At the outset he bore testimony to the great value which attached to British administration. Great Britain, he said, had influenced the world for good in [a] way in which no other nation had done."[45] But even good government had detrimental effects on indigenous society.[46] As Andrew Porter has noted, evangelicals were aware of the presence of sin in government as well as of the potential helpfulness to missions of British rule.[47] So, in terms of evils within British territory, there was still, in the era of the so-called new imperialism, a wariness of empire that weighed against a desire to harness it for good.

There was a much more marked alteration in attitudes on the question of extending British authority over fresh lands. Evangelical Anglicans had far less scope than Nonconformists for change on this point. Most evangelicals in the Church of England had long been politically aligned with the Conservatives, who, at least from Disraeli's speeches around the passing of the Second Reform Act, had been sympathetic to imperial growth.[48] Although in 1894 Prebendary Webb-Peploe, one of the most prominent evangelical clergymen, sat on the executive council of the Arbitration Alliance, which implied a public commitment to the principle of nonaggression, the alliance was overwhelmingly dominated by Nonconformists.[49] The bulk of chapel-goers

43. A. F. Painter, to the editor of the *Record*, 6 January 1899, p. 25; *Record*, 10 June 1910, p. 558.

44. *Christian World*, 16 April 1891, p. 305; 7 October 1897, pp. 7f. Samuel Smith, *My Life Work* (London, 1902), p. 298. *Christian World*, 3 March 1904, p. 2.

45. *Record*, 24 March 1905, p. 269.

46. "H. E. Fox at C.M.S. Centenary Celebration," *Record*, 14 April 1899, p. 386.

47. Andrew Porter, pp. 382-83.

48. Freda Harcourt, "Disraeli's Imperialism, 1866-1868: A Question of Timing," *Historical Journal* 23 (1980): 87-109.

49. "The Arbitration Alliance," enclosure with R. W. Perks to Lord Rosebery, 10 August 1894, MS 10050 f. 5, Rosebery Papers, National Library of Scotland.

shared the Gladstonian Liberal Party's respect for peace alongside retrenchment and reform. Their leading weekly organ, the *Christian World,* regularly criticized military adventures on the fringe of empire. In an editorial of 25 November 1897 headed "A National Crime," for example, it denounced the slaughter on the northwest frontier of India. Although yielding to none in its desire for the extension of British civilization, culture, and religion, the newspaper was prepared to accept the taunt of "Little Englander" rather than endorse unnecessary bloodshed.[50] There was particular alarm among some Nonconformists about the aggrandizement of chartered companies. In 1894, for example, James Hirst Hollowell arraigned Cecil Rhodes for provoking the Matabele War.[51] And even if the Peace Society was a weak organization, its pacificist (rather than pacifist) views retained some lingering support in the chapels.[52] Although the Wesleyans were less inclined to resist a spirit of conquest than the other Free Churches,[53] the general view among Nonconformists was that jingoism was a thoroughly bad thing.

Their consensus that Britain must abstain from imperial aggression received a jolt when, in 1882, Alexandria was bombarded and the occupation of Egypt ensued. John Bright resigned from the government, but the rather bewildered Nonconformists were rallied by most of their representative men to support the actions of a Liberal government. "In vindicating the rights of its own subjects against a bandit chief," wrote Guinness Rogers, "Great Britain is only discharging a duty of police to which the Khedive is unequal."[54] Like most Liberals, the Nonconformists became used to justifying government policy and consequently an addition to global responsibilities.[55] Other factors were pushing them in the same direction. They had long regarded Christian soldiers as figures to be admired and emulated, and the pervasive cultural ideal of chivalry was having its effect on them.[56] The emergence in 1878 of the Salvation Army, with its array of aggressive rhetoric and elaborate command structure, was symptomatic of an increasing willingness to blend the religious and the military. The cult of Oliver Cromwell, a national hero Nonconformists

50. *Christian World,* 25 November 1897, pp. 10-11.

51. *Christian World,* 29 November 1894, p. 896.

52. Henry Richard, to the editor of the *Christian World,* 15 October 1888, p. 778.

53. Koss, "Wesleyanism and Empire."

54. J. G. Rogers, "The Egyptian Difficulty," *Congregationalist,* August 1882, p. 626.

55. R. C. Mowat, "From Liberalism to Imperialism: The Case of Egypt, 1875-1887," *Historical Journal* 16 (1973): 109-24.

56. Olive Anderson, "The Growth of Christian Militarism in Mid-Victorian Britain," *English Historical Review* 86 (1971). Mark Girouard, *The Return to Camelot: Chivalry and the English Gentleman* (New Haven, 1981).

could claim as their own, was a further sign that inherited inhibitions about the use of force in a good cause were wearing thin. When in the mid-1890s news reached Britain of Turkish atrocities among the Armenians to rival those among the Bulgarians two decades before, something snapped. "One almost wishes," declared the *Christian World*, "that CROMWELL would rise again, and bring the SULTAN to his knees as he did the DUKE OF SAVOY."[57] Nonconformists demanded, as they had refrained from doing over the Bulgarian question, that Britain should intervene to protect the Armenian victims. When Turkey suppressed a rebellion in Crete in 1897, again the Nonconformist policy was that Britain should use force on the side of the Cretans.[58] There was in both cases a sense of outrage that their country was not taking measures to deal with a crying evil. These events were what prepared Nonconformists to support Joseph Chamberlain's policy in the run-up to the Boer War. In this instance, at last, the British government was willing to redress apparently flagrant wrongs — the denial of civil rights to the Uitlanders in the Transvaal. The Boers, announced the *Christian World*, were revealed as "guilty of the very political injustices that roused the English Puritans of the seventeenth century to revolt."[59] An evil over the imperial frontier justified a war of aggression. In the last two decades of the nineteenth century, Nonconformists performed a volte-face. By the Boer War most of them were no longer seeing a forward policy on the limits of empire as an iniquity to oppose.

The wrongs suffered by the Uitlanders formed an example of the type of sin outside the empire that now induced evangelicals in general to favor the advance of British rule as the remedy. The continuing slave trade was another. If variants of slavery within the empire were intolerable, the slave trade beyond its bounds was a wrong that Britain could extinguish by extending a protectorate over the regions affected. This consideration was a powerful element in the evangelical psyche, well illustrated by the Scottish Free Church evangelist Henry Drummond. In his *Tropical Africa* (1888), an account of his expedition into what is now Malawi, he is strongly preoccupied with the slave trade. He makes the apparently extraordinary remark that "the sooner the last elephant falls before the hunter's bullet the better for Africa." The explanation is that slaves are needed to carry the ivory to the coast. "The extermination of the elephant, therefore, will mark one stage at least in the closing up of the slave-trade."[60] Drummond's publicity for the area was one of the fac-

57. *Christian World*, 10 January 1895, p. 21.
58. *Christian World*, 25 February 1897, p. 10.
59. *Christian World*, 5 October 1899, p. 2.
60. Henry Drummond, *Tropical Africa* (London, 1888), pp. 20-21.

tors behind the successful Scottish campaign for a protectorate over Malawi.[61] Likewise the abolition of the slave trade was a reason why Evangelical Anglicans rejoiced when Uganda came under the British flag,[62] and why Nonconformists similarly celebrated the annexation of Fulah to Nigeria in 1904: "Although the aggrandisement of the British Empire is a necessary consequence, it was not the primary object; it was imperative on us, placed as we were, to break the powers of darkness and rescue the millions, who lived under the shadow of the accursed slave-trade, from the terrible evils it involves."[63] Although this comment may verge on self-deception, it does reveal the extraordinary extent to which the elimination of the slave trade was seen as a humanitarian enterprise justifying imperial advance.

An even more potent factor vindicating the acquisition of new territory, however, was the need to protect the inhabitants from false religion. Evangelicals were conscious of a rivalry for converts with Islam, but their minds were far more haunted by the specter of Roman Catholicism. It was an epoch when at home the Roman threat was apparent in the demands of the Irish for a Catholic university and their steadfast resistance to proposals for the inspection of convent laundries. Catholic hostility was symbolized by the (understandable) opposition of Irish MPs to a statue in the precincts of Parliament commemorating Cromwell.[64] "Rome on the Rates" was the rallying cry of the protracted Nonconformist struggle over the funding of elementary education while Evangelical Anglicans were resisting the steady advance of Romanizing ritual within their own church. In overseas affairs there was enormous sympathy for the American side in the struggle of 1898 with effete and popish Spain and strong resentment over a longer period at the French takeover of Madagascar, a field of the London Missionary Society (LMS), in 1885.[65] Indeed, the chief vehicle for the Catholic peril abroad seemed to be the growth of the French Empire. The Third Republic was not likely to give active support to Catholic missions, but where the French flag went the White Fathers or their equivalent followed, and Protestants soon found life difficult. The LMS work in Tahiti had effectively been suppressed following the island's occupation by France in the 1840s, and fears of similar policies fueled demands for the British annexation of the New Hebrides in 1885 and of New Guinea a year later.[66] The

61. McCracken, pp. 156-58.

62. *Record,* 3 May 1895, p. 443.

63. *Christian World,* 2 April 1903, p. 2.

64. *Christian World,* 17 March 1898, p. 6; 11 March 1909, p. 23; 1 March 1900, p. 2.

65. *Christian World,* 14 April 1898, p. 10; 16 May 1895, p. 358.

66. A. A. Koskinen, *Missionary Influence as a Political Factor in the Pacific Islands* (Helsinki, 1953), pp. 230-33, 207.

acquisition of territory by Britain was therefore seen as a preemptive strike against a power that would erect barriers to world evangelization.

There is an instructive parallel with the well-attested attitude of merchants to empire in the period. When other powers began imposing protective tariffs on trade in the territories they were acquiring, commercial interests began to call for Britain, while maintaining its own free trade principles, to occupy regions that might otherwise fall to its rivals.[67] In the same way, the churches became convinced that their country, while continuing an even-handed policy toward Protestant and Catholic missions, should anticipate France by expanding the empire in order to prevent discrimination against the gospel. Suspicion of French ambitions became deep-seated. This feeling helps account for an extraordinary scene at the Congregational Union autumn assembly in October 1898. Two speakers were commissioned to welcome the czar's proposals for a peace conference, but both found themselves condemning the unfurling of the French flag at Fashoda on the upper Nile. France, they insisted, must retire. This, said Dr. Goodrich, "was not the speech he had prepared, but it was the speech he wanted to make." His sentiments boiled over: "he wished to say that he was not a Jingo, and they were not Jingoes; but, he added, amid cheers, 'We are Englishmen.'"[68] The xenophobia evident in Goodrich's outburst was closely bound up with an anti-Catholicism that had been rekindled earlier in the year during the Spanish-American War. The malign force of Romanism must not be allowed an advantage under French rule. Thus the capacity of the empire to neutralize the Catholic threat, combined with its ability to suppress slavery, operated as powerful motives for the growth of imperialism in the churches.

Consequently there was a shift in the balance of forces playing on the attitudes of evangelicals toward empire. Although their view of the evils in British territory remained ambiguous, there were discernible transformations in the other two categories of sin. Inhibitions about imperial expansion weakened among Nonconformists, and a sense of the value of British authority as a force for righteousness grew. The overall effect was to turn the bulk of evangelicals into ardent imperialists in time for the opening of the Boer War. The *Record* spoke for Evangelical churchmen in its first issue after the outbreak of war: "Now that the issue is clearly defined there can be no possible doubt as to our duty. We must end once and for all the rule of the Boer oligarchy. Its gross corruption, its toleration of systematic vice, its open brutality, its interference with the course of justice, its restrictions on education, its policy to-

67. M. E. Chamberlain, *The New Imperialism* (London, 1970), pp. 26-27.
68. *Christian World,* 20 October 1898, p. 12.

wards the natives, and its endeavour to procure the ascendancy of Dutch rule over British in South Africa, must cease." It was a struggle of darkness against light: Britain must "vindicate the cause of righteousness and freedom."[69] The majority of Nonconformists took the same course. When the pro-Boer Hirst Hollowell alluded at the Congregational Union autumn assembly that month to the force of the British Empire being used to "assassinate" the Transvaal, Hubert Arnold protested that the empire had been forced to go to war. Arnold's intervention was received with great cheering, accompanied by hissing.[70] That was the approximate division of Nonconformist opinion throughout the struggle: although a vocal minority was critical of Britain's part in the war, the majority was entirely favorable. In the latter stages of the conflict, the Wesleyan leader Hugh Price Hughes went so far as to credit Britain for relieving Boer commandos of their domestic duties by setting up concentration camps for their families.[71] The general endorsement of the war fairly represented evangelical enthusiasm for empire.

The Anglicans in the evangelical constituency were to become even keener imperialists. In the Edwardian period they grew aware that colonial officials were increasingly supportive of missions, which were seen as civilizing agencies that bolstered the administration. A turning point came in 1905 when Lord Cromer actually invited the CMS to take up work in the Sudan, the first occasion on which the imperial authorities took the initiative in summoning missionaries. By 1910 it was acknowledged that the best friends of missions were found among government officials.[72] But on the score of attitudes to government, the change among Nonconformists was far greater. Their mid-nineteenth-century skepticism about the state had given way to a belief that government had great potential for doing good. The social gospel that was in vogue from the late 1880s onward saw public authority as the instrument for building the kingdom of God on earth. The growing understanding of the Old Testament prophets as fiery castigators of public wrongs encouraged Nonconformists to insist that the state should advance the cause of social righteousness. It was easy to cast government in a more activist role overseas as well as at home. Already by 1890 Hughes had been swept along by that tide. Nonintervention, which at that date he still supported in a qualified way, did not mean, he claimed, a neglect of international duties. "A nation," he declared,

69. *Record,* 13 October 1899, p. 981.

70. *Christian World,* 26 October 1899, p. 13.

71. *Christian World,* 28 November 1901, p. 1. Cf. J. H. S. Kent, "Hugh Price Hughes and the Nonconformist Conscience," in *Essays in Modern English Church History in Memory of Norman Sykes,* ed. G. V. Bennett and J. D. Walsh (London, 1966), pp. 198-203.

72. *Record,* 31 March 1905, p. 295; 10 June 1910, p. 558.

"as well as an individual, must play the noble part of the Good Samaritan."[73] John Clifford, the Baptist leader who was to become a pro-Boer, nevertheless wrote in 1897 a series of articles celebrating "our vast and growing empire."[74] Although he concentrated on the settler colonies, Clifford appreciated the worldwide phenomenon as a power for good. It is clear that the novel commitment of the Nonconformists to empire, superseding their earlier passive acceptance of it as a providential responsibility, was a major transformation.

The imperialism of the evangelical community shared much common ground with its counterpart in other groups at the same period. There was, for example, frequent recapitulation of the secular benefits of British rule. On one occasion Bishop Tugwell specified "liberty, security to life and property, and administration of justice"; on another F. B. Meyer, a prominent Baptist just returned from India, explained that he had been impressed by British achievements in "making railways, telegraphs, roads, diverting rivers, etc."[75] Yet various spokesmen often insisted that the form of imperialism they advocated was not to be confused with its normal current manifestation. They did not stand for gloating over numbers of soldiers and sailors, the bishop of North Queensland told the Colonial and Continental Church Society in 1899, or over the amount of the empire's imports, but for the "Imperialism that may give openings for spreading the Word of God."[76] Likewise in 1906 the Congregational journalist W. T. Stead wrote a whole book to contrast the jingoistic attitude to empire with a view that stressed voluntary involvement by self-governing nations, virtually dominions within a commonwealth. "What Antichrist is to Jesus of Nazareth," he exclaimed, "Jingoism is to true Imperialism."[77] The British Empire, these champions held, was distinctive because it stood for Christian values as against militarism, triumphalism, and oppression. It existed to confer benefits on its inhabitants. The *Record* stressed "the responsibility which these possessions cast upon us" in endorsing the celebration of Empire Day in 1905.[78] Here was the doctrine of trusteeship in the making. John MacKenzie has remarked that those who controlled imperial propaganda in the interwar years deplored jingoism and were fervent "moral" imperialists.[79] That style of discourse had its roots before the First World War

73. H. P. Hughes, "Non-intervention," in his *The Philanthropy of God* (London, 1890), p. 131.

74. John Clifford, *God's Greater Britain* (London, 1899), p. 4.

75. *Record,* 3 November 1899, p. 1080; 21 April 1899, p. 407.

76. *Record,* 5 May 1899, p. 458.

77. W. T. Stead, *The Best or the Worst of Empires: Which?* (London, 1906), p. 11.

78. *Record,* 26 May 1905, p. 497.

79. MacKenzie, *Propaganda and Empire,* p. 10.

in the religious rhetoric of empire to which evangelicals contributed so largely.

At the tercentenary celebrations of Cromwell's birth in 1899, the *Record* regretted that Nonconformists had tried to monopolize the occasion and, on behalf of its Anglican readers, applauded the Puritan spirit. Urging that Cromwell held "essentially Imperial" instincts, it argued that a "sense of religious responsibility . . . gives much of its strength to the Imperial feeling of to-day."[80] It was a sound verdict. The evangelical churches of Britain — Anglican, Nonconformist, and Scottish Presbyterian too — participated fully in the upsurge of imperialist sentiment that marked the late 1890s.[81] That body of feeling would no doubt have emerged without them: popular imperialism, after all, developed in this period in Continental countries where evangelicals in the British sense were very few in numbers. But the churches tried to temper their confidence in Britain's global destiny with a sense of responsibility, disregarding the jingoism of the music halls in the process. That ecclesiastical attitude undoubtedly extended beyond the confines of the evangelical world.[82] What was distinctive to evangelicals was their spontaneous analysis of public issues in a framework dominated by the notion of sin and their consequent political participation through agitations targeting flagrant wrongs. These campaigns were what mobilized the evangelical constituency on imperial questions, rousing its members to oppose instances of wickedness within existing British territory, in its aggrandizement, or beyond its perimeter. The changing weight attached to different forms of iniquity molded their attitudes to empire. There was, after the last years of the nineteenth century, less compunction about expansion and more expectation of benefits from colonial rule. Hence evangelicals became more enthusiastic about the moral possibilities of British power abroad. There was an evolution of public opinion that deserves coverage in studies of popular imperialism and even in general surveys of imperial history. Empire, like the atonement, came to be seen as a means of redeeming human beings from slavery to sin.

80. *Record,* 28 April 1899, p. 426.

81. Richard Koebner and H. D. Schmidt, *Imperialism: The Story and Significance of a Political Word, 1840-1960* (Cambridge, 1964), pp. 207-16.

82. Lang, pp. 166-73.

Imperial Christianity? Bishop Montgomery and the Foreign Missions of the Church of England, 1895-1915

STEVEN MAUGHAN

I

"These are great times and one feels the stir of an Imperial [Christ]ianity. Thank God it is good to live in these days." Thus did Henry Hutchinson Montgomery, bishop of Tasmania, express his feelings to his friend and brother bishop Randall Davidson, of Winchester, six days after the relief of Mafikeng in the South African War.[1] In this passage Montgomery, soon to be appointed to lead the High Church Anglican Society for the Propagation of the Gospel (SPG), voiced a sentiment that resonated with the cresting wave of popular imperialism in the 1890s: that there was an organic connection between the religion of Britain and the success of its empire.[2] When elevated to the leadership of the SPG fourteen months later, Montgomery avowed he would use this connection to reorder High Church and, indeed, all Anglican missions. In many ways this was a romantic and enthusiastic plan, redolent

1. Lambeth Palace Library, Randall Thomas Davidson Papers, vol. 519, fols. 248-56, Montgomery to Davidson, 24 May 1900.

2. John Wolffe, *God and Greater Britain: Religion and National Life in Britain and Ireland, 1843-1945* (London and New York, 1994), pp. 222-25.

I wish to thank participants at the Northwest Conference on British Studies at the University of Puget Sound, 14-15 November 1997, and the consultation of the North Atlantic Missiology Project at Westminster College, Cambridge, 7-9 April 1998, on "The Imperial Horizons of British Protestant Missions, 1880-1914," for their helpful comments on earlier versions of this piece. I am particularly indebted to Brian Stanley for his suggestive written response at the latter meeting.

with the sentiments of Kipling and other popularizers of empire. He intended to transform the SPG into a popular organization that would lead the church consciously into a program of imperial duty. While for decades the SPG had languished in comparison to mainstream evangelical missionary societies, and especially its sister Anglican society, the evangelical Church Missionary Society (CMS), Montgomery aimed to draw the higher varieties of Anglicanism back into the world of missions, make explicit the connection between British religion and British empire, and establish the Church of England as the leader of British missions. Ultimately this bid to weld Christianity and empire into a single popular program failed, and Montgomery's efforts might be considered no more than a quixotic episode in the history of Anglicanism and popular imperialism. Closer inspection of this subject, however, illuminates several difficult problems in the history and interrelationship of Christian missions and the British Empire. Here I examine the dynamics that theology, party identity, local feeling, and the imperatives of missions in the field brought to the complex relationship of Christianity and empire in Britain.

Montgomery's story belongs as much to the history of popular imperialism as it does to that of foreign missions. Of the ubiquity of imperial culture in late Victorian Britain there can no longer be any doubt. In recent years investigation of the culture of empire has produced a detailed corpus of work illuminating the various forms of enthusiasm and support for empire that characterized the late nineteenth and early twentieth centuries.[3] These studies have exposed the pervasiveness and persistence of imperialism as an "ideological cluster" by examining realms of culture such as commodity exchange, popular journalism, and travel and tourism.[4] Curiously, however, one of the most important Victorian realms of culture and ideology, religious belief and practice, has not been examined with the same intensity. The relationship of religious belief and empire, or the specifically religious dimensions of the imperial urge, have more often than not been ignored while missionaries, one of the largest, loudest, and most influential groups involved in the affairs of the British overseas, have attracted little detailed study from students of imperialism.[5] This lacuna in the scholarship of imperialism, as

3. Most notably the Manchester University Studies in Imperialism series edited by John M. MacKenzie, now numbering over twenty volumes, launched with his *Propaganda and Empire: The Manipulation of British Public Opinion, 1880-1960* (Manchester, 1984) and edited volume *Imperialism and Popular Culture* (Manchester, 1986).

4. For a recent review of this literature, see Dane Kennedy, "Imperial History and Post-Colonial Theory," *Journal of Imperial and Commonwealth History* 24 (1996): 345-63.

5. Where mentioned, they have been treated primarily as vehicles for advancing pro-imperial agendas: MacKenzie, *Propaganda and Empire*, pp. 32-33, and *Imperialism and*

Andrew Porter has recently noted, is surprising given the ease with which the concerns of the missionary project can be fitted into current conceptualizations of "cultural imperialism."[6] Perhaps the problem resides in the fact that missionaries tended to be problematic imperialists, pursuing many goals not strictly imperial, and sometimes clashing with colonial officials in pursuit of their particular spiritual agendas.[7] Yet imperialists of all persuasions had diverse motives, and it is more likely, as Jeffrey Cox suggests, that the dominant forms of imperial history cast missionaries as marginal actors in empire.[8]

That missionaries were not marginal to the British Empire, however, is attested by the scope of their resources and activity. Missionary societies were prominent among British imperial institutions and directly affected large numbers of people in Britain itself: by the turn of the century the British missionary movement was a truly imposing undertaking involving over nine thousand female and male missionaries, sixty missionary societies, and roughly £2 million annually. Missionary presses accounted for a substantial outflow of "missionary intelligence" on the empire and its "regions beyond." The largest society, the CMS, alone distributed 2.5 million magazines and 5 million papers and tracts in 1899.[9] That many churchmen at the turn of the century hoped to forge stronger links between missionary enterprise and imperial activity is evident from the articles and books by Angli-

---

Popular Culture, which completely ignores the subject of religiously motivated pro-imperial popular culture. The situation is paralleled in postcolonial treatments of imperial culture, following Edward Said's bald assertion that missions had "a complex apparatus" to achieve a simple goal: aiding European expansion and trade: *Orientalism* (New York, 1979), p. 100.

6. Andrew Porter, "'Cultural Imperialism' and Protestant Missionary Enterprise, 1780-1914," *Journal of Imperial and Commonwealth History* 25, no. 3 (1997): 368-71.

7. For the complexity of missionary motives, see Brian Stanley, *The Bible and the Flag: Protestant Missions and British Imperialism in the Nineteenth and Twentieth Centuries* (Leicester, 1990), pp. 11-31 and passim.

8. Jeffrey Cox, "Audience and Exclusion at the Margins of Imperial History," *Women's History Review* 3, no. 4 (1994): 504-6.

9. James S. Dennis, *Centennial Survey of Foreign Missions* (Edinburgh and London, 1902), pp. 257-60; CMS Archives, G/CC b 15, "Report of the Centenary Review Committee. Section XI," in *Centenary Review Reports* (private printing, 1899), p. 78. Anglican figures suggest that this amount represents about 12.5 percent of total church contributions. From 1860 to 1884 Anglican giving to foreign missions of £10,100,000 placed them as the third-largest Anglican charity, behind £35,175,000 for church building (43.1 percent) and £21,362,041 for elementary education (26.2 percent). *Official Yearbook of the Church of England, 1888* (London, 1889), p. xv. Proportions were similar within the Congregational churches. Hugh McLeod, *Religion and Society in England, 1850-1914* (New York, 1996), p. 147.

cans.[10] However, John Wolffe's conclusion, that by the end of Victoria's reign religious aspirations had given "moral and spiritual legitimacy" to the imperial project, does little to answer one crucial question that faces the historian of missions: "what was the precise relationship between Western religion and imperialism?"[11]

The answer to this question, of course, has as many dimensions as there were different mission fields, but the question is also relevant to the relationship of empire and mission in domestic British culture. Here variations in denominational outlook and theology alone substantially complicate the picture. In Bishop H. H. Montgomery we have a concrete example of a churchman and his followers who attempted to transcend the Anglican party to construct within the Church of England a missionary program that would embrace imperial involvement as a crucial component of the Anglican communion.

On the surface an easy identification between religion and empire would predict success for Montgomery's program, and his work as the secretary of the SPG should by no means be adjudged a complete failure. But beyond the simple renewal of the Edwardian-era SPG, the leaders of the Society were ultimately frustrated in their plan to use "support of empire" as an effective motivation for missionary action. Despite Montgomery's enthusiasm to construct an "imperial Christianity" and the support he received from the highest authorities in the church, he failed to attain his most ambitious goals. Thus the case of the SPG is especially instructive; while the Society was home to the most ardent missionary imperialists at the turn of the century, the disappointments suffered by Montgomery demonstrate that the equation between support of empire and support of missions was not an automatic one, and that the conversion of diffuse imperial enthusiasm into concrete support and action proved to be unexpectedly difficult. Bishop Montgomery and his supporters discovered that the construction of clear and proactive imperial policies in missions was unsustainable precisely because the contested discourse on empire, nationality, and race reinforced persisting divisiveness over theology, religious authority, and religious identity both in Britain and in the empire.

10. See most prominently, for example, G. Robert Wynne, *The Church in Greater Britain* (London, 1901); Henry H. Montgomery, *Foreign Missions* (London, 1902), pp. 1-2; John Ellison and G. H. S. Walpole, eds., *Church and Empire: A Series of Essays on the Responsibilities of Empire* (London, 1907); and the flurry of articles in the missionary magazines of the CMS and SPG.

11. Wolffe, p. 222.

II

Throughout the nineteenth century, both within the Anglican Church and throughout Britain, missionary effort was led by the ("Low") evangelical CMS. Its sister society, the High Church SPG, lagged far behind in income, enthusiasm, and influence. In the 1890s the CMS had particular success, adding hundreds of new missionaries and tens of thousands of pounds per year in contributions to its resources, culminating in what missionary observers all agreed was a spectacularly successful centenary celebration in 1899.[12] CMS successes and the more general "holiness" revivalism of the late Victorian period that drove them have drawn scholarly attention.[13] Less widely known, however, is that the CMS's achievements spurred efforts among its intrachurch rivals at the SPG to revitalize High Church missions in the 1890s and 1900s. The High Church party, which by then included the Anglo-Catholic heirs to the Oxford Movement and older varieties of Anglicanism impressed by tradition and episcopal authority, favored the SPG over the evangelical CMS.[14] Yet not all could comfortably support the SPG. Extreme Anglo-Catholics instead funneled their support toward missionary agencies that embraced an anti-Erastian episcopal independence and zealous devotion to ritual, most notably the Universities' Mission to Central Africa (UMCA), the Cambridge Mission to Delhi, and the Oxford Mission to Calcutta.[15] Because other High Churchmen disapproved of the more radical ritualism of

12. Between 1880 and 1903 the CMS missionary rolls increased from 256 to 977; centenary gifts amounted to £212,297; and between 1887 and 1899 CMS annual income advanced from ca. £200,000 to over £300,000. E.[ugene] S.[tock], "The Position of the Society," *Church Missionary Intelligencer*, n.s., 28 (December 1903): 883; Eugene Stock, *The History of the Church Missionary Society: Its Environment, Its Men, and Its Work*, 4 vols. (London, 1899 and 1916), 4:14, 16. In contrast, between 1887 and 1900 SPG income increased by only £10,000 to about £100,000 per annum, and one-fifth was raised of the bicentenary fund target of £250,000: C. F. Pascoe, *Two Hundred Years of the S.P.G.: An Historical Account of the Society for the Propagation of the Gospel in Foreign Parts, 1701-1900*, 2 vols. (London, 1901), 2:832d, and table p. 832.

13. For example, Andrew Porter, "Cambridge, Keswick and Late Nineteenth Century Attitudes to Africa," *Journal of Imperial and Commonwealth History* 5, no. 1 (October 1976): 8; Porter, "Evangelical Enthusiasm, Missionary Motivation, and West Africa in the Late Nineteenth Century: The Career of G. W. Brooke," *Journal of Imperial and Commonwealth History* 6, no. 1 (October 1977): 23-46.

14. Peter Benedict Nockles, *The Oxford Movement in Context: Anglican High Churchmanship, 1760-1857* (Cambridge, 1994), pp. 19, 25-43.

15. Steven S. Maughan, "Regions Beyond and the National Church: Domestic Support for the Foreign Mission of the Church of England in the High Imperial Age, 1870-1914" (Ph.D. diss., Harvard University, 1995), pp. 85-95.

such enthusiasts, the SPG became a haven for moderate and nonpartisan varieties of High Churchmanship. Moderates — mostly High Church and Anglo-Catholic, but also some traditional Low Churchmen — found reason to maintain the older SPG tradition of claiming to be above party by articulating a set of nonsectarian church principles. On either side of the SPG rested more extreme ideals of church governance: the voluntary ideal embraced by the CMS that shaded over into "Puritan" sympathy with Nonconformists and the anti-Erastian separatism suggested in the independent episcopal governance of the UMCA.

Prior to the 1890s Anglicans from the High and Low traditions had been bitter combatants over issues of doctrine and church order. By the end of the century, however, damaging party strife had led to the evolution of powerful moderate parties in both camps and a growing desire within these to broker a reconciliation in the interests of church unity.[16] At the center of these developments were several English bishops, many of the younger clergy, and university students who as part of a growing student missionary movement advocated ecumenism and "scientific" methods of missionary planning.[17] Supporting this movement among Anglican students and younger clergy were the largely evangelical and increasingly ecumenical Student Volunteer Missionary Union (SVMU) and the activist Junior Clergy Missionary Association (JCMA) of the SPG. In particular, the JCMA held strong ideals of church unity, imperial engagement, and enthusiastic activism — uncharacteristic emphases within the conventional "high and dry" party the SPG had strongly represented in the past.[18] Because of this unconventional enthusiasm, and also the association of many of its leaders with Anglo-Catholicism, the JCMA was perceived by secretaries at the SPG as challenging the traditional appeal of the society, its deference to church hierarchy, and its commitment to cooperation with the British state. During the 1890s the JCMA clashed repeatedly with the professional staff of the SPG and its traditionalist secretary, Prebendary Henry Tucker, who sus-

16. Owen Chadwick, *The Victorian Church,* 2nd ed., 2 vols. (London, 1970-71), 2:357; Eugene Stock, "Concerning Some Misconceptions," *Church Missionary Intelligencer,* n.s., 29 (January 1904): 31-37; Maughan, pp. 509-12, 523-30.

17. Maughan, pp. 393-433.

18. The JCMA, led by John Ellison, thought of itself as "progressive" and generated increasing friction with an "old Brigade" at the SPG: Davidson Papers, vol. 68, fols. 243-44, Ellison to R. Davidson, 11 April 1901. As Bishop M. R. Neligan of Auckland recalled, JCMA members were thought of as "hot-headed, inexperienced, upsetting young men," but they brought a gradual change in attitude at the SPG toward imperial service: "New Zealand: An Ill-Constructed Quadrilateral," in Ellison and Walpole, eds., *Church and Empire,* p. 188.

pected the JCMA of desiring to transform the SPG into an organ for spreading Anglo-Catholic ritual.[19]

Despite resistance from Tucker, the JCMA party gained considerable influence with the bishops and the SPG Standing Committee by recruiting talented university graduates and revitalizing SPG local organization. It carried its program at the SPG when, after the failure of the SPG bicentenary in 1901, a commission of bishops determined to place a new secretary at the Society. The moderate High Churchman and imperial enthusiast Bishop Henry Montgomery was selected in 1901 with JCMA support by a committee of six English bishops and given a mandate to "remake" the SPG.[20] His larger dream, however, was to reinvigorate the church itself by directly linking the fortunes of Anglicanism with the British Empire. Through a missionary program relying heavily on episcopal authority, Montgomery and his JCMA supporters hoped to effect a reconciliation between the parties of the church while marshaling party energy against the religious doubts bred by the modern world. In pressing this vision of an imperial missionary church, the "progressives" at the SPG sought to force a sweeping reconsideration of the role of the Church of England in the empire.

Montgomery's plan to transform the Church of England's imperial role appeared more realistic than it otherwise might have because of troubles at the CMS following its centenary. The CMS, previously the undisputed leader of church missions, experienced financial deficits brought on by its rapid extension of overseas work, and a new wave of attacks by evangelical radicals who condemned it for tolerating ritualism in the church. A crisis of confidence at the CMS resulted from a perceived "pause in missionary progress."[21] This CMS crisis reinforced a new sympathy with cooperative Anglican missionary ventures that had been growing through the 1890s between Anglican missionary agencies, and with the articulation of an imperial vision for the Society.[22] With Evangelicals at the CMS thus more receptive to cooperation

19. Maughan, pp. 434-56.

20. The bishops, headed by Randall Davidson, recruited Montgomery to generate enthusiasm; Davidson in particular was Montgomery's pilot through the dangerous shoals of English church politics: Davidson Papers, vol. 151, fols. 335-44 and 348-51, Montgomery to Davidson, 4 October and 13 December 1901.

21. E. Graham Ingham, "Why Should There Be a 'Pause'?" *Church Missionary Review* 60 (May 1909): 257.

22. This cooperative spirit toward empire was strengthened by successes in Uganda under imperial protection. It received clear articulation by T. A. Gurney in a groundbreaking article in the CMS's "serious" magazine, which for the first time approached imperialism as a topic in itself for consideration in relation to foreign missions: "Modern Imperialism and Missions," *Church Missionary Intelligencer*, n.s., 27 (July 1902): 485-86.

than they had ever been, Montgomery launched his bid for leadership of an Anglican imperial program, drawing the previously separatist High Church SPG into the mainstream of British foreign missions for the first time.[23]

Educated at Harrow as a "Broad Church Evangelical" by F. W. Farrar and trained for ordination as a conservative High Churchman by Charles Vaughan, Montgomery's diverse religious background encouraged him to strive for unity in the Anglican communion.[24] Born in India to an influential East India Company official of the "Punjab School" and strongly influenced by the environment of his first episcopal appointment, the white settlement colony of Tasmania, Montgomery developed an elevated view of British imperial power.[25] Prior to his appointment to the secretaryship of the SPG, he had agitated for missionary activity in the Australian church, and although he agonized over abandoning his colonial bishopric after only twelve years of work, with encouragement from the English bishops he saw the SPG appointment as an opportunity to transform the church itself.[26] His imperial fervor came to maturity in the 1890s, when public support for imperial ideologies, both in England and in the white settlement colonies, was at a historic high point.

Both the party of the Liberal Imperialists led by Lord Rosebery and the conservative Tariff Reformers under Joseph Chamberlain suggested that empire could help relieve the social problems of an urban industrialized England. Montgomery transferred these assumptions to the church by arguing that missions could excite denominational unity, defuse party tensions at home, and encourage the acceptance of the status quo in matters of church authority.[27] He made these plans public with his book *Foreign Missions* —

23. Following the conventions of the day, the terms "evangelical" and "evangelicalism" will be capitalized when they refer to Anglican Evangelicals, who made up a distinct party in the wider evangelical world.

24. Geoffrey Stephens, *H. H. Montgomery — the Mutton Bird Bishop,* University of Tasmania Occasional Paper 39 (Hobart, 1985), pp. 1-2.

25. India Office Library, MSS. Eur.D.1019/2, Robert Montgomery Family Correspondence, 1842-87, vol. 2, H. H. Montgomery, "Robert Montgomery of the Punjab. From 1839 to 1857," typescript.

26. Fearing criticism of abandoning difficult colonial work, Montgomery requested an "order" from the bishops: Lambeth Palace Library, Frederick Temple Papers, vol. 49, Montgomery to Temple, 7 June 1901, fols. 30-35; Maclagan to Temple, 7 June 1901, fols. 37-38; Montgomery to Temple, 17 June 1901, fols. 51-56. See also M[aud] M[ontgomery], *Bishop Montgomery: A Memoir* (London, 1933), pp. 47-48.

27. Bernard Semmel, *Imperialism and Social Reform: English Social-Imperial Thought, 1895-1914* (Cambridge, Mass., 1960); Andrew Porter, *European Imperialism, 1860-1914* (London, 1994), pp. 31-38.

written on his England-bound steamer journey in 1901 from Tasmania — wherein he made explicit his conviction that "[t]he clergy are officers in an imperial army" who, when "full of the Imperial spirit, not merely of the empire of England, but of something still greater, the empire of Christ," could remove the primary obstacles to missionary success, "party spirit" and a "want of missionary zeal."[28] Fulsome imperial sentiments were not isolated or even novel at this time, but they held a new significance coming from Montgomery because of the specific religious program to which he attached them. He imagined himself an "Archbishop of Greater Britain," with the "dearest dream to make S.P.G. the 'centre of reconciliation'" in the church.[29]

Montgomery's enthusiasm marked him as a natural candidate for the secretariat of the SPG; however, by the time he was appointed in 1901, the new century was already presenting unanticipated challenges. After the South African War the flood of missionary and imperial enthusiasm characteristic of the 1890s began to recede as attention shifted among advocates of empire to the need for social improvements at home.[30] Within the church, the parties were forced to confront the new religious challenges posed by theological modernism and declining levels of worship in English society. Montgomery sought to meet these challenges by coordinating SPG efforts with those of Anglican Evangelicals and advocating an outspoken imperialism that would link missions and the formal empire in explicit and concrete ways. Thus the SPG under Montgomery attempted to replace the evangelical enthusiasm for revivals and conversions, a style that was repugnant to High Churchmen, with a new enthusiasm for the British Empire.[31]

By 1905 Montgomery had reorganized the SPG, paying special attention to the integration of women into its home organization.[32] His efforts led to

28. H. H. Montgomery, *Foreign Missions*, pp. 1-2, 10, 145.

29. The larger argument, of course, was that a strengthened church would have more resources for expansion on all fronts: Davidson Papers, vol. 151, fols. 284-87, H. H. Montgomery to R. Davidson, 27 May 1901.

30. For the role of "Broad Church" Anglicans, see G. R. Searle, *The Quest for National Efficiency: A Study in British Politics and Political Thought, 1899-1914* (London, 1971), pp. 97-98.

31. For enthusiastic support from the younger clergy unions of both SPG and CMS, which met jointly from 1899 onward, see CMS Archives, G/AC 4/5175, typescript, speech of Rev. Ernest N. Coulthard, 7 February 1899.

32. Under Montgomery, the Women's Missionary Association (WMA) (founded as the Ladies Association in 1866) became the Committee for Women's Work (CWW), with a degree of autonomy and influence that women at the CMS regarded with envy. United Society for the Propagation of the Gospel [USPG] Archives, H 3, box 2, typescript, H. H. Montgomery, "Survey of My Stewardship. 1902-1918," pp. 2-6; CWW 90, Report, Annual

increased income at a time when many missionary societies saw stagnant contribution levels, and a strong perception of increased "warmth" in the Society.[33] Under Montgomery the SPG, which had never attracted levels of support comparable to the CMS, and still fell short of doing so, nonetheless began to usurp the reputation of the CMS as the most innovative and influential missionary force in the church. Montgomery's plans facilitated levels of Anglican collaboration that would have been unthinkable in the midst of earlier ritualist controversies. The close connection he had from 1903 to the new archbishop of Canterbury, Randall Davidson, further strengthened SPG influence.[34] The CMS was not, of course, severed from evangelical culture, nor could its influence as the largest missionary society in Britain be completely appropriated, but its troubles led CMS leaders to emphasize their moderate loyal churchmanship as a strategy to consolidate the loyalties of "respectable" Anglicans. Their moderation created a more favorable atmosphere for Montgomery's bid for leadership.

During this period of rising religious difficulties, many churchmen, accustomed to thinking of colonies as a defense of nation, came to imagine foreign missions as a potential defense of the church.[35] After the turn of the century, churchmen almost unanimously proclaimed foreign missionary activity vital to the Church of England's life and health.[36] To prosper, the church had to address questions of imperial scope. In a letter to Randall Davidson in 1899, after praising the enthusiasm of the CMS, Montgomery commented "[h]ow interesting it is too to see how the devotion of the CMS party is in one channel & *does not touch* great *social questions.* It doesn't come into their ho-

---

Conference, 30 April 1903, Special Sub-Committees and Reports of Conferences, Minute Book, 1898-1930; CWW 71, "Report of the Special Committee on the Relations between the W.M.A. and the S.P.G.," 2 April 1903, pp. 2-3, Women's Home Organisation Advisory Group, Minute Book, 1903-9.

33. When Montgomery arrived in 1902, regular annual income at the SPG was £88,586; when he left in 1918, it had risen to £148,381, or 68 percent. Pascoe, 2:832, and H. P. Thompson, *Into All Lands: The History of the Society for the Propagation of the Gospel in Foreign Parts, 1701-1950* (London, 1951), p. 722. Also USPG Archives, H 3, box 2, typescript, H. H. Montgomery, "Survey of My Stewardship. 1902-1918."

34. Davidson was the first primate with long and demonstrated support for foreign missions: G. K. A. Bell, *Randall Davidson: Archbishop of Canterbury,* 2 vols. (London, 1935), 1:46.

35. For an earlier example, see James Johnson, ed., *Report of the Centenary Conference on the Protestant Missions of the World held in Exeter Hall,* 2 vols. (London, 1888), 1:435.

36. Charles Gore, leader of the Anglo-Catholic party, and Hensley Henson, the chief exponent of Anglican modernism, also emphasized the imperial mission of the church as a primary concern: H. H. Montgomery, *Foreign Missions,* p. 11; Roger Lloyd, *The Church of England, 1900-1965* (London, 1966), pp. 68-70.

rizon." The natural conclusion for one preoccupied with healing the church and extending its influence in British society was: "Truly the marriage of High & Low is needful."[37] Through such a marriage the enthusiasm of evangelicalism could be absorbed and redirected to the benefit of church projects at home as well as abroad. As he wrote in one of his early statements of purpose: "The expansion of SPG which is to be the new factor in this century is in a sense to revolutionize Church ideals and make the ancient Church of England more completely an Imperial Church — the unit being the world and not the United Kingdom."[38]

Strikingly, the primary purpose of Montgomery's plans was not to advance evangelistic conversion: much as secular imperialists looked to empire as a realm of salvation for England,[39] success at the SPG meant that the Society "might help to check the falling off in men in Holy Orders in England as well as supplying the world." Similarly, leaders at the CMS such as Eugene Stock came to embrace more fully the idea of using missionary societies to ameliorate church party strife. Montgomery's goal was the creation of a "Pax Evangelica" in which the supporters of the missionary societies would be "indirectly banded together" against the English Church Union, Confraternity of the Blessed Sacrament, and Church Association.[40] In this way Montgomery could also imagine the SPG, previously home of the old "high and dry" churchmanship, reestablishing its historic claim as the truly nonsectarian representative of Anglican missions, a claim implied in its practice of choosing its missionaries through the Archbishops' Board. Furthermore, in an atmosphere where the increasing radicalism of extreme Anglo-Catholics was beginning both to destroy what post–Oxford Movement unity had been achieved among High Churchmen and to erode traditional High Church belief, Montgomery's imperial program can be seen as an attempt to move the SPG beyond reliance on an older constituency and claim a broad Anglican middle ground opening between Anglo-Catholicism and "holiness"-inspired Evangelicalism. Because the CMS had so strongly identified itself with the enthusiastic, undenominational impulses of Keswick evangelicalism, while at

37. Davidson Papers, vol. 519, fols. 244-47, H. H. Montgomery to R. Davidson, 12 July 1899.

38. Davidson Papers, vol. 151, fols. 322-23, H. H. Tasmania [Montgomery] to the Standing Committee of the SPG, 17 August 1901.

39. MacKenzie, *Propaganda and Empire,* p. 2.

40. Davidson Papers, vol. 151, fols. 348-51, H. H. Montgomery to R. Davidson, 13 December 1901. The first step in this program, Montgomery asserted, would be to arrange that neither the SPG nor the CMS would have any paid members belonging to any partisan society.

the same time the most stridently Anglo-Catholic societies like the UMCA had broken free from the SPG umbrella and insisted on local episcopal autonomy, this strategy held considerable appeal. Even the JCMA, for all its apparent radical enthusiasm, ultimately eschewed the logic of separate diocesan-based societies embodied in the UMCA and stood, as supporters of the SPG, for a nonpartisan central Anglicanism.

Montgomery was exceedingly talented in articulating an ideal of imperial cooperation that appealed to the enthusiasm of young High Churchmen. However, while he developed the SPG ideal of "imperial Christianity" and in the process revitalized the Society, his larger project to unify the church through an appeal to the empire was less successful. Very little materialized out of Montgomery's program beyond his successful agitation for the international and comprehensive Pan-Anglican Congress of 1908. Montgomery wanted to direct the attention of a troubled home church overseas, and thereby create an area of consensus. However, he had no means of compelling acceptance of his imperial rhetoric, especially in a church that was home to historically antagonistic parties, and which had largely ceded independence to overseas bishops in their dioceses long before.[41] One of the chief difficulties of Montgomery's scheme, which Davidson realized from the beginning, was that a vision of church unity achieved through an engagement with empire was frightening to many in the church who prized the independence which the historically broad Anglican communion provided. Moderate High Churchmen and Evangelicals alike desired a more unified communion, but there was no explicit agreement on the basis of this union. Montgomery implied something close to imperial federation. Eugene Stock of the CMS advocated something nearer to cooperative evangelization. Archbishop Davidson favored worldwide Anglican concord through consultation. All hoped for a Christian community in which deep involvement with foreign evangelization would erase domestic controversy; none put forward clear and open plans. Their fellow churchmen, trained in an individualist and often confrontational communion, remained wary.

Within ten years, Montgomery's imperial missionary bid to unify the church and infiltrate the empire had collapsed. There appear to be three major reasons for its failure. First, the old divisions between Evangelicals, Anglo-Catholics, and "rigid" High Churchmen flared up, despite their common ab-

41. Hans Cnattingius, *Bishops and Societies: A Study of Anglican Colonial and Missionary Expansion, 1698-1850* (London, 1952), pp. 188-91, 195-229. On the strained relations between overseas bishops and missionary societies, see William Shenk, *Henry Venn — Missionary Statesman* (Maryknoll, N.Y., 1983), pp. 35-37; T. E. Yates, *Venn and Victorian Bishops Abroad,* Studia Missionalia Uppsaliensia 33 (Uppsala and London, 1978).

horrence of the threat of liberal theological modernism. Second, the Anglican clergy remained preoccupied with domestic problems. Third, churchmen disagreed over the proper basis for meaningful Christian imperial engagement. Montgomery's program was launched with several practical steps: the SPG itself was reorganized, the JCMA relaunched its Council for Service Abroad to attract clerics to colonial service, and plans for the Pan-Anglican Congress were undertaken. From 1903 the new archbishop of Canterbury assisted, emphasizing Lambeth Palace as a clearinghouse for worldwide episcopal correspondence, and publicly campaigning to raise scholarship money for study at Oxford or Cambridge to encourage promising public school boys "to offer themselves as Missionaries in the Imperial work of the Church of England."[42] Such moves were visionary, but the world in which the SPG operated — especially as conditioned by the limitations imposed by church parties, local preoccupations, and the imperatives of missionaries in the field — redirected his program and diluted his efforts. The most obvious reason for the ultimate failure of Montgomery's program is easy to identify: in an age of defensiveness in both the High and Low Church parties, foreign activity, itself contested on many levels, had a limited ability to displace the local concerns on which the social reality of religiosity in England was based.

III

One of the greatest obstacles to any program for Anglican Church unity resulted from the stubborn persistence of party divisions within the communion. For generations competition and sectarian identity had been a primary factor in generating missionary support.[43] Doubtful as Montgomery's original premise was that missionary preoccupations could heal party rifts within the church, even more doubtful was the idea that unity within the church would increase levels of support for foreign missions. Long experience suggested instead that it was precisely competition and sectarian identity that most strongly animated supporters. Because so much of the Victorian missionary ethos had been based on this competition, it was risky to dilute the core of individualist evangelicalism that had underpinned the Victorian missionary

42. Davidson Papers, vol. 151, fols. 348-51, H. H. Montgomery to R. Davidson, 13 December 1901; Bell, 1:715-16; M. Montgomery, p. 53.

43. Stuart Piggin, "Sectarianism vs. Ecumenism: The Impact on British Churches of the Missionary Movement to India, c. 1800-1860," *Journal of Ecclesiastical History* 27 (1976): 387-402. Cf. David Savage, "Evangelical Educational Policy in Britain and India, 1857-60," *Journal of Imperial and Commonwealth History* 22 (1994): 432-61; Wolffe, pp. 40-42.

movement. If many Evangelicals were becoming more comfortable within the church, and embraced the novel idea that the use of episcopal influence could strengthen Evangelicalism, the ever closer relations between the CMS and the SPG also reirritated old wounds originally inflicted in the battles over ritual. Strikingly, the chief opposition that arose to Montgomery's "Archbishop of Greater Britain" rhetoric came not from anti-imperialists, but from three different religious quarters: from Evangelicals who imagined that he had been "appointed by a set of Ritualists to advocate Ritualism all round the world," from Anglo-Catholics associated with the *Church Times* who opposed any move perceived to increase the power of central church authority above the level of the diocese, and from exclusivist supporters of the SPG itself who resisted cooperation and association with Evangelicals and Nonconformists.[44] It was this party identity that the system of independent voluntary missionary societies served. Bishops such as Davidson found that the situation required them to restrain enthusiasts who envisioned abolishing the societies to create a unified church missionary structure to serve a unitary empire. To one such JCMA enthusiast, Davidson suggested that "it must always be remembered that the real supporters of Missions in the Church of England have for generations past been mainly those who belong to the Evangelical School. Even now, for one High Church layman who is really aglow with belief in Foreign Missions, you have ten or twenty Evangelical laymen." Trust Bishop Montgomery quietly to advance unity in church missions, Davidson advised his correspondent, but respect the societies for their function of raising both interest and funds, while waiting in the knowledge that unified church missionary boards were the ultimate, if long-range, goal of the episcopate.[45]

Continuing divisions manifested themselves in familiar ways. "Rigid churchmen" at the SPG, for example, despite Montgomery's pleading, resisted ecumenical cooperation outside the communion. These actions increased tensions with Evangelicals, particularly when the most unbending of High Churchmen accused them of fostering "pan-Protestantism" and Anglo-Catholics criticized them for hindering progress toward achieving reunifica-

44. Davidson Papers, vol. 151, fols. 324-25, 333-34, 335-44, H. H. Montgomery to R. Davidson, 21 August 1901, 8 September 1901, and 4 October 1901.

45. Davidson Papers, vol. 68, fols. 300-301, R. Davidson to A. W. Bedford (chairman, London JCMA), 15 October 1901. The history of controversy over unified Anglican missionary boards extended back to the 1870s. CMS Archives, G/AC 1/18, Henry Wright to W. T. Bullock (SPG secretary), 19 February 1873; G/AC 1/19, Wright to E. Sturgis, 6 July 1874; and G/AZ 1/7, no. 52, H. Fuller, Eastern District, Lincolnshire and Nottinghamshire, *Association Secretaries' Reports, 1895*, p. 10; Eugene Stock, *My Recollections* (London, 1909), p. 234.

tion with the Eastern churches and Rome.[46] Notably, the secretary of the SVMU, Tissington Tatlow, was able only by both threats and persuasion to secure SPG participation, first in his own conferences, then in the ecumenical Edinburgh World Missionary Conference held in 1910. Along with the other societies, the SPG had become dependent on the student movement for its best recruits, yet only after Tatlow threatened to "wash my hands of the S.P.G." if delegates were not sent to the 1907 SVMU Conference, was Montgomery able to persuade the Standing Committee to acquiesce.[47] The Standing Committee did not, however, abandon its more traditional reticence toward contact with Nonconformists: in December 1908 the attitude of "the more rigid churchmen" reasserted itself when the Standing Committee refused the invitation to be officially represented at Edinburgh, although ultimately this decision was reversed.[48]

Party identities also took on new meaning in the age of theological modernism. The burgeoning student volunteer movement was ironically involved in the reemergence of party strife, because although it emphasized ecumenical cooperation, through its advocacy of "scientific" missions it questioned both biblical infallibility and the emotionalism of "holiness"-based evangelicalism. These positions added fuel to the fires of controversy ignited by the advance of theological modernism.[49] The original intent of the evangelical student movement had been, like Montgomery's imperial program, to dissolve party difference in the work of mission. But instead, student activity served to publicize the new set of fault lines emerging in British religious culture. At the SPG one of Bishop Montgomery's primary goals was to integrate as many "advanced" students as possible and reconstruct the Society as modern, open, and progressive. This meant taking an open, even adventurous approach to missionary problems. *The East and the West,* the SPG's new "issues and problems" publication, was launched to engage the SPG with the concerns that drove the student missionary move-

46. Stock, *History,* 4:26.

47. Tissington Tatlow, *The Story of the Student Christian Movement of Great Britain and Ireland* (London, 1933), pp. 308-9; USPG Archives, X 366, p. 483, Montgomery to Tatlow, 12 June [190]7.

48. The SPG made the decision to send official delegates to the Edinburgh conference only under intense pressure and at the last moment: USPG Archives, CWW1, "Monthly Summary. May 24, 1910," Committee for Women's Work Secretary, Monthly Summaries and Reviews, 1910-1918. The issue was confused enough for both Archbishop Davidson's biographer and H. P. Thompson's authorized history of the SPG to suggest that SPG delegates did not attend: Bell, 1:573-74; Thompson, p. 487.

49. Maughan, pp. 514-17.

ment, but instead brought the wrath of traditional constituencies down on the Society. Two articles in the journal's first issue, in October 1903, explored biblical criticism, the most theologically sensitive of subjects.[50] The response was an immediate denunciation of the SPG for promulgating "sceptical theories."[51] Montgomery was forced to back down, and a public expression of regret by the SPG "settled" the matter.[52] A serious obstacle had arisen to Montgomery's missionary program, as he suggested in a circular letter explaining the SPG position:

> We found ourselves met by two very strong parties: in one sense these parties represented the old and the young — surely a very interesting fact. My correspondence has proved to me that there are a great many of the older men who have been made very unhappy by the discussion of views in regard to what is called the Higher Criticism in S.P.G. Magazines. Their letters showed me that their alienation would lead to a large withdrawal of money from the Society unless some means could be discovered to comfort them without in any way compromising our position, which of course is as broad as the Church.[53]

The whole episode was testimony to how older issues of party had been transformed by modernism, and how they operated on a plane separate from, but also connected to, imperial issues. The youthful imperial enthusiasms of university-based Christians were essential to any Anglican imperial program, yet the concerns of those same Christians to engage "modern" subjects, both theological and imperial, were increasingly at odds with the anxieties felt by the deeply orthodox lay and clerical supporters of the traditional missionary societies. Growing generational differences were making

50. James Monroe, "The Teaching of the Higher Criticism Incompatible with Missionary Work, *East and the West* 1 (October 1903): 413-20, and X. P., "The Higher Criticism Considered as an Aid to Missionary Work," pp. 426-37 in the same volume. Critics assumed that X. P. was the editor, Charles Robinson.

51. USPG Archives, H 37, folder 1 (labeled X1481), J. C. Sharpe, "The 'Higher Criticism' and the S.P.G.," *Church Times,* 18 November 1904. The SPG archives contain about forty letters of opposition to the article, and about seventy signed, preprinted forms supporting a joint letter of protest sent in March 1903.

52. A special SPG session produced "a most dramatic scene" where the objectors demanded among other things a disavowal of modernism in all forms. They had to be satisfied with a resolution expressing the regret of the Society over the controversy. Despite the trouble, the majority present supported the apologetic Society. Davidson Papers, vol. 98, fols. 22-25, H. H. Montgomery to R. Davidson, 3 November 1904.

53. USPG Archives, H 37, folder 1 (labeled X1481), circular letter, 15 December 1904.

Montgomery's bid to reassert the nonsectarian ideals of the SPG even more problematic.

A second factor undermining Montgomery's program was the continuing preoccupation of most bishops and clergy with the domestic problems of the church. From the beginning, many doubted the realism of Montgomery's plans, none more so than Montgomery's own commissary for thirteen years, F. D. Cremer. Cremer objected to Montgomery accepting the post of SPG secretary because he believed Montgomery could do little in it: "Have you weighed up the exact value of my friend's high-sounding phrases," he asked Archbishop Temple, "'Archbishop of the World of Missions,' 'Worldwide oversight'? Are they not a trifle inflated? Is the office of Secretary to *one* of our great Mission Societies anything of the sort?? Ought it to be?"[54] Cremer questioned the visionary nature of Montgomery's ambitions, but he also hinted at a deeper problem: that clerics were unlikely to focus so closely on missions when the church was facing important domestic challenges. This became rapidly evident to Davidson upon his elevation to Canterbury in 1903. Home problems demanded immediate attention, including the needs both to reconcile orthodox conservatives (both High and Low) to theological modernism and to attract qualified clergy and laity alike to the church.[55] These problems revived older criticisms that foreign missions drained much-needed clerical resources from the home shores, making it more difficult for Davidson to support missionary schemes when the promised waves of new church enthusiasm did not issue from SPG efforts.

By 1905 Davidson and the bishops regarded the plans of "imperial" Anglicans with increasing skepticism. When the JCMA requested from the bishops another "authoritative" call for foreign missionaries, Davidson resisted. He asked John Ellison, leader of the JCMA, to imagine what might happen if an authoritative call were made:

> I wonder if you can yourself picture what would occur if I as Archbishop were to send, say, to the Bishop of Worcester, or Hereford, or Norwich, a definite request for, say 10 or 12 of his best younger men to be sent up within a year for me to despatch them over the world. . . . Or, if this be an unfair presentation of what is desired, let us say that [a] committee is to make a claim on England now for say 60 men, who must be young and keen and presumably unmarried, and that in the name of the Church they are to be summoned to go abroad. Are the Colonial

54. F. Temple Papers, vol. 49, fols. 63-66, F. D. Cremer to F. Temple, 10 July 1901.

55. Lloyd, pp. 75, 102, 131, 148.

> members of this committee to take into account or to disregard English needs and English conditions? Or is England simply to be a region whereon they draw, leaving the home authorities to arrange the details for meeting the demand?[56]

As the pragmatic leader of a church governed largely through consent and good will, Davidson was forced to question the grandiose imperial rhetoric of both the JCMA and Montgomery and to recognize the fundamentally local nature of religious experience in England.

Looking backward from 1905, Davidson had to assess how successful the imperial strategy at the SPG had been. A program launched by the JCMA in 1898 to rotate curates through an imperial appointment was a case in point: "I rather gather," Davidson wrote, "that the Council for Service Abroad, which we used to believe was going to do so much, is now regarded by the junior clergy generally as a self-assertive interloping authority which ought to be snubbed or abolished."[57] What Davidson understood was exactly that principle which Evangelicals had asserted throughout the nineteenth century: in a broad Anglican communion concerned first and foremost with local affairs, the prosecution of foreign missions had to operate as an act of persuasion rather than an act of compulsion. At the heart of much missionary persuasion was a distinctive, individualist evangelical spirituality, which militated against any narrow programmatic imperial vision. Regardless of the expansive rhetoric of Ellison and Montgomery, the attention of the home episcopate, which largely controlled the training and assignments of non-Evangelical clergy, was never deeply or consistently engaged with an imperial missionary program. Montgomery's arrival at the SPG and his prosecution of a self-important program for the Society did not change this. The matters that the English bishops dealt with, not surprisingly, were overwhelmingly domestic, as the agenda sheets of Lambeth Palace bishops' meetings show.[58] In the end, the heartfelt rhetoric of the late 1890s had not produced significantly higher levels of missionary commitment among High Churchmen. By 1905 the impressive-sounding initiatives of Montgomery and the JCMA had clearly begun to wear thin, and critics within the JCMA itself noted the lack of action. The association, with 5,524 members in 1906, had sent roughly 1

56. Davidson Papers, vol. 106, fols. 237-39, R. Davidson to J. Ellison, 17 October 1905.

57. Davidson Papers, vol. 106, fols. 237-39, R. Davidson to J. Ellison, 17 October 1905.

58. Between 1897 and 1902 the monthly assembly of English bishops typically considered one item of significance to foreign missions among fifteen to thirty items. From 1902 onward, even this level of attention diminished: Lambeth Palace Library, Bishops' Meetings, 1897-1907, BM 4.

percent of its members, 56 persons, abroad in the previous year, and at most of its meetings, Edgar Rogers complained, "the only inspiration was tea and a pipe, with clerical gossip afterwards."[59]

The problem of how precisely to define the nature of imperial missionary engagement — in the face of both conflict in British politics and the rise of colonial nationalisms — provided the third and final straw that broke Montgomery's program. Increasingly the nature of the British Empire was becoming a topic for debate and division in the missionary world. The SVMU was again implicated in the disturbance through criticisms made by some of its prominent leaders of British imperial practice. Such criticism divided student leaders from many at the SPG, and is perhaps best exemplified by the evolving ideas of Frank Lenwood, the Congregationalist student leader who vigorously pushed the SVMU in the "modernist" direction, became a missionary, and then, in 1912, the foreign secretary of the London Missionary Society.[60] From his Indian experience Lenwood came to believe the operation of the British Empire was deeply flawed due to a want of sympathy with indigenous peoples. Although no anti-imperialist and quite prepared to criticize the "Indian character" and Indian culture, Lenwood developed an equally harsh assessment of the cold, hierarchical, and bureaucratic operation of the Raj in India. While many missionaries were at fault, their attitudes were only a small part of a larger problem among Indian civil servants and English "sahibs" in general. Unless this attitude was conquered, progressive student leaders suggested, the empire would be misgoverned, and perhaps lost.[61]

Thus student leaders forwarded a criticism of the cold, formal, distant imperial policy of colonial rulers, emphasizing instead the need for "a Christianized world with a juster and nobler order of society."[62] While Lenwood's missionary liberalism retained social Darwinist assumptions about established racial hierarchies, racial difference was not his primary emphasis.[63] Instead he called for sympathetic friendship with indigenous Chris-

59. "The Junior Clergy Missionary Associations: A Plea for Development," *East and the West* 4 (October 1906): 400-401, 403.

60. Tatlow, pp. 202, 220, and passim.

61. Council for World Mission Archives (LMS), Home: Personal, Box 7, folder 6, Frank Lenwood, circular letter, 26 February 1908, Agra. For a similar response from onetime JCMA member and missionary to India in the Cambridge Mission to Delhi, C. F. Andrews, see Daniel O'Connor, *Gospel, Raj, and Swaraj: The Missionary Years of C. F. Andrews, 1904-14* (Frankfurt am Main, 1990), pp. 32-33 and passim.

62. Dr. Cairns, quoted in Tatlow, p. 250.

63. Brian Stanley, "Manliness and Mission: Frank Lenwood and the London Missionary Society," *Journal of the United Reformed Church History Society* 5 (1996): 465-69.

tians. This appeal seemed dangerously naive to more strident imperialists at the JCMA and the older stalwarts at the SPG offices. Uncritical imperial sympathizers emphasized the "responsibilities" of rule and the "backwards" nature of colonial subjects.[64] Firmness and morality at home were paralleled by the assertion that firmness and Christianity were the backbone of imperial rule and missionary activity.[65] These divisions over how to conceptualize imperial relations were reinforced by political agendas as well: for missionary progressives like Lenwood, the rejection of unpalatable forms of imperial control was implied by the liberalism swept into office by the 1906 election. This liberalism reacted against "the doctrine of efficiency which Rosebery and other such had been preaching"; rejected "Toryism, by its very essence, always considering the system, the machine, their efficiency"; and embraced a "real Liberalism always . . . thinking first of the well being and above all the free development of the individual."[66] While these styles of "liberal imperialism" were hardly the stuff of anti-imperial radicalism, the well-known predilection of Anglicans for Conservative politics did not mesh well with liberal trends among student missionary leaders.

In essence, church leaders discovered that a real imperial policy, as opposed to vague support for the idea of empire, could be a dividing rather than a unifying force. Thus when John Ellison wrote enthusiastically to Archbishop Davidson in 1905 that the Church of England should publicly join the rising bandwagon of support for Lord Meath's "Empire Day," Davidson's response was cautious.[67] To Meath's own importunities that the church should vigorously support the celebration, Davidson replied that changes in the political situation could turn involvement by the church into a political liability.[68]

Davidson's reticence over one of those popular imperialist rituals that became so common in the early twentieth century indicates his assessment that for a broad and comprehensive institution like the Church of England, much like a political party, an empty rhetoric of empire was far safer than any con-

64. E.g., former JCMA member, later bishop of Auckland, M. R. Neligan, in Ellison, ed., p. 180 and passim.

65. W. T. Gaul, bishop of Mashonaland, "South Africa: The Anglican Church and Imperialism," in Ellison, ed., *Church and Empire*, p. 239.

66. Council for World Mission Archives (LMS), Home: Personal, Box 7, folder 10, typescript, [Frank Lenwood], "The British Government of India," 22 March 1911.

67. Davidson's caution was striking because the idealism and rhetoric of Meath's Empire Day were in many ways so similar to those of the missionary movement: Davidson Papers, vol. 115, fols. 187-88, printed sheet, "Empire Day" [Address of Lord Meath in Saint James's Hall, London], 24 May 1904.

68. Davidson Papers, vol. 115, fols. 207 and 208, Davidson to Lord Meath, 8 December and 15 December 1905.

crete imperial policy. He agreed, nevertheless, to circularize the foreign bishops to help make a decision on church promotion of Empire Day, and discovered that in Montreal, Melbourne, and Rupert's Land, Empire Day had rapidly become a popular "public holiday." In other colonies less heavily influenced by English immigration and settlement like Jamaica and particularly India, it was not only less popular but Anglican leaders perceived its celebration as positively detrimental to the interests of the church.[69] This information sealed the issue; Davidson decided the church would not officially support Empire Day.

The problems raised in securing church unity under the banner of empire were reinforced in 1908 when Montgomery's scheme to draw the entire church together to face its challenges corporately materialized in the form of the Pan-Anglican Congress, the "special 'child'" Montgomery advocated in his first SPG Annual Sermon in Saint Paul's.[70] But, as Eugene Stock openly acknowledged, the congress, originally conceived of as advancing foreign missions, came to focus primarily on the internal order of the Anglican communion and the home problems of the church.[71] After the Pan-Anglican Congress, Montgomery could no longer ignore the fact that imperial rhetoric, which roused JCMA gatherings, was more difficult to sell as relevant to solving the diverse problems of the entire communion. The concerns of the congress came to revolve around continuing social challenges and the declining power of the church at home, to which missions had been presented as a potential, but by 1908 evidently inadequate, solution.

Furthermore, given emergent colonial nationalisms, the rhetoric of an imperial church produced problems of definition in the "white settlement" colonies and positive hostility in India.[72] Bishop G. A. Lefroy wrote frankly in preparation for the congress that educated Indian sentiment found "the very word and thought of Imperialism . . . in the highest degree obnoxious," and that widespread fears existed among Anglo-Indian Christian thinkers regarding the outcome for the church if ideas associated with "Empire and Imperialism" spread within it. The Indians, Lefroy commented, "resented bitterly the claim of racial superiority" and "coldness" in English manners.[73] In this

69. Davidson Papers, vol. 115, fols. 217-19, 222-28, 239, 243, replies of W. B. Montreal (Bond), S. P. Rupertsland (Matheson), H. L. Melbourne (Clarke), E. Jamaica (Nuttall), R. S. Calcutta (Copleston), and others.

70. M. Montgomery, pp. 57-58.

71. Stock, *History,* 4:549.

72. On colonial nationalism, see S. C. Donaldson, archbishop of Brisbane, "Australia," in Ellison, ed., *Church and Empire,* pp. 152-68, and Neligan, "New Zealand," pp. 169-91.

73. G. A. Lefroy, "Our Indian Empire," in Ellison, ed., *Church and Empire,* pp. 66-68;

respect, a clear weakness in Montgomery's position was its openly racist basis: while he encouraged "sympathy" toward other races, he also insisted upon each race occupying "the place reserved from the beginning for it" — implying a clearly subordinate position for all outside the "Anglo-Saxon" race.[74] Montgomery also expressed horror at the prospect of miscegenation, going so far as to propose a "new Table of Prohibited Degrees" in the Prayer Book to police marriages between "races too far apart."[75]

Despite the problems that emphasizing such a clear construct of racial hierarchy produced in the mission field among non-European peoples, a language of race allowed Montgomery to shape a strong rationale for church unity. For Montgomery, in addition to demonstrating the spiritual unity of humanity, foreign missions also illuminated racial hierarchies within Christianity at large. With this emphasis he could begin to explain sectarianism in the history of Christianity as a manifestation of racial temperament. While he imagined the "imperial church" to be an expression of Christian unity through worldwide Anglicanism, he also imagined this union to be racially divided, with the British "church of the race" analogous to the Church of England. Anglicanism could embrace many races, but could be led by only one. Once the church of the race, the Church of England, was educated to the essential reality of its Anglo-Saxon racial unity, internal divisions could be vanquished, the church could fully embrace its fated duty to lead, and division with the world Anglican communion could be diffused by a patronizing tolerance of racial difference by the church's "natural" leaders.[76] Awareness of racial hierarchy, then, formed the basis of an understanding that could unify the church, strengthen the empire, and brace the loyalty of its subjects. Such open theorizing about the fixity of race and the hierarchy of functions that it set for the various Anglican "racial" churches of the world was not unusual at this time, but was more characteristic of High Church than of evangelical mission theorists. Rapid changes in the mission field, however, ensured that Montgomery's program would suit neither indigenous Christians, whose le-

---

O'Connor, pp. 76-79; Jeffrey Cox, "George Alfred Lefroy 1854-1919: A Bishop in Search of a Church," in *After the Victorians: Private Conscience and Public Duty in Modern Britain: Essays in Memory of John Clive,* ed. Susan Pedersen and Peter Mandler (London and New York, 1994), pp. 55-76.

74. H. H. Montgomery, introduction to *Mankind and the Church, Being an Attempt to Estimate the Contribution of Great Races to the Fullness of the Church of God,* ed. H. H. Montgomery (London, 1907), p. xii.

75. H. H. Montgomery, *Service Abroad: Lectures Delivered to the Divinity School of the University of Cambridge* (London, 1910), pp. 9-10.

76. H. H. Montgomery, introduction to *Mankind and the Church,* pp. xxvii-xxviii.

gitimacy in places like India was contested by nationalists, nor missionaries in the field who, like G. A. Lefroy, embraced the wisdom of crafting missionary ideologies that would not unnecessarily antagonize the ethnic, racial, or national identities of the proselytized.

IV

Bishop Montgomery's imperial vision was attractive to many in 1899, but it had grown out of Australian conditions. His primary assumption was that the reflexive support of empire characteristic of Australian Anglicans could be easily extended throughout England and the empire. As the debate over what sort of empire the British should have unfolded in the Edwardian period, Montgomery advanced an ideal of imperial federation in which colonies would be tied with the bonds of Anglican spiritual loyalty to the mother country. But he miscalculated the appeal of this program because of his misperception, in part as a colonial, that Britain could operate as a powerful metropolitan engine of empire if only its people could be educated to their duty. This misperception was reinforced at the SPG, which, supporting comparatively few missionaries in tropical Africa and India, worked more than other societies in areas dominated by settler populations. The SPG's relative underexposure to non-Western peoples and Montgomery's colonial experience combined to support an imperial vision much more concentrated on common cultural, national, and racial identity than those developed by many evangelicals.

Following the Pan-Anglican Congress Montgomery drew back from agitating for an "imperial church." By 1910 the obvious course open to leaders of Anglican foreign missions was to attempt to reclaim the Victorian strategies that had gathered support in the past. Hopes that Anglican unity would be achieved through the actions of university students, ecumenical cooperation, and imperial progress were thwarted by university heterodoxy, reemerging party factionalism, and discomfiture with contending imperial models. While the core ideologies of the Victorian Anglican missionary movement, rooted heavily in an evangelical impulse and a parallel High Church reaction, continued to have a force and resilience through the Edwardian period, the bid to unify foreign missions in the shape of heroic imperial Anglicanism had failed.

In June 1915 Bishop Montgomery gave a revealing address to the home workers of the Society at the SPG summer school in Eastbourne. He explained that the Anglo-Saxons were an impatient race from a temperate climate advancing through the lethargic tropics; as they progressed, they were constantly diverted by the internecine squabbles of a people ruthlessly critical not only of others, but of themselves. This critical British nature expressed itself nowhere more virulently than in the most important project the race was undertaking: the planting of churches in every land. While Montgomery had not abandoned his imperial and racial paradigms for explaining missions, he had reversed his stand on imperial church unity, suggesting instead that restless, critical, individualistic chauvinism was at the heart of British strength.[77]

The reemergence of old disputes between High Churchmen and Evangelicals after 1910 forced the SPG to draw back from its Edwardian commitment to cooperation and ecumenism — to reassert its traditional principles and ideals — for fear of losing the support of "eager, fervent, convinced Churchmen" in the midst of the lukewarm religious moderation that ideals of imperial church unity seemed to have produced.[78] This constituted an admission of the failure of Montgomery's ambitious imperial dreams. The shift in course was undoubtedly influenced by the Anglican infighting that resulted from the 1913 Kikuyu Controversy, in which the Anglo-Catholic bishop of Zanzibar accused the Evangelical bishops of Mombasa and Uganda of heretically ecumenical associations with Nonconformists.[79] The partisan rhetoric unleashed by Kikuyu helped to reestablish the overriding importance of maintaining an identifiable and distinctive religious identity at the SPG. Maintaining openness to Protestant ecumenism was increasingly incompatible with holding the allegiance of the SPG's Anglo-Catholic constituency. With this last prewar controversy, Montgomery's hope for building church unity through imperial enthusiasm was finally and irrevocably dashed.

The CMS experienced similar problems at this time, as the advanced thinking of university progressives began to cause widening rifts in its Evangelical constituency. The problem, quite simply, was that reforms which included strong imperial linkages, introduced both by Montgomery and by student enthusiasts at the CMS, were not widely popular. The personal motivation of local organizers was crucial, and their most constant motivation was religious party loyalty or spiritual enthusiasm. This religious motivation was open to influence by imperial ideas only when those ideas did not erode spiritual inspiration or party identity.[80]

77. Henry Montgomery, *The S.P.G.: Its Principles and Ideals* (London, 1915), pp. 3-6.

78. H. H. Montgomery, *Principles and Ideals*, p. 6.

79. Stock, *History*, 4:409-24; Bell, 1:690-708; Herbert Maynard Smith, *Frank, Bishop of Zanzibar: The Life of Frank Weston* (London, [1926]), pp. 145-70; Roland Oliver, *The Missionary Factor in East Africa* (London, 1965), pp. 222-30.

80. USPG Archives, H 138, Home Organisation, Rough Minutes Book, 1910-1928, Meeting, Home Organisation Sub-Committee, 10 October 1910, "Report of the Membership Secretary," 1 October 1910.

In a fundamental way Bishop Montgomery's imperial program represented an attempt to draw the experience of holiness-inspired activism and enthusiasm outside the subculture that produced it. Anglican missionary leaders tried to shift from a missionary movement that focused on religious identity to one that focused on the wider role of missions in imperial and national life. However, removing foreign missions from the important place they had assumed in the debate over church identity, spirituality, and theology, thus disconnecting them from party passions, ran counter to the defining role played by party in the Victorian church. Missionary strategists, focusing on the leadership supplied by university recruits, allowed the concerns of the university — most prominently, religious innovation and imperial efficiency — to redefine the missionary movement. Yet the event that in 1913 finally saved the financial situation of the CMS after years of growing deficits was not a manifestation of programs for church unity, imperialism, or missionary cooperation, but a return to the style and language of Victorian revivalism. For in that year, with the CMS in the midst of crisis, the Society organized a meeting of local association officers, conducted on the model of a holiness prayer meeting, and appealed to its supporters to provide direction for the Society. The appeal within the revivalist idiom worked. Evangelicals rallied at the 1913 Swanwick Conference to promise immediately 1,000 gifts of £100 each, clearing the accumulated deficit and placing the CMS on a new financial footing.[81]

It was the Pan-Anglican Congress of 1908 that had been the turning point in the fortunes of Bishop Montgomery's Edwardian missionary bid. For that congress demonstrated that foreign missions could not form the focal point of church renewal. Quite to the contrary, the Pan-Anglican demonstrated that domestic issues of worship and religious observance remained paramount with the church hierarchy. The plan to implement a student-driven "imperial Christianity" had not united the church, but rather further divided it: traditional communities of the faithful were distressed by the issues of theology that church unity raised. Additionally, direct engagement with troubled questions of imperial rule raised fears that missions would be implicated in the worldly doings of traders, secular officials, and the military. Perhaps as important, the new strategy did not significantly increase missionary recruitment or funding. Imperial ideas were useful when general and amorphous, but could not bear the weight of a concrete program because just as Victorian Christians could not agree on dogma, they could not agree on what "imperial Christianity" should entail. The attempt to redefine an essentially evangelical

81. Stock, *History,* 4:481-85.

missionary movement for pan-Anglican purposes after 1900 instead generated more sectarian feeling and activity within the church, returning the movement to its Victorian footing on the eve of the great social and theological changes that would emerge after the First World War.

Church, State, and the Hierarchy of "Civilization": The Making of the "Missions and Governments" Report at the World Missionary Conference, Edinburgh 1910

BRIAN STANLEY

I

Recent academic interest in the celebrated World Missionary Conference held in Edinburgh in June 1910 has focused on Commission IV, "The Missionary Message in Relation to Non-Christian Religions."[1] No such detailed attention has been devoted to the other seven commissions which reported at Edinburgh, and none at all to Commission VII, concerned with the relations of missions to governments. The report of Commission VII is the slimmest volume of the nine produced by the conference. It is also one that will disappoint any modern commentator who approaches the text in the hope that it might concentrate on the issues of ethical principle raised by missionary association with Western imperialism. The report discussed at length the extent to which missionaries might legitimately appeal to the civil power, utilize the privileges of extraterritoriality, and claim compensation for loss of life or property. These topics, however, were treated as technical questions of international relations rather than as expressions of a fundamental disequilibrium of power between the Western and non-Western worlds. Moreover, the language and very structure of the report supply plentiful ammunition for the case that the

1. K. Cracknell, *Justice, Courtesy, and Love: Theologians and Missionaries Encountering World Religions, 1846-1914* (London, 1995), chap. 4; J. S. Friesen, *Missionary Responses to Tribal Religions at Edinburgh, 1910* (New York, 1996).

I owe particular thanks for assistance and permission to cite from their respective archives to: Ms. Cynthia Frame, formerly Preservation Librarian, Burke Library, Union Theological Seminary, New York; and M. Pierre Beffa, Librarian, World Council of Churches, Geneva.

mainstream Protestant missionary enterprise as it neared its peak was saturated with the racial assumptions of the age of high imperialism. Nevertheless, this paper will seek to show that there was more to Commission VII than meets the eye.

The selection of missions and governments among the eight constitutive themes of the 1910 conference was claimed as innovative and potentially controversial, not least because of the strain it might impose on the unity of the conference.[2]

The international committee that planned the Edinburgh conference made a decision that was to prove significant for the construction of the report of Commission VII. In each case, those members who resided in the same country as the chairman of the commission were to form an executive committee, with the members resident on the other side of the Atlantic forming an advisory and cooperative council under the guidance of the vice chairman of the commission.[3] It is clear from the example of Commission VII that this procedure, whether intentionally or not, marginalized the Continental European members of the commissions: the report of Commission VII was the product of a British-American axis. It is equally clear that the numbers of serving missionaries on the commissions were kept low, not simply by the practical difficulties of securing their attendance at the commission's meetings, but also by a principled decision, presumably reflecting the view of the conference chairman, John R. Mott, that "it was obviously desirable that the main body of each commission should consist of those whose outlook upon the world field was detached from special experience or interest in a particular country."[4] For Commission VII, that principle appears to have inclined Mott to look first for distinguished laymen of wide experience in public and foreign affairs, and only secondarily for missionaries whose work had brought them into frequent contact with government.

The president of the World Missionary Conference, Lord Balfour of Burleigh, was appointed chairman of Commission VII. "B. of B.," as he was frequently known, was a prominent layman in the Church of Scotland, but married to an Anglican. Secretary of state for Scotland in A. J. Balfour's Conservative administration from 1902 to 1903, he was a stout defender of the

2. World Missionary Conference, 1910, *Report of Commission VII: Missions and Governments* (Edinburgh and London, n.d.), p. 173 (hereafter *MG*); W. H. T. Gairdner, *"Edinburgh 1910": An Account and Interpretation of the World Missionary Conference* (Edinburgh and London, 1910), pp. 154-55. In fact, the topic of missions and governments had received some brief attention at the ecumenical missionary conference held in New York in 1900.

3. *Addresses and Papers of John R. Mott*, 6 vols. (New York, 1946-47), 5:6-7.

4. *Addresses and Papers of John R. Mott*, 5:7.

principle of church establishment, and of established institutions generally.[5] His presidential role in the conference as a whole was largely decorative, and his influence on the report of Commission VII appears to have been scarcely more substantial. Far more influential was the secretary of the commission, Dr. Andrew Blair Wann of the Church of Scotland Foreign Mission Board. Wann had been educated for the Church of Scotland ministry at the University of Edinburgh under Robert Flint, a theologian who reconciled Calvinism with an optimistic and evolutionary view of human history as the story of humanity's progress toward truth, freedom, and justice.[6] Wann then served in India as a higher educational missionary from 1886, becoming principal of the Church of Scotland College in Calcutta in 1904, and then first principal of the united Scottish Churches College there from 1908 to 1909.[7] Wann wrote all of part I and significant sections of part II of the report. He was the author, for example, of the opening theoretical statement asserting that "the consideration of the relations between Governments and Missions may be theoretically regarded as a study of one aspect of the great problem of the relation between the Church and the State, and the discrimination between their respective spheres."[8] For Wann, as also, one suspects, for Lord Balfour, the topic of mission-government relations was primarily a geographical extension of the historic concern of Western political theory with the lines of demarcation between church and state. The other British members of the commission were not particularly noteworthy, with the exception of Sir Robert Hart, by now retired from his post as inspector general of the Chinese imperial customs service.[9] There is, however, no evidence that he exerted any in-

5. On Lord Balfour of Burleigh, see *Dictionary of National Biography; Dictionary of Scottish Church History and Theology,* ed. N. M. de S. Cameron (Edinburgh, 1993); Lady Frances Balfour, *A Memoir of Lord Balfour of Burleigh K.T.* (London, n.d.).

6. Wann took his MA in 1881, and BD in 1884; he received an honorary DD from Edinburgh in 1909. On Flint, professor of systematic theology at Old College, 1876-1903, see A. P. F. Sell, *Defending and Declaring the Faith: Some Scottish Examples, 1860-1920* (Exeter, 1987), pp. 39-63.

7. See A. B. Wann, *The Message of Christ to India: With a Memoir and Appreciations of the Author,* ed. J. Morrison (Edinburgh and London, 1925), pp. xii-xxii.

8. *MG,* p. 2.

9. Other British members included: Wellesley Bailey, founder of the Mission to Lepers in India (now the Leprosy Mission); Sir Andrew Wingate, a retired member of the Indian civil service; Bishop E. G. Ingham, former bishop of Sierra Leone and home secretary of the CMS; George Cousins, a former LMS missionary in Madagascar, and joint foreign secretary of the LMS, 1898-1909; Lawson Forfeitt, a BMS missionary on the Congo from 1889 to 1909; and Marshall Hartley, a member of the secretariat of the WMMS since 1888, who had previously served in the Methodist home ministry.

fluence on the text of the report. The European continent was represented, somewhat unevenly, by three Germans with strong colonial connections and one Norwegian.[10]

With a British chairman, an American was required for vice chairman to preside over the American "advisory council." Mott's choice (if, as seems probable, Mott did the choosing) was Seth Low, a New York merchant and Episcopalian. Temple Gairdner described Low as "a man whose name is honoured all over the States as one who has stood and fought for civic and political righteousness."[11] Low, however, was no radical but a pillar of the municipal and mercantile establishment in New York. He had made his fortune in the Far Eastern silk trade, and served as Republican mayor of Brooklyn from 1882 to 1885, and subsequently as mayor of New York from 1901 to 1903.[12] As vice chairman, Low had responsibility for issuing a questionnaire to the North American mission boards and using the responses to present a report from the advisory council to the British executive committee. This American questionnaire (app. B below) differed significantly from that sent out by the Edinburgh conference office to selected individual missionaries (app. A below).

Although Seth Low had an important role in determining the stance taken by part II of the report on certain controversial points, a much more substantial contribution to the text of part II came from another member of the American advisory council, Rear Admiral Alfred Thayer Mahan, naval strategist, historian, and another Episcopalian. Mahan is remembered today as the architect of the strategic doctrine of American sea power, articulated through his highly influential work *The Influence of Sea Power upon History, 1660-1783* (1890) and a string of later publications on British and American naval history.[13] He was a global political thinker who saw East Asia and the Pacific Rim as the key to global security and the potential source of catastrophic conflict between East and West. That threat could be averted only by the extension of American power and its corollary, Christian civilization, to the Far East and the Pacific. Mahan was a fervent believer in the providential

10. The Continental members were: Max Berner, president of the Berlin Missionary Society, and since 1903 "Private Counsellor of the German Government in Missionary Affairs"; Professor Gottlieb Haussleiter of Halle; Carl Mirbt, professor of church history at Marburg; and Lars Dahle, missionary in Madagascar, 1870-88, and from 1889 secretary-general of the Norwegian Missionary Society.

11. Gairdner, p. 53.

12. *Dictionary of American Biography,* 20 vols. (New York, 1927-36) with seven Supplements (New York, 1944-81), and B. R. C. Low, *Seth Low* (New York and London, 1925).

13. R. Seager II, *Alfred Thayer Mahan: The Man and His Letters* (Annapolis, Md., 1977).

destiny of nations and consistently defended the use of force in international relations. Events such as the American annexation of the Philippines in 1898 were, in his view, part of a divine strategy for the incorporation of East Asia within Christendom.[14] In 1909, the same year he contributed so substantially to the Commission VII report, he published a devotional book, part of which argued that the English race, like Israel on her entry into Canaan, had been authorized by God to "redeem" American territory from the Red Indian and set it apart for a distinctive mission of universal salvation.[15] Mahan was, quite simply, an unashamed Anglo-American Christian imperialist.

A letter Mahan wrote to Low on 12 August 1909, reflecting upon the replies from the American mission boards to Low's questionnaire, was the near verbatim source for substantial sections of the report.[16] In addition, three of the eight findings of the commission, with which the report concluded, owed their origin directly or indirectly to his letter.[17] The letter so impressed Low that he adopted it as the core of the advisory council's report to the British executive committee of the commission, supplemented by a series of memoranda written by other members of the council in response to the letter. Portions of the memoranda also found their way into the final report. Though these memoranda, including Low's own, disagreed with Mahan on certain points, Mahan had thus set the agenda for the bulk of the interpretative section of the Commission VII report. It should also be noted that most of this section (part II) reflected the responses of the North American mission boards alone: Mahan's letter and the memoranda it elicited were written without any knowledge of the other two sets of responses — those of the British and European missions and the forty-one individual missionaries — which were considered solely by the British executive committee.[18]

14. R. N. Leslie, Jr., "Christianity and the Evangelist for Sea Power: The Religion of A. T. Mahan," in *The Influence of History on Mahan: The Proceedings of a Conference Marking the Centenary of Alfred Thayer Mahan's "The Influence of Sea Power upon History, 1660-1783,"* ed. J. B. Hattendorf (Newport, R.I., 1991), pp. 127-39.

15. A. T. Mahan, *The Harvest Within: Thoughts on the Life of the Christian* (Boston, 1909), pp. 118-24.

16. New York, Union Theological Seminary, Burke Library, Missionary Research Library Collection, World Missionary Conference, Edinburgh 1910, Box XVIII (microfilm in the Henry Martyn Centre, Westminster College, Cambridge; hereafter UTS, Box XVIII). Mahan's letter forms the first item in the printed report of the advisory council, entitled "Documents Submitted by the American Members of Commission VII" (hereafter "Documents Submitted"), and is the source of pp. 97-104, 106-8, and 111-14 of the printed report.

17. These were no. 2, "The right of entry for Christian missions" (p. 119); no. 7, "The Belgian Congo" (p. 121); and no. 8, "Preparation of a statement of principles" (p. 121).

18. Only four British missions replied to the questionnaire: the British and Foreign

With a part I based on an unusually small sample of missionary correspondents, and a part II composed largely in ignorance of those correspondents' replies, the report of Commission VII was shaped as much by metropolitan perspectives as by those from the field. In comparison with the British members, the North American arm of the commission was both more distinguished in political terms and also conspicuously lacking in members with firsthand mission experience. In addition to Low and Mahan, it included R. L. Borden, leader of the Conservative opposition in the Canadian parliament and later prime minister of Canada, and John Watson Foster, the lawyer and diplomat who served briefly as American secretary of state in 1892-93, and a significant figure in the American annexation of Hawaii. Borden made virtually no contribution to the commission. Foster, on the other hand, submitted a significant memorandum in response to Mahan's letter, and was instrumental in securing a statement from the solicitor to the U.S. State Department entitled "The Government of the United States and Foreign Missionaries," which was printed as appendix A to the final report.[19] The American churches were represented by William Lawrence, bishop of Massachusetts, chairman of the House of Bishops of the Protestant Episcopal Church and a personal friend of Theodore Roosevelt, and by Rufus M. Jones, the historian of Quakerism. In contrast to the British arm of the commission, there was only one representative of the American mission boards: the Reverend Dr. Thomas S. Barbour, foreign secretary of the American Baptist Missionary Union and the person chiefly responsible for introducing E. D. Morel's Congo Reform campaign to the United States.[20] His contribution to the report was considerable: a memorandum in response to Mahan was reproduced in the report, partly in the main text and partly as an appendix.[21] Of the seven North American members of the commission, only Low, Bishop Lawrence, and Barbour attended the conference.

Bible Society; the China Inland Mission; the Presbyterian Church of England Foreign Missions Committee; and the Sudan United Mission. It is possible that the executive committee decided not to send questionnaires to the larger denominational missions, but rely on individual responses.

19. *MG*, pp. 123-34. On Foster, see the *Dictionary of American Biography.*

20. W. R. Louis and Jean Stengers, eds., *E. D. Morel's History of the Congo Reform Movement* (Oxford, 1968), pp. 154, 183. In 1910 the American Baptist Missionary Union changed its name to the American Baptist Foreign Mission Society.

21. UTS, Box XVIII; "Documents Submitted," pp. 26-36. Much of Barbour's memorandum appears in *MG*, pp. 108-10 (to the end of sec. 3), and as app. D, pp. 140-41.

II

Three themes stood out in the report of Commission VII. The first was that the question of how missions should relate to governments must be approached with reference to the degree of "civilization" attained by both the people and the government of the territory concerned. The introduction to the report lamented the difficulty of making meaningful generalizations about the variety of governments with which missions had to deal, and concluded with a passage whose very construction revealed the view taken of the hierarchical nature of the range of human societies and polities. It is worth quoting in full:

> In Japan, *e.g.*, a fully civilised native Government rules over a civilised and yet non-Christian people; in its neighbour, China, the Government is both antiquated in methods and defective in policy, according to European standards, and is therefore to some extent limited in its actions by European influences; in India a foreign Christian Government controls the destinies of 300,000,000 Hindus and Mohammedans; in Mohammedan lands the law of Islam, which, strictly interpreted, absolutely prohibits conversion to Christianity, is applied with various degrees of rigour; in European protectorates over uncivilised regions the amount of control varies infinitely, and Government policy varies with it; and in barbarous lands, still independent, the caprice of the chiefs, checked only by ancient usage and hereditary superstition, modifies the relations between them and the missionaries day by day.[22]

Part I of the report then proceeded to survey the different mission fields in the descending order of hierarchy set out by this sentence: Japan; China, India, and the Dutch East Indies; the Islamic world; and finally, sub-Saharan Africa. The Caribbean and the Pacific islands were ignored altogether by Commission VII, and almost entirely by the other commissions, presumably because they were regarded as fully Christianized.[23] The exclusion of Latin America from the horizons of the conference for similar, but more ecclesiastically sensitive, reasons is better known.[24] Responsibility for both the text and

22. *MG*, p. 3.

23. Commission I described the Pacific islands as fully Christian, yet with much scope for continuing missionary work, whereas for the West Indies it regarded only the Hindu and Muslim population as relevant to its objects. See World Missionary Conference, 1910, *Report of Commission I: Carrying the Gospel to All the Non-Christian World* (Edinburgh and London, n.d.), pp. 132, 251.

24. W. R. Hogg, *Ecumenical Foundations: A History of the International Missionary Council and Its Nineteenth-Century Background* (New York, 1952), pp. 131-32.

construction of part I lay with Dr. Wann.[25] The concept of a hierarchy of civilization and polity appeared again in an alternative format in the opening sentences of part II, which were also written by Wann. "The differences in government with which the Commission is concerned are seldom political or constitutional, but arise from the nature of the religion and the stage of civilisation of the countries concerned." Part II then differentiated five categories of mission lands:

a. those of low civilization, but independent;
b. those of higher civilization, and independent;
c. those of low civilization, under Christian rule or influence;
d. those of higher civilization, under Christian rule or influence;
e. those of the highest international rank.[26]

The various mission fields surveyed in part I were then allocated to these five categories. Japan belonged to category (e); India to (d); the European colonial empires in Africa to (c); whilst China and Persia were examples of (b). But what of (a)? Whereas the scale at the beginning of part I had implied that "barbarous lands, still independent" were a continuing reality in which missionaries had to cope with "the caprice of the chiefs, checked only by ancient usage and hereditary superstition," part II now declared category (a) to be vacant: "The absolutely independent savage chief, representative of group (a), has disappeared; and the ethical and prudential rules governing the dealings of missionaries with such potentates, though intensely interesting as a study of character, need not occupy the attention of this Commission."[27] It is a mark of just how comprehensive was the partition of the tropical world undertaken by the European powers since 1880 that such a bold statement could in 1910 be made without fear of challenge. The significance of the declaration that group (a) had vanished from view lay, however, primarily in its implications for (c) — Africa under colonial rule.

Missions in African protectorates or colonies, according to part II, could expect the encouragement of the civil power on the ground of the proven value of the missionary enterprise to civilization, peace, and humanity. In such countries, the report went on, "there is no independent Government to be respected; there is no sensitive community, united by a great history or a great religion, to be approached with circumspection. Civilisation and reli-

25. *MG*, pp. 147, 184.
26. *MG*, p. 88.
27. *MG*, pp. 88-89.

gion come to them almost indistinguishably from the one power, and Missions and Governments may work in the closest sympathy."[28] The fact that tribal authorities had failed to survive as independent political entities posed a question mark against the right of those that remained as dependencies of European powers to command the obedience due to sovereign "governments."[29] As part I observed in relation to German East Africa, the "legal powers" of subject native chiefs were "somewhat indeterminate," confronting missionaries with the dilemma of deciding how far their authority was to be obeyed.[30] The report here was drawing on the testimony of Karl Axenfeld, *Missionsinspektor* of the Berlin Missionary Society. Axenfeld's reply to question II of the questionnaire had discussed the delicacy of a situation in which some chiefs exerted real authority and others a purely nominal one. If, for example, all orders from chiefs forbidding people to migrate to mission stations were to be respected, the labor market would be sabotaged and the industrial development of the protectorate imperiled. If, on the other hand, their orders were to be flouted with impunity, mission stations would become asylums for the disaffected and the chiefs rendered helpless as political authorities.[31]

Part II of the report gave some acknowledgment to the equilibrium maintained by such views as Axenfeld's by asserting that those forms of native chieftainship under European suzerainty which continued to command popular affection, preserve order, and "conserve national and tribal life" were lawful powers which deserved respect.[32] The main drift of its discussion of Africa was, however, in a contrary direction. Barbarous lands were, by definition, those whose authorities had failed to meet the ends which the Scriptures laid down as the purpose of civil government, namely, the maintenance of law and order. In many cases, the report noted, it was missionaries who had stepped into the governmental vacuum left by barbarism. Now that "civilised rule" had followed them, missionaries were well equipped to mediate between colonial governments and "the suspicious native races, resentful of in-

28. *MG*, p. 90. Wann, in an earlier draft, had included after "circumspection" the words "and a voluntary abandonment of the prestige of the ruling race" (UTS, Box XVIII).

29. See W. Ross Johnston, *Sovereignty and Protection: A Study of British Jurisdictional Imperialism in the Late Nineteenth Century* (Durham, N.C., 1973), passim.

30. *MG*, p. 79.

31. Geneva, Ecumenical Centre library, bound volume 280.215 W893cVII (hereafter "Commission VII replies"), pp. 557-59. On Axenfeld, see G. H. Anderson, ed., *Biographical Dictionary of Christian Missions* (New York, 1998), p. 34; H. Gründer, *Christliche Mission und deutscher Imperialismus 1884-1914* (Paderborn, 1982), pp. 42-43, 102-3; and M. Wright, *German Missions in Tanganyika, 1891-1941* (Oxford, 1971), pp. 121-25, 130.

32. *MG*, pp. 90-91, 93.

terference with their ancient ways, evil and good alike."[33] The normal expectation in category (c), therefore, was that missions and colonial governments should work in harmonious partnership toward the civilization of the population; indigenous authorities had little role to play in the process.

Wann was typical of those whose mission experience was limited to Asia in denying that African societies possessed any "sensitive community, united by a great history or a great religion." However, such cultural and racial myopia was not representative of responses to the questionnaire from Africa missionaries. The most striking examples of insistence on respect for the integrity of African cultures came in responses from French missionaries, and it may be that the French colonial policy of cultural assimilation provoked missionaries to adopt in reaction more self-conscious strategies of cultural indigeneity than many of their colleagues working in British colonial contexts.[34] Part II of the report noted such statements, and indeed used them to claim that "the reproach that missionaries desire to Europeanise the inhabitants of mission lands, if ever true, is now absurdly false."[35] Yet such evidence from the replies was not permitted to affect the fundamental categorization of cultures that provided the organizing framework for the report itself.

The report's division of mission lands according to their supposed position on the scale of civilization and good government was seen by the British arm of the commission to require clear emphasis.[36] The American advisory council, on the other hand, though not objecting to the hierarchy on principle, was anxious to stress that its validity was purely temporary: "In the references made to existing social and political distinctions, we would be carefully on our guard against the peril of creating the impression that, in our judgment, or in the judgment of missionaries, the existing distinctions are in so far of divine appointment that genuine aspiration for advancement is to be repressed or regretted."[37] This comment suggests that American Protestant thought may have been even more inclined than its British counterpart to filter evolutionary concepts of race through the mesh of a continuing firm commitment to ideals of a universal human capacity for progress. However, the majority of the commission — whether American or British — viewed the purpose of the scale not in didactic or theoretical terms, but as a prag-

33. *MG,* pp. 96-97.

34. Commission VII replies by E. Haug and F. Vernier, pp. 355-56, 415-16.

35. *MG,* p. 94.

36. UTS, Box XVIII, minutes of meeting of Commission VII, 17 December [1909], pp. 1-2.

37. UTS, Box XVIII, points submitted for consideration by Dr. Low in preparing reply to British members of Commission VII, p. 2.

matic rule of thumb to guide missionaries in decisions about the exercise or voluntary suspension of their political rights. This was made most explicit in a section of the report taken from Barbour's memorandum. The lower the position on the scale of advancement occupied by the country in which missionaries worked, the less appropriate it would be for them to insist on recompense for injuries suffered. On the other hand, in higher civilizations where freedom of religious belief and practice was protected by law, to cooperate with government in its duty of exacting just reprisals was quite legitimate.[38] The way the report applied the idea of a hierarchy of civilization was indebted to the debate provoked among the American members by Mahan's letter to Low. Mahan subordinated American orthodoxy on the separation of church and state to an exalted view of the divinely imposed duties of governments. He argued in favor of missionaries appealing to the civil (i.e., imperial) power for protection and redress, and demanding indemnities from native authorities in compensation for loss of property or even life. Such action, he maintained, was necessary to satisfy the universal claims of justice and public order.[39] Mahan's view, however, was not shared by the American members as a whole nor endorsed by the report. In what were termed the "peculiar" circumstances of China, where missionary replies differed over the propriety of making use of the privileges secured by the "unequal" treaties, the report came down on the side of discouraging appeals to the civil power.[40] By contrast, in countries where a high civilization guaranteed the rule of law in association either with Christian rule, as in India, or with a commitment to religious liberty matching that of Christian nations, as in Japan, resort to the civil power was encouraged.[41] In practice, as the report acknowledged, "vexatious questions" between missions and government were extremely rare in both India and Japan.[42] Hence the obligation to invoke the rule of law in support of religious freedom remained virtually redundant in "civilized" countries; if they were civilized enough to make the appeal to the rule of law possible, they were civilized enough to make it largely unnecessary.

In practice, therefore, the concept of an evolutionary hierarchy of race

38. *MG*, p. 108; see also Lord Balfour's comments in *World Missionary Conference, 1910*, vol. IX: *The History and Records of the Conference* (Edinburgh and London, n.d.), pp. 144-45.

39. UTS, Box XVIII, "Documents Submitted," pp. 8, 11-12. For Mahan's view of church-state relations, see R. Seager II and D. D. Maguire, eds., *Letters and Papers of Alfred Thayer Mahan*, vol. 3, *1902-1914* (Annapolis, Md., 1975), pp. 501-3, 507-9.

40. *MG*, pp. 7-22, 105.

41. *MG*, p. 105.

42. *MG*, pp. 4-5, 23.

and civilization was used to restrict rather than extend the contexts in which missions were encouraged to shelter under the umbrella of imperial power. The most blatant imperialist on the commission — Mahan — made no use of the concept in his submission to Low, and indeed seems to have been unsympathetic to using such distinctions as a guide for policy: for him, there was one set of absolute moral and legal norms to be applied globally. Africa, however, remained the problem for the commission's attempt to regulate missionary relations to government to the scale of civilization. According to Thomas Barbour's criteria, its indigenous authorities were insufficiently "civilized" to attract the "supporting public sentiment" that made it possible for missionaries to appeal to them to punish wrongs.[43] But equally those governmental structures were insufficiently "civilized" to provide security for the Christian convert. In such extreme conditions, an appeal by the missionary to the colonial power on behalf of the indigenous Christian community was sometimes, according to the report, the only avenue by which justice could be secured: "[U]nder some conditions even the intervention of the missionary to secure justice for the convert — a thing forbidden by European Ministers and deprecated by Mission Boards in the case of China — may be a necessary part of the missionary's work, as in European Protectorates over barbarous regions in cases where native chiefs tyrannise or European officials have not yet grasped the situation."[44]

III

The second recurring theme of the report was its claim that field opinion was "practically unanimous" that missionaries, confronted with the awakening of political and social aspirations throughout the world, "should have nothing to do with political agitation" but rather teach obedience to the "settled government." Although it was also reported that missionaries uniformly acknowledged their duty to press governments, particularly colonial ones, for the "removal of gross oppression and injustice," the report added this qualification: "provided that in so doing they keep clear of association with any political movement."[45] These assertions of Dr. Wann were reinforced in still more absolute terms by Seth Low when he introduced the report to the conference on 20 June 1910: "There is one . . . point on which . . . the missionaries

43. UTS, Box XVIII, "Documents Submitted," pp. 31-33; *MG*, pp. 109-10.

44. *MG*, p. 105. This section was apparently written by Wann.

45. *MG*, p. 95.

are absolutely at one, and that is that everywhere a missionary is under a moral obligation to abstain entirely from politics. There is absolutely no exception, I think, to the expression of that opinion, and I am quite confident that the Conference will share it."[46]

Most answers to question VI of the British questionnaire (app. A) were predictably hostile to any overt identification by missionaries with movements professedly critical of established governments.[47] This was especially so among the ten China missionaries, most of whom cautioned against any close association with the reform movement in the Chinese Empire.[48] Yet there were minority voices — Gilbert Reid and Timothy Richard — who assessed the reform movement favorably.[49] Only six questionnaire replies were received from India missionaries.[50] Whilst they certainly counseled against any identification with "agitation," most also revealed more active sympathy with national aspirations constitutionally expressed than might be deduced from the report. Thus Herbert Anderson, the Baptist Missionary Society (BMS) India secretary, warned against missionaries gaining a reputation for political activity, yet proclaimed his personal sympathy with the politicians of the "Indian Moderate School."[51] D. A. Rees, a British Wesleyan missionary in Bangalore, similarly advised missionaries to take no active part in politics themselves, but also stated that Indian Christians should have "the fullest liberty to espouse any political cause they deem good."[52] Perhaps the most remarkable of the India replies was from Andrew Low, serving with the United Free Church of Scotland in Rajputana, who presented the case for a total severance of all mission schools from government grants-in-aid. Low argued not from principled commitment to voluntaryism, but from the standpoint of how Indians must inevitably perceive the funding of a foreign religion by a conquering government. Imagining a Buddhist power taking control of the British Isles, establishing Buddhist schools, and endowing them so lavishly as to overshadow entirely the ill-equipped existing schools, he concluded that, in such a situation, "there is no doubt but that our sympathies would be most

46. *MG*, p. 149.

47. Low's American version contained no such question (cf. apps. A and B).

48. E.g., Arnold Foster of the LMS; Commission VII replies, pp. 21-22.

49. Commission VII replies, pp. 105-6, 95.

50. Although it is possible that more questionnaires were sent out than were returned, the unusually small number of India correspondents for Commission VII suggests that the commission may have decided in advance that in India the subject was too straightforward to need much investigation.

51. Commission VII replies, p. 177.

52. Commission VII replies, p. 196.

heartily with them in objecting to the *status quo*."[53] No such attempt to adopt the perspective of the indigenous observer can be found in the report.

These expressions of sympathy with moderate nationalist aspirations may be thought to have little political significance, but in 1909-10 sufficient numbers of missionaries were declared supporters of the Indian National Congress for their presence to be hard to ignore, even by those to whom it was unwelcome.[54] Hence Wann's original draft of the section on social and political aspirations in India contained the observation: "In past days a few missionaries have thrown themselves with enthusiasm into the Congress movement; possibly they were more than balanced by others who regarded the Congress with suspicion, if not aversion. And certainly the approbation of the Missionary body, as a whole, was not with them."[55] Wann's comment attracted the disapproving notice of members of the American advisory council, who made representations to Seth Low that it would be wise to avoid any reference to the "attitude of missionaries to the movement in India for native independence" on the grounds that, from the perspective of American views of British colonial rule, it was desirable to avoid either "championship of this rule on the one hand" or "arraignment of it on the other."[56] The objection in this instance was almost certainly to anything that might be construed as indicating missionary condemnation of British rule, though it is not easy to conceive how Wann's dismissive allusion to missionary support for the Congress could be read in this way. This section of the report ended by roundly applauding Indian Christians as a shining example of "loyalty to a Government which they recognise as now ruling in India under God's Providence for the ultimate restoration of India to its place among the nations." The Americans raised no objection to *that* markedly pro-British statement, whereas the offending passage about support for the Congress movement was omitted from the final report.[57] All that remained about missionary attitudes to Indian nationalism was an assertion that, whilst most missionaries agreed that "a transfer of power to the natives of the soil should proceed *pari passu* with their advance

53. Commission VII replies, p. 207.

54. A. Mathew, *Christian Missions, Education, and Nationalism: From Dominance to Compromise, 1870-1930* (New Delhi, 1988), pp. 125-44; G. A. Oddie, "Indian Christians and the National Congress, 1885-1910," *Indian Church History Review* 2, no. 1 (June 1968): 47-48; G. Thomas, *Christian Indians and Indian Nationalism, 1885-1910: An Interpretation in Historical and Theological Perspectives* (Frankfurt, 1979), pp. 123-33.

55. UTS, Box XVIII, Drafts by Dr. Wann, Series 4:A, pp. 41-42, and 4:C, p. 19.

56. UTS, Box XVIII, Points submitted for consideration by Dr. Low, p. 2.

57. *MG*, p. 35. The offending statement was removed from the end of the first paragraph, p. 34.

in enlightenment and moral stability . . . very few indeed consider it part of their duty to spend any part of their time and thought in propagating the idea."[58] Whilst this claim was doubtless accurate, it served to accentuate the monochrome tone of this section of the report in comparison with the more variegated character of the questionnaire replies from India.

The majority of the Africa correspondents, like those from other fields, gave answers to question VI on the questionnaire that balanced respect for the authority of colonial governments with some form of statement of the priority of African interests.[59] In some replies the juxtaposition of imperial loyalty and higher Christian commitment was stark.[60] Where the colonial government was neither British nor Protestant, the missionary replies to question VI still maintained a similar equilibrium, although positive enthusiasm for empire was replaced by theological affirmations about the need to obey legitimate authority. Thus from Portuguese Congo (Angola), R. H. Carson Graham of the BMS referred to the intrinsic tendency of Protestantism to generate social and political freedom, while emphasizing that this could only be along lines of "Christian Evolution rather than Revolution" (an interesting phrase coming from an Ulster Calvinist in the Spurgeonic tradition). Nonetheless, Graham was at pains to stress that Baptist missionaries in Angola had always taught obedience to the Portuguese government, and indeed claimed that, if the BMS mission were withdrawn, the Portuguese would require three times their present soldiery to hold the country and collect revenue. "Yet it is said," commented Graham wryly, "that Missionaries meddle unwarrantably with politics."[61]

Two of the Africa responses were extensively cited in the report — those from Frederick B. Bridgman, an American Board missionary in Natal, and Bishop Alfred Tucker of Uganda. Bridgman we shall consider below. Tucker's response reviewed the history of the Church Missionary Society Uganda mission in order to explain how it was, "through the necessities of the case, that the missionaries became mixed up with the politics of the country." Tucker proclaimed that "as a general principle I am entirely opposed to missionaries mixing themselves up in the political affairs of the country in which their lot is cast." The Uganda circumstances were "exceptional." The natives were already bound to the missionaries by "very close ties of affec-

58. *MG*, p. 34.

59. E.g., Robert Laws of Livingstonia; Commission VII replies, p. 380.

60. E.g., W. R. Miller; Commission VII replies, pp. 391-92.

61. Commission VII replies, pp. 331-34. On Graham see his *Under Seven Congo Kings* (London, n.d.); also my *The History of the Baptist Missionary Society, 1792-1992* (Edinburgh, 1992), pp. 340, 343.

tion and duty," and it would have been "a grave dereliction of duty" by the latter to refuse to offer the political guidance that was sought.[62] All this Wann reproduced in the report, as if Uganda could be presented to the conference as the single exception that proved the rule of "no politics for missionaries." What Wann did not include, however, were Tucker's answers to question VI about political aspirations:

> Sympathy with the political aspirations of the people among whom the Missionary is working, so long as it does not involve taking sides in political controversy, I should regard as almost a duty. The national spirit which has recently shown itself in Bunyow [Bunyoro] and Toro in Central Africa, is a case in point. The longing for the fullness of national life in these countries is all for good and involves no political controversy. The Missionery's [*sic*] duties and sympathies in a case like this are, in my view, really identical. But when political controversy is involved the Missionary should rigorously hold aloof. His mission is to both parties and to take sides would be to fail in one of the primary duties of his calling.[63]

Tucker, like many Christian imperialists of his generation, combined fervent enthusiasm for the British Empire with a readiness to champion indigenous interests in a mixture that challenges modern preconceptions. He had recently, for example, successfully contested proposals from the governor of Uganda to introduce Indian settlers to Busoga which, he argued, would be fatal to the Basoga, who were still recovering from a sleeping sickness epidemic.[64] Tucker's prohibition on pastoral grounds of missionaries from taking partisan stances on disputed issues should not, therefore, be taken as evidence of absolute political quiescence. It has to be said that the commission's bland reiteration of the "no politics" rule failed to communicate to the conference the complex variety and not infrequent subtlety of the political responses displayed by those who had to grapple firsthand with how to relate mission activity to colonial governments and their dependent indigenous authorities. It also reflected an extraordinarily narrow view of what constituted "politics" and a deliberate blindness to the major role missionaries frequently played in the introduction of Western codes of law and order.

62. *MG*, pp. 73-75.

63. Commission VII replies, pp. 406-7. Tucker had toured Bunyoro and Toro earlier in 1909.

64. A. P. Shepherd, *Tucker of Uganda: Artist and Apostle, 1849-1914* (London, n.d.), pp. 183-84.

IV

The report's third predominant theme was articulated by Mahan in his letter to Low of 12 August 1909: "With the single glaring exception of the Congo State, and probably of the Portuguese African possessions, there can be elicited, I think, a concensus [*sic*] of opinion that the missionary cause on the whole has been gaining, and continues to gain, in the esteem and favour of Governments, both Christian and non-Christian."[65] This confident assertion was incorporated in the report, apart from the opening clause, which was replaced by "in spite of certain grievances, some of which have been illustrated in Part I. of this Report."[66] Conference delegates would certainly have left Edinburgh with the impression that almost all colonial governments viewed missionary activity with benevolent approval. The conference received an official message from the Imperial German Colonial Office, recording its "satisfaction and gratitude that the endeavours for the spread of the Gospel are followed by the blessings of civilisation and culture in all countries."[67] In the debate on Commission VII's report, delegates received reassurance from Seth Low that "the good understanding between Missions and Governments is increasing," and were even told by Lord Reay, a former governor of Bombay Presidency, that "missionaries in India, I consider, are auxiliaries of Government."[68]

This picture of growing harmony between missions and governments had some basis in fact. The General Acts of the Berlin Conference of 1884-85 and the Brussels Conference of 1890 had committed the European powers, albeit in vague terms, to the support of missions as part of a wider program for the civilization of Africa.[69] Now that colonial frontiers were largely settled, missionaries seemed more frequently an asset than a threat. Within the British Empire, the main exceptions to this were in countries predominantly Muslim. The only sections of the report openly critical of British colonial policy related to Egypt, the Egyptian Sudan, and northern Nigeria. In each case, the report complained, the administration was in practice inclined to favor Islam at Christianity's expense.[70] Similar views had been expressed by several of the

65. UTS, Box XVIII, "Documents Submitted," p. 15.

66. *MG*, p. 112.

67. Gairdner, p. 45.

68. *MG*, pp. 149, 154.

69. Article 6 of the Berlin Act, cited in A. B. Keith, *The Belgian Congo and the Berlin Act* (Oxford, 1919), p. 304; and articles 1 and 2 (clause 3) of the Brussels Act, in E. Hertslet, comp., *A Complete Collection of the Treaties and Conventions . . . between Great Britain and Foreign Powers*, XIX (London, 1895), pp. 281-82.

70. *MG*, pp. 51-57, 58-60.

American mission boards and in Mahan's letter to Low. Nevertheless, criticism of Lord Cromer's administration for excessive sensitivity to Muslim scruples proved too strong for most American members of the commission, who felt that such "caustic criticism" was "incongruous in the report of a joint commission."[71] These objections were overruled by the British, and the animadversions on Cromer remained. Low felt obliged in presenting the report to assure the conference that if the commission's words on this subject gave pain, they were to be treated as "the wounds of a friend."[72]

There were, in addition, the more "glaring exceptions" referred to by Mahan. Although his reference to the Congo and Portuguese Africa was cut from his opening summary of the replies to question VIII, the report still noted that "the most crying scandals enumerated in the replies" occurred under the "nominal Christian" governments of the Belgian Congo and Portugal. It also adopted verbatim Mahan's text recommending that the conference appeal to the signatories to the Berlin Act to take action to halt the continuing violation of the claims of humanity in the former Congo Free State.[73] Temple Gairdner recorded that "almost the only real anger" manifested at the conference was in relation to the three "great national wrongs" of the opium and liquor traffic and forced labor, which were allocated their own section in part II of the report.[74] Similarly, the conference broke into "very loud applause" during the debate of the report when C. E. Wilson, foreign secretary of the BMS, promised that "we are *not going to give up* our divinely appointed task to work for the emancipation and uplifting of the down-trodden and oppressed people of the Congo."[75] The passion expended on the Congo and Portuguese Africa derived its force from a conviction that these so-called Christian nations had reneged on "the only possible justification" of colonial annexations, namely, the duty to adopt "a deliberate, steadfast, and thorough policy" for the education and uplift of those described as "the more backward races of mankind."[76] Again, it should be noted that evolutionary concepts of racial hierarchy were foundational to the argument of this most outspoken and "radical" section of the report.

Two qualifications must be added to the report's picture of a generally harmonious relationship between missions and governments. First, the re-

71. UTS, Box XVIII, Points submitted for consideration by Dr. Low, p. 2; see "Documents Submitted," p. 16; and series 6, passim; see also p. 80 below.

72. *MG*, p. 148. The Americans had objected to pp. 69-70 of the draft (UTS, Box XVIII, Series 4:A), but they appeared unamended in the final report.

73. *MG*, pp. 114, 121.

74. Gairdner, p. 168; *MG*, pp. 116-17.

75. Gairdner, p. 175; *MG*, p. 182.

76. *MG*, pp. 115-16.

port itself gave no indication of the real divergence of views within the commission on how appropriate it was to include forthright criticism of colonial governments on any matters not self-evidently connected to religious liberty. Wann's early drafts, for example, were virtually silent on the question of forced labor. His section in part I on Portuguese Africa had originally said, "We have in this Commission nothing to do with troubles in connection with forced labour." The American advisory council objected, and Wann revised his text to read "We cannot discuss matters indirectly affecting mission work, such as the troubles in connection with forced labour, etc."[77] Moreover, the section in part II identifying the "great questions" of national wrong on which missions had been compelled to make repeated representation to government had not originally mentioned forced labor alongside the opium and liquor trades.[78] The meeting of the British executive committee in December 1909 insisted that, in view of opinions expressed by members of the commission, the section be rewritten by Wann and J. H. Oldham to include reference to forced labor (this, incidentally, appears to be the only point at which Oldham exerted any direct influence on Commission VII).[79]

Similarly, some of the American boards did not mince words in condemning the British government for its "political enthronement of Islam" in Egypt and the Sudan.[80] As seen above, the final report was a generally faithful reflection of such sentiments. Mahan and Barbour went further, voicing criticisms of British policy toward missions in India and China.[81] Such criticisms, however, failed to carry the majority support of the American members of the commission.

A second and consequent qualification, therefore, is that the divergent political stances revealed in compiling the report corresponded only to a limited extent to divisions of nationality. Disagreements amongst the commission's American members were as significant as those separating the Americans as a whole from their British colleagues. Yet it may not be coincidental that replies to the British questionnaire reporting quite serious tension or even confrontation with British officials, notably in Africa, came from non-British missionaries.[82]

77. UTS, Box XVIII, Points submitted for consideration by Dr. Low, p. 2; *MG*, p. 72.

78. UTS, Box XVIII, Series 4:C, draft report of section A, p. 17.

79. UTS, Box XVIII, minutes of meeting of Commission VII held on 17 December [1909], p. 2.

80. UTS, Box XVIII, Series 6, Folder III, Response 1.

81. UTS, Box XVIII, "Documents Submitted," pp. 16, 35.

82. See the case of Karl Cederquist in Commission VII replies, pp. 297-317, very selectively summarized in *MG*, pp. 57-58.

The most comprehensive indictment of British colonial policy contained in the questionnaire replies was that of Frederick Bridgman. Bridgman, it is true, enjoined absolute loyalty to the colonial government; he also took pride in the fact that missionaries of the American Board of Commissioners for Foreign Missions, as members of "the great Anglo-Saxon family," had always been regarded by the British as "fellow citizens of the Empire," and had thus been able to mediate between the native population and the authorities.[83] To dismiss Bridgman on this evidence as a typical Anglo-Saxon racist would be a grave mistake. Recent writing has identified him rather as a pioneer of a politically and socially aware approach to the problems of urban South Africa.[84] Alongside these markedly pro-imperial statements, his answers to the questionnaire contained a perceptive analysis of Ethiopianism in Natal and telling criticisms of British policy on African lands and the freedom of missions to operate in native reserves.[85]

Bridgman's indignant account was incorporated in the report, but in emasculated form, with the invective cut out. His advocacy of African land rights was grossly misrepresented by a mere passing reference to "other difficulties" in Natal with "mission lands."[86] On the other hand, a passage in which he stressed missionaries' duty to "inculcate absolute loyalty to Government" and teach the native "the necessity of his proving his worthiness" to receive the privilege of political responsibility, became virtually the entire section of the report devoted to political aspirations in South Africa.[87] The report did not print the immediately ensuing portion of Bridgman's text, in which he urged that *British* missionaries "should be bold to declare themselves according to their convictions of truth and justice" on questions of African rights; missionaries who were not British subjects, whose status in the country was that of guests by courtesy of a government not their own, had to act with greater reserve and moderation.[88]

Bridgman also contributed to the conference debate on the Commission VII report, spurred to his feet by the claim of the preceding speaker, a missionary of the Dutch Reformed Church, that missionaries in South Africa were able to proclaim the gospel "without let or hindrance."[89] This,

83. Commission VII replies, p. 278.

84. P. B. Rich, "Albert Luthuli and the American Board Mission in South Africa," in *Missions and Christianity in South African History*, ed. H. Bredekamp and R. Ross (Johannesburg, 1995), pp. 192-93.

85. Commission VII replies, pp. 279-92.

86. *MG*, pp. 82-83.

87. *MG*, pp. 83-84.

88. Commission VII replies, p. 295.

89. *MG*, p. 169.

Bridgman protested, had not been the case in Natal, though he was able to tell the conference that there were now hopes that government restrictions on native evangelists would soon be removed. The record of the South African colonies fell well short of the Golden Rule — "they had not done to the natives as they would be done by. I feel in some respect that there has been a sad lack of a deep sense of responsibility on the part of the ruling race for the welfare of the weaker race." From the new Union of South Africa, Bridgman hoped for better things, but he went on to spell out the agenda — beginning with the "bed-rock issue" of the land question — which must be pursued if white responsibility to the black race were to be adequately discharged.[90] This conjunction between acceptance of race theory and accurate perception of the real political issues confronting the African population of South Africa is striking. It was precisely because blacks were the "weaker race" that the standards of imperial duty had to be so strictly enforced. Bridgman's speech prompted Seth Low, in concluding the morning session of the debate, to hasten to correct the impression "that I fear may have been created that the British Government is, in relation to Missions, either lukewarm or unfriendly."[91]

V

How far the report of Commission VII shaped the subsequent relations between missions and governments is hard to establish. It made few specific recommendations. One it did make — the proposal of an appeal to the European powers to take action over human rights in the Congo — was effectively stymied by the decision (apparently taken in planning the conference) that no formal resolutions should be passed. As Gairdner observed, the conference debate on "the red horror of the Congo" ended on a necessarily inconclusive note.[92] Public pressure for Congo reform was, in any case, ebbing following the death of Leopold II on 17 December 1909.[93] Some general observations are, however, appropriate.

The report's acceptance of A. T. Mahan's recommendation, that the conference take steps for the appointment of a committee to draw up "a brief statement of recognised principles which underlie the relations of Missions to Governments," bore fruit in the Continuation Committee's adoption of

90. *MG*, pp. 171-72.

91. *MG*, p. 172.

92. Gairdner, pp. 175-76.

93. S. J. S. Cookey, *Britain and the Congo Question, 1885-1913* (London, 1968), pp. 262-63.

such a statement at its fifth meeting at The Hague in 1913. The statement was concerned primarily with defining the legal rights of missionaries, and differentiating these from spiritual obligations.[94] It said nothing about the moral obligations of governments toward subject peoples. Nevertheless, both the Conference of British Missionary Societies and the Foreign Missions Conference of North America established advisory committees on missions and governments in the wake of Edinburgh 1910. For all its deficiencies, Commission VII paved the way for the concerns of missionary statesmen with the questions of nationality and internationalism raised by the First World War and the postwar mandates. It is plausible to suggest that the Commission VII report laid the theoretical foundations for the campaigns waged so assiduously by J. H. Oldham on issues such as forced labor in Kenya after the war. The one section of the 1910 report that was in part Oldham's work dealt with the "public questions" of opium, the liquor trade, and forced labor. In 1919 Oldham intervened to ensure a reference was inserted in article 22 of the League of Nations covenant to the peoples, "especially those of Central Africa," who were "at such a stage" that the mandatory powers must be prepared to guarantee "freedom of conscience or religion, subject only to the maintenance of public order and morals."[95] That statement owed its parentage to article 6 of the Berlin Act of 1885.[96] It may also be indebted to the emphasis Commission VII had placed on religious liberty as a distinguishing mark of civilization, yet a survey published in 1931 made no reference to the 1910 commission.[97] Just how significant the Commission VII report was for the years that followed must, therefore, remain an open question.

The First World War made many of the report's assertions about the compatibility between the respective objectives of missions and governments look theadbare, as the pressures of war exposed the profoundly self-interested national agenda concealed beneath the high-sounding professions by colonial

94. The provisional statement was printed in the *International Review of Missions* 2 (1913): 563-66, and adopted without amendment by the Continuation Committee at its meeting from 14 to 20 November 1913. Geneva, IMC archives, microfiches H-10,000, 26.0003-4, Minutes of the Continuation Committee of the World Missionary Conference 1910-1913, and papers for Continuation Committee, November 1913. Members of Commission VII drafting the statement were Lord Balfour, Low, Mahan, Barbour, Max Berner, and Lars Dahle.

95. G. K. A. Bell, *Randall Davidson: Archbishop of Canterbury,* 2nd ed. (London, 1938), pp. 944-45. On Oldham, see Keith Clements, *Faith on the Frontier: A Life of J. H. Oldham* (Edinburgh and Geneva, 1999).

96. See Keith, p. 304.

97. M. Boegner, "Missions et gouvernements: de l'acte de Berlin au traité de Versailles," *Le Monde Non-Chrétien* 1 (1931): 59-78.

governments that had so impressed the members of Commission VII. The war also marked the beginning of the end of the era in which subjects such as the relations of missions to governments could be debated out of earshot of representatives of the indigenous populations of Asia and Africa.[98] Even those missionaries who tried to see matters from the perspective of the indigenous populations among whom they worked, such as Andrew Low or F. B. Bridgman, were, as we have seen, given short shrift by the commission report. Wann acknowledged at Edinburgh that "there has been a great deal of combustible material which we have had to keep outside of the Report," and admitted that "a very large number of Missions and missionaries" had used the questionnaires to vent particular grievances against governments.[99] The commission's decision to omit such material resulted in a document that can easily mislead historians who have not consulted the sources that lie behind it.

It remains the case that the disagreements rumbling beneath the dominant harmonies of the Commission VII report were all variations on an agreed imperial theme. Those variations of view cannot be neatly arranged into patterns determined by nationality. Whilst it is possible to conclude that non-British missionaries were more likely than British ones to find fault with British colonial administration, it is also true that most American members of Commission VII were less prepared than their British counterparts to criticize British colonial governments in the text of the report, despite considerable evidence in replies from the American boards justifying such criticism. This reluctance is explained less by national affiliation than by the fact that the American arm of the commission tended more toward governmental perspectives and the British members more toward the missionary viewpoint. The Christian imperialism of the missionary movement was primarily an international rather than a national ideology, even though it was frequently seduced by the rhetoric of those whose agenda was a nationalistic one.

Of greater significance for the historiography of the missionary relation to imperialism is the complex relationship between political stances and racial theory apparent among both commission members and their missionary correspondents. This paper has suggested that the commission employed the concept of a hierarchy of race and civilization to insist that missionaries grade their political expectations and claims to civil rights according to the degree

98. Only one non-Western voice was heard in the debate on Commission VII — that of Dr. C. T. Wang of China — in a speech which Gairdner described as "a revelation of the Chinese point of view": Gairdner, p. 164; *MG*, pp. 154-56.

99. *MG*, p. 173.

of "civilization" possessed by the people and government of the field in which they worked. The report argued that appeals by missionaries to governments to grant redress for contravention of rights of freedom of religious belief and practice were least appropriate in countries toward the bottom end of the scale of civilization. This might appear to imply that the report anticipated that the relations of missions and governments would be at their most distant in the African continent. In point of fact, of course, it took the opposite view. The paradox is explained by the way concepts of race were put to political use. Those missionaries who were most outspoken in asserting indigenous interests — such as Bridgman — often defended their position by appeal to the extent of moral obligation created by the differential between the "higher" and the "lower" races. For such missionaries the utility of evolutionary race theory was precisely that it could be used to enforce the obligations owed by colonial governments to haul their subject populations up the rungs of the ladder of civilization. Bridgman contrasted his own position with that of Natal's white settlers, concerned to keep the native "down and under" in perpetuity.[100] Similarly Wann, for all his deeply conservative instincts, employed categories of racial development in the section of the report on national duties to the more backward races of mankind to argue against those who doomed the "coloured" races to "perpetual national servitude" and to insist on policies of "native uplift" as the only possible justification for empire.[101]

It was thus no accident that most of the report's more politically radical statements related to Africa. Here, where racial differentials were held to be widest, lay the most pressing need for the vacuum of civilization to be filled by the closest possible cooperation between missions and colonial governments. Missionaries in Africa were indeed not to expect much from governments in defense of their own civil rights, but they were to expect open acknowledgment of the civilizing imperative. In the minds of mission theorists, Africa should have supplied the most admirable examples of government collaboration with the missionary enterprise. The fact that not infrequently the reverse was the case led Commission VII to abandon its prevailing timidity and adopt more adventurous political pronouncements. The paragraph on forced labor, inserted into the concluding section of the report at a late stage, condemned the practice as one tending "to the oppression and virtual enslavement of helpless races," and called on all "civilized Governments" to aim at its speedy and complete suppression.[102] Whilst the report failed at crucial

100. Commission VII replies, p. 279.
101. *MG*, pp. 115-16, 119.
102. *MG*, p. 117.

points to reflect the range and passion of missionary opinion from the field, it still in some measure set the direction for the more fundamental Christian challenges to the operation of colonial rule in Africa led by Oldham in the interwar years. Philip Curtin long ago pointed out that evolutionary racism could lead to diametrically opposed colonial policies. He suggested, however, that the missionary movement by the early twentieth century had succumbed to notions of the intrinsic inferiority and hence permanent wardship of the African race.[103] Much recent writing similarly blames pseudoscientific theories of racial hierarchy for the fractures of mission-church relationships on the field in this period. The evidence from Edinburgh 1910 points in a different direction: these same unpalatable theories, albeit cast in developmentalist form, were intrinsic to the missionary endeavor to hold colonial governments true to their professions of imperial trusteeship. As Oldham's *Christianity and the Race Problem* (1926) would make clear, the argument over imperial trusteeship was not over the centrality of the category of race — which almost all accepted — but over the relative importance of "nature" and "nurture" in determining the perceived pattern of racial development.[104] The Protestant missionary movement absorbed theories of racial hierarchy into its existing paradigm of progress and civilization without fundamental readjustment of mental categories.

Appendix A: British Questionnaire

I. What subjects have led in recent years to important communications between your Mission and the Government authorities in the district in which it is working? Kindly state the result of any such negotiations and the way in which that result affects missionary work.

II. To what extent and in what circumstances is it advisable for missionaries to appeal to the civil authorities for protection and assistance in such matters as danger to life and property, persecution of converts, compensation for damage to property or loss of life, etc.?

If your Mission acting as a body, or if a United Conference of Missionaries working in your field, has made any pronouncements regarding the attitude

103. P. D. Curtin, "'Scientific' Racism and the British Theory of Empire," *Journal of the Historical Society of Nigeria* 2, no. 1 (1960): 49-50.

104. J. H. Oldham, *Christianity and the Race Problem* (London, 1926), p. 75 and passim.

of missionaries to the civil authorities in these or similar questions, kindly send us a copy of such pronouncements.

Is it possible, in your judgment, to lay down any clear guiding principle in the matter?

In countries in which there is a native Government, kindly distinguish clearly between appeals to the native authorities and appeals to the representatives of the Government of which the missionary is himself a subject.

In discussing the advisability of such appeal, kindly quote in illustration as many definite instances as possible, showing favourable or unfavourable results.

III. Is there anything in the attitude, policy, or regulations of the Government under which you are working which restrict[s] or hinder[s] the success of Missions?

Have you any practical suggestion to offer as to the way in which a remedy should be sought?

Kindly deal as fully as possible with particular instances.

IV. Is it desirable that there should be some representative missionary body in each field through which matters of common interest can be laid before the local Government and which can advise individual missionaries in important cases?

V. To what extent have missionaries been able to exert any influence in the shaping of legislation in such matters as education, marriage laws, the language question, etc.?

VI. What attitude, in your judgment, should be taken by missionaries towards the social and political aspirations of the people among whom they are working?

VII. Can you give instances in which missionaries have been able to render important services to Governments through geographical exploration, scientific research, linguistic work, or through facilitating the conduct of the administration?[105]

Appendix B: American Questionnaire

I. What are the chief matters which have led, in recent years, to important communications between your Board and the Government authorities in the various districts in which it is working?

II. In matters affecting converts and their property, do you advocate resort

105. UTS, Box XVIII, Series 1, Instructions to correspondents.

to the civil authority, and, if so, in what cases? What should be the guiding principle? In what cases ought the missionary to resort to the civil power for help or protection?

III. Discuss the limits of Government interference with missionary activity, either by general prohibition or on particular occasions. How far is Government justified in forbidding a missionary to cross a frontier? Discuss instances.

IV. Should missionaries take advantage of extra-territorial rights?

V. Is it advisable to claim or accept compensation for damage to mission property, or loss of life?

VI. What are the circumstances which, in your opinion, justify missionaries in extending protection to religious or other refugees?

VII. Is it not desirable that there should be some representative missionary body in each field through which matters of common interest can be laid before the local government, and which can advise individual missionaries in important cases?

VIII. Is the attitude of any government under which you are working in any respect inimical or unfavourable to missionary work? Or does the attitude in any way militate against its success? If so, what government, and in what respects?[106]

106. UTS, Box XVIII, Series 6, Subseries A, summary of replies from missionary boards and churches.

Christian Missions and the Mid-Nineteenth-Century Change in Attitudes to Race: The African Experience

ANDREW C. ROSS

A Chartered Company is not a government and never can be. To be ruled by such is to be ruled for commercial ends by absentee directors shareholders whose real interests are only served by tangible dividends.[1]

Very little ground in Cape Colony belongs to the natives and no advance has been made without some Kaffir War. We have here very different antecedents and very different relations, and we look forward to the settlement of questions in this land without wars and without bloodshed.[2]

But in order to put down the slave trade you must have a proper doctrine of humanity, a true appreciation of the slave. Just as Christ took upon Him the form of a slave long ago, so He takes upon Him the form of Africa today. Africa bears the sins of the world's rulers. How long are we as a nation going to lay our selfishness, our meanness, our falsehoods, our lusts, yea, and the whole burden of our sins upon this Lamb of God?[3]

I

When I first read these words and many others written by David Clement Scott, the builder of Blantyre Church and father of the Blantyre Synod of the

1. *Life and Work in British Central Africa,* October 1890, p. 3.
2. *Life and Work in British Central Africa,* August 1891, p. 2.
3. *Life and Work in British Central Africa,* August/December 1897, p. 8.

Church of Central Africa Presbyterian,[4] I thought, "Here is a man years before his time." Apart from the members of his own family serving with him in Blantyre and a very few colleagues like Alexander Hetherwick and Neil MacVicar, no other white in central Africa[5] at that period — missionary, settler, or government officer — spoke like that. On burrowing more deeply into the history of the nineteenth century, I found that it was quite the opposite. David Scott and his allies were essentially old-fashioned. They were continuing to articulate and act upon an attitude to Africa, its people, and its future that was long out of date. Their attitude belonged to the evangelicalism of the late eighteenth century and the early decades of the nineteenth, with its mixture of biblical piety and Enlightenment principles, a classic example of which is John Wesley's *Thoughts on Slavery* published in 1774. There Wesley switches without any hesitation or sense of "changing gears" from a passionate appeal to God to have compassion on the slave and to bring forth his judgment on the slaveholder, to a firm insistence on the Enlightenment principle that "Liberty is the right of every creature, as soon as he breathes the vital air; and no human law can deprive him of that right which he derives from the law of Nature."[6]

In the earliest days of Protestant mission in Africa, we find this belief in the essential equality of all human beings irrespective of race clearly proclaimed in the letters, petitions, pamphlets, and books of Dr. John Philip, resident director of the London Missionary Society in southern Africa from 1819 till 1851. In a letter to the American Board of Commissioners for Foreign Missions, he wrote, "So far as my observation extends, it appears to me that the natural capacity of the African is nothing inferior to that of the European. At our schools, the children of Hottentots, of Bushmen, of Caffres and of the Bechuanas,[7] are in no respect behind the capacity of those of European parents: and the people at our missionary stations are in many instances superior in intelligence to those who look down upon them."[8] It was the same Philip who, in 1828, had called for equal civil rights for all His Majesty's subjects. "We ask for nothing unreasonable, nothing illegal, and nothing new. We have nothing to say to politics. The question under discussion is a mere question

4. The Presbyterian church in Malawi.

5. Malawi, Zambia, and Zimbabwe.

6. John Wesley, *Thoughts on Slavery* (London, 1774), p. 4.

7. The normal terms used at that time for, respectively, the Khoi, San, Xhosa, and Tswana peoples.

8. Printed in the journal of the American Board, the *Missionary Herald* 29 (November 1833): 414, quoted from Andrew Ross, *John Philip (1775-1851): Missions, Race, and Politics in South Africa* (Aberdeen, 1986), pp. 95-96.

of civil rights. . . . We have offered no particular directions about the machinery of government desirable in such a country. We have recommended no checks but such as are necessary to prevent one class of British subjects from oppressing and destroying another."[9]

Until the 1850s this belief in the oneness of humanity was widespread; it was a powerful influence on many, though not all, evangelical Protestants on both sides of the Atlantic. An unambiguous statement of this belief was the constitution that the American Antislavery Society adopted at its inaugural meeting in 1833. This document called not only for the immediate freeing of the slaves but also for them to receive their full civil rights as U.S. citizens. In Africa another striking example of this understanding of the nature of humanity appears on the first two pages of David Livingstone's first major publication, *Missionary Travels and Researches in South Africa.* It is particularly significant in the context of our discussion because not one of his many biographers between his death and the 1930s, the heyday of the influence of the racial understanding of history and culture, takes any serious notice of it. What Livingstone said was: "My great-grandfather fell at the battle of Culloden, fighting for the old line of kings, and our grandfather was a small farmer in Ulva, where my father was born. . . . when he [grandfather] was on his deathbed, he called his children around him and said, '. . . I leave this precept with you: Be honest.' . . . This event took place at a time when the Highlanders, according to Macaulay, were much like the Cape Caffres."[10]

Many of the first evangelical missionaries of this era shared this sense of oneness of humanity. There were cultural differences between groups, which neither could be nor were denied. However, whether we look at a Scot like Livingstone, an Englishman like James Read of Kat River, or an American like Theodore Weld, "Lane Rebel" and leader of the Antislavery Society in the West, we find that they saw these differences as analogous to those between Livingstone and his grandfather. What Christianity and education had done for the tribal Gael, it could do for the Xhosa.

Philip Curtin, in his seminal study *The Image of Africa,* refers to this attitude in the years up to the 1850s as "conversionism."[11] A confirmation of how widespread this view was even beyond the confines of evangelicalism comes from a scholar working in a different historical field. D. Lorimer's work on Victorian Britain appears to indicate that people in Britain tended to treat "people of

9. John Philip, *Researches in South Africa,* 2 vols. (London, 1828), 1:xxv-xxvi.

10. David Livingstone, *Missionary Travels and Researches in South Africa* (London, 1859), pp. 1-2.

11. Philip D. Curtin, *The Image of Africa: British Ideas and Action, 1780-1850* (London, 1965), pp. 259-61, 414-16, 424-28, 473-76.

color" in terms of class rather than by skin color or race until the 1850s.[12] Other attitudes to race were current during this period even among evangelical missionaries — witness Philip's difficulties with colleagues such as Henry Calderwood[13] — but the "conversionist" understanding was the most influential.

It is important to note that this tradition was something acted out and indeed institutionalized in various places. In the Eastern Cape, for example, missionaries of the Glasgow Missionary Society (GMS) founded the Lovedale Institution, a nonracial school educating boys (later girls also) of all races up to university entrance level. In Sierra Leone, the Church Missionary Society (CMS) organized Fourah Bay College in 1827 on the same philosophical basis. It was this worldview that let Tiyo Soga go to Glasgow University to graduate in arts and divinity and return with his Scottish wife as a full member of the GMS mission to the Eastern Cape. The promotion of Fourah Bay to university college level, Henry Venn's continued support for Samuel Ajayi Crowther, and the work of Scott and Hetherwick in Nyasaland all indicate that egalitarian ideas were not entirely eliminated within church circles even in the last decades of the century. In the world of politics, however, egalitarianism was already defeated. The low-qualification, nonracial franchise granted for the new Assembly of the Cape Colony in 1853 and the attempt at "Reconstruction" of the defeated rebel southern states of America between 1865 and 1871 were the last flings in public policy in the English-speaking world of this older view of humanity. We will note later in the paper how these particular experiments were viewed in the early decades of the twentieth century. However, by the 1890s people like David Scott were fighting a losing battle against the growing domination of the English-speaking intellectual world by a new understanding of the nature of humanity and its history. This understanding was represented by a family of ideas that took a number of different forms but all agreed on the fundamental importance for the understanding of history and human culture of what they saw as immutable racial differences.

II

Scholars like Curtin, Lorimer, Bolt, and Gossett[14] all agree that the 1850s was the pivotal decade for this change of intellectual climate in the English-speaking

12. Douglas A. Lorimer, *Colour, Class, and the Victorians: English Attitudes to the Negro in the Mid–Nineteenth Century* (Leicester, 1978), pp. 67-68.

13. Ross, pp. 219-20.

14. Christine Bolt, *Victorian Attitudes to Race* (London, 1971); T. F. Gossett, *Race: The History of an Idea in America* (New York, 1996).

world. Of course, from the time of Edward Long's two-volume *History of Jamaica* (1774) there had been writers of some seriousness and popularity who tried to prove that humanity was not one but divided into discrete and incompatible species. These species were usually ranked on an ascending scale by both moral and intellectual ability, the European always at the top and the African always at or near the bottom, whatever other variations in the order there were among the various writers. This family of views was, until the 1850s, one of several, and it was less influential than the egalitarian one, which was fed from both evangelical Christian and Enlightenment sources. However, in the middle decade of the century a massive shift began to take place in the world of ideas.

By 1850 the application of science was transforming life in western Europe and North America at an increasing rate. This helped give science an increasingly dominant authority in the world of ideas, particularly in Britain and the USA, the leading industrial powers. Already in 1850 Robert Knox, who, before his disgrace over body snatching in the Burke and Hare case, was a most distinguished anatomist, had published *The Races of Man.* This was based on a series of lectures he had been giving around Britain since 1846. Like the French Count Gobineau, Knox was building on intellectual foundations already laid by other thinkers, but the scholarly consensus is that it was his book that had the long-term impact rather than those earlier writers. Knox insisted that a scientific understanding of race was the key to understanding history and culture. This position came to dominate thought in the English-speaking world in the subsequent decades up to the 1930s. "Race is everything, literature, art, science, in a word, civilisation depend on it" was his key assertion.[15] Science was changing the world for the better at an astonishing rate before people's eyes, and so the support for this idea by so many leading scientists of the day had a profound effect on the English-speaking world. This racial pattern of thinking was further reinforced in its influence by the Anglo-Saxon/Teutonic understanding of history that universities such as Oxford and Harvard were to propound during the last thirty years of the century. However, in illustrating the threat true civilization was under, Knox chose not the African as the threat but the Celt, thereby showing how science and Anglo-Saxonism were coming together even before the emergence of Bishop Stubbs and the Oxford school of history.

> 700 years of absolute possession has not advanced by a single step the amalgamation of the Irish Celt with the Saxon English: the Cymbri of

15. Robert Knox, *The Races of Men: A Philosophical Enquiry* (London and Philadelphia, 1850), preface.

> Wales remain as they were: the Caledonian still lingers in diminished numbers, but unaltered on the wild shores of his lochs and firths. . . . Transplant him to another climate, a brighter sky, a greater field free from the trammels of artificial life, the harnessed routine of European civilisation; carry him to Canada, he is still the same: mysterious fact. . . . If you seek an explanation go back to France, go back to Ireland, and you will find it there: it is race: the subject will one day test the Declaration of Independence for the Celt does not understand what we Saxons mean by independence.[16]

Although much of the scientific evidence brought to support this family of race-based ideas between the 1850s and the 1930s is today referred to as pseudoscience, it was then propounded by the leading scientists and thinkers of the time. The racial basis of civilization appeared universally supported by the findings of modern science, the new science of anthropology as well as zoology and biology. Humanity was not one: the fair-skinned, fair-haired European, whether called Saxon, Teuton, or Aryan, was the true human, and all other forms represented, as it were, earlier evolutionary stages in the development of humanity. In the late nineteenth century the new school of historians led by Bishop Stubbs, Edward Freeman, and J. R. Green was supported by Professor Adams at Harvard and Professor Burgess at Columbia, in asserting that modern civilization was the creation of the Saxon/Teutonic race.[17] When these outstanding scholars, leaders in the disciplines of history and politics, agreed that race theory was the key to history, then the intellectual victory of race thinking was close to complete.

Of course, not all who felt they had no alternative but to accept the conclusions of science and history went on to accept the ruthless policy outcomes that some writers and politicians insisted flowed from them. J. M. Bowker, the leader of the British 1820 settlers in the Eastern Cape, an avid reader of Carlyle and Knox, proclaimed in a famous speech that the Xhosa were destined to give way and disappear before the advance of the superior race just as the springbok had done.[18] Knox made explicit what Bowker meant when he wrote, "What signify these dark races to us? Who cares particularly for the Negro, or the Hottentot or the Kaffir? These latter have proved a very troublesome race, and the sooner they are put out of the way

16. Knox, p. 18.

17. Green's *Short History of the English People* (1874) was still recommended in British universities as late as 1945.

18. *Speeches, Letters, and Selections from Important Papers of John Mitford Bowker* (Grahamstown, 1864; reprint, Cape Town, 1962), p. 125.

the better."[19] Or again, as a *Times* editorial commented about Commandant Pretorius's massacre of approximately one thousand Tswana:

> We doubt very much if as many Kafirs have fallen by the bullets or bayonets of our troops in the last three wars, as were destroyed in this single expedition of Pretorius. It would be hard indeed to argue that such an example should be followed; but of this we are convinced, — if the colonisation of South Africa is to be continued, the savage tribes of our frontier can only successfully be encountered, like the savages of all other regions, by acts resembling their own. The backwoodsmen of Kentucky pursued the Red Indian as the Red Indian pursued them, and the victory in the end fell to the superior race.[20]

This was the attitude which led to the acting out on too many occasions of the saying "the only good Indian is a dead Indian" and the killing or extinction of the entire aboriginal population of Tasmania.

As Kenan Malik points out in his book *The Meaning of Race,* the celebrated Thomas Huxley represents the majority who accepted the fundamental truth of race thinking but shied away from what they saw as Knox's extremism.[21] However, Huxley, perhaps one of the most distinguished scientists of his age, the defender of Darwin against Bishop Wilberforce in the famous British Association debate, was a key proponent of the scientific basis of race thinking. It was his writings that for many confirmed the immutability of race difference and its importance in understanding culture and history. Like all the scientists and anthropologists of the day, he could not settle on an exact definition of race, but also like them, he nevertheless asserted its crucial importance.

The power of race thinking can be seen in the way it remained authoritative into the 1930s, something clearly reflected in the way racial stereotypes were simply taken as given in the novels of a humane man like John Buchan. Scientists of repute in the 1920s were still endorsing it. Thomas Huxley's brilliant scientist grandson, Julian, wrote articles for the *Spectator* late in 1924 on life in the United States. While he accepted that there was still no scientifically agreed-upon definition of race, he insisted that such agreement would come, and that the fact of race difference was indisputable. "You only have to go to a nigger camp-meeting to see the African mind in operation — the shrieks, the

19. Knox, pp. 23-24.
20. *Times* (London), 17 March 1852.
21. Kenan Malik, *The Meaning of Race* (London, 1996), pp. 89-90.

dancing and yelling and sweating, the surrender to the most violent emotion, the ecstatic blending of the soul of the Congo with the practice of the Salvation Army. So far, no very satisfactory psychological measure has been found for racial difference: that will come, but meanwhile the differences are patent."[22] As we have suggested, a majority of people — like the Huxleys — sheered away from the brutality of genocide, and supported instead the attitude called by Curtin and many others "trusteeship." This rested on the assumption that while the various non-Anglo-Saxon races were inferior, that did not justify their ill treatment; indeed, the superior race was obliged to accept its responsibility and ensure that inferior peoples were governed fairly and justly. It was an attitude most famously expressed in Kipling's poem *The White Man's Burden* (1899).

The all-pervasiveness of this belief in race as the key to history, culture, and civilization itself affected people across the whole spectrum of political positions, left as well as right. British-born and ideologically committed socialist trade union leaders led white miners through the streets of Johannesburg in 1922 under banners that read "White Workers of the World Unite." Just as striking is the commitment to a racial understanding of human reality of the socialist writer Jack London. T. F. Gossett believes the vast sales of London's books gave a significant boost to the authority of race thinking among ordinary people in both North America and Britain.[23] In a famous interview London made a deliberate statement about race and socialism, which was a miniconfession of faith. He insisted socialism was a system for the superior races and that brotherhood could not be extended to the weaker races. Although some socialist leaders sincerely advocated brotherhood with the weaker races, he felt it pointless because the stronger races would inherit the earth: "it is the law." London, like so many from Knox onward, also included the darker Europeans as a separate group inferior to the Anglo-Saxons.[24]

What many today have so much difficulty in accepting is that it was the radical and modern thinkers who shaped and led this all-embracing intellectual movement. To oppose it was to appear reactionary, indeed irrational. The extent of the influence of race thinking over the English-speaking world is illustrated graphically by the leaders of the Social Gospel movement, Washington Gladden, Josiah Strong, and Walter Rauschenbusch. These men were completely dedicated to achieving justice for the poor and rejected, yet they failed completely to engage with the contemporary imposition of "Jim Crow"

22. Julian Huxley, quoted in Malik, p. 124.

23. Gossett, p. 199.

24. Joan London, *Jack London and His Times*, pp. 212-13, quoted in Gossett, p. 206.

legislation in the American South and the growth in the number of lynchings of African Americans.

It is appropriate at this juncture to see how liberal intellectuals in the early twentieth century viewed the Cape Constitution of 1853 and Reconstruction in the American South. That great liberal statesman Woodrow Wilson, idealistic founder of the League of Nations, wrote that Reconstruction's enfranchisement of the ex-slaves had led to utter ruin until the whites, the true citizens, took over again.[25] If one looks at the all but forgotten attempt at legal nonracialism in the Cape Colony, one finds a similar reaction. It was a reforming British Liberal government that, after the great victory of 1906, laid the foundations of the domestic welfare state but also in effect betrayed the Cape by agreeing to the creation of the Union of South Africa. This plan absorbed the Cape, where the old nonracial legal traditions had been struggling to survive the pressure from Cecil Rhodes and others, into union with the three segregationist colonies, the Transvaal, the Orange Free State, and Natal. In the new nation the franchise was extended to all adult white males. Those African and "Coloured" people of the Cape who already had the vote under the old Cape education or property qualifications could keep it. In the old Cape franchise, these qualifications had applied to everyone so that the black vote had been a significant factor in Cape politics. In the new union these black Cape voters became the marginalized relics of a discredited experiment. In 1909, when a delegation representative of all the Cape's peoples went to London and appealed to the Liberal government against the racial injustice of the constitution of the proposed union, they were told that the proposed white parliament could be trusted to look after the welfare of the black majority. A form of trusteeship had triumphed. What the new Union Parliament could be trusted to do was seen in the discriminatory laws passed in the next ten years that brought Cape society more into line with the rest of the new Union of South Africa.[26]

III

What was the impact of this intellectual consensus in the English-speaking world upon the workings of the Protestant missionary movement? A movement so vast by the last quarter of the nineteenth century is impossible to en-

25. *Atlantic Monthly* 87 (January 1901), quoted in Gossett, p. 284.

26. M. Wilson and L. M. Thompson, eds., *The Oxford History of South Africa*, 2 vols. (London, 1970), vol. 2, chap. 7, passim. Cf., most recently, David E. Torrance, *The Strange Death of the Liberal Empire: Lord Selborne in South Africa* (Liverpool, 1996).

compass here. Nevertheless, one can look at some areas of British missionary activity in Africa and consider to what extent these experiences were typical of the wider situation. The episcopates of Bishop Crowther in West Africa and of Bishop Tucker in Uganda, the work of the Scottish missions in Malawi, and some features of the missionary biography "industry" of the period from 1880 to 1939 will be discussed. These examples indicate, I believe, that trusteeship was a powerful influence in Protestant missionary thought by the beginning of the twentieth century. As was clear in David Scott's words, quoted at the beginning of the chapter, the old conversionist views were not entirely eliminated in the 1890s, but they were going against the stream.

Modern scholars agree that Henry Venn, the CMS secretary, wanted Samuel Adjai Crowther to be bishop of the growing indigenous church among his own Yoruba people. The decision of 1864 that gave him episcopal control only over those areas of the Yoruba church with no European missionaries was only temporary. The restriction of his authority to the Niger Mission, where he was primarily a missionary and not bishop of a diocese, stemmed from the opposition of the missionaries within Yorubaland on the basis of race to serve under him. Venn hoped that when things changed, Crowther could be the "native" bishop over a "native" self-governing, self-supporting, and self-propagating church, and the crown of all his work for Africa. Venn died in the same year as Livingstone, and thus, like the Scot, had lived on into an era in which his beliefs were becoming seen as inappropriate and out of date. His plan for Crowther had to be developed in the peculiar way it did, in what Ajayi characterized as "a comic, Gilbertian situation," because of racism.[27]

More recent work has shown that race thinking alone is too simplistic an explanation of the subsequent attacks on Crowther and his work. However, the conclusions of the new research do not mean that race was not an issue. As we have attempted to show, racial difference had come to pervade the English-speaking world's understanding of reality, and could take many forms. The racism that affected the work of the CMS in West Africa was not the racism of a Bowker or the bitterly anti-African missionaries in Malawi who resigned because of their opposition to David Scott's policies. However, the young volunteers who joined the CMS and were sent to the Niger in the 1880s and made sad the last years of Bishop Crowther were not immune from the all-pervasive influence of race thinking.

27. T. E. Yates, *Venn and Victorian Bishops Abroad,* Studia Missionalia Uppsaliensia 33 (Uppsala and London, 1978), pp. 155-63; J. F. A. Ajayi, *Christian Missions in Nigeria, 1841-1891* (London, 1965), chap. 7, passim; E. A. Ayandele, *The Missionary Impact on Modern Nigeria, 1842-1914* (London, 1966), chaps. 6 and 7.

The bishop's strange position had been made more difficult by the CMS decision in 1878 to send out J. A. Ashcroft to be in charge of the temporalities of the Niger Mission. This decision, it has been pointed out, was in keeping with the new theological approach that was having an increasing impact on the CMS and many other missionary agencies.[28] Donald Fraser of Loudon, for example, was one of its prominent representatives in the Free Church of Scotland Mission in Nyasaland. Thinking that could be categorized as that of a "holiness" movement shaped this new approach. Its great emphasis was the possibility of the elimination of conscious sin from the life of even the ordinary Christian. One of the results of the influence of this theological approach in the CMS was the belief that clerical mission staff such as Bishop Crowther should be freed from worldly concerns so as to concentrate on spiritual matters. That was so, but it also must not be ignored that this action took away also a great deal of power from the bishop. What is more, it put power into the hands of a white newcomer who was ready to relay to London criticisms of Crowther's African staff made by European traders, some of which were justified, but some not.

It was into this situation that the new missionaries arrived. This holiness movement radiating from the Keswick Conventions, as Porter has shown, had a profound influence on these young men. The holiness approach to the Christian life saw the removal of all conscious sin and a purification of one's character as essential before any worthwhile work could be achieved. Indeed, this religious pattern of thought concentrated on what someone *was* rather than on what someone achieved as the key to judging that person's worth. This understanding also saw the achievement of a high degree of personal holiness as a necessary preliminary to the effective spreading of the Christian gospel.[29] From this perspective, one shared by many of the CMS leaders in England, Bishop Crowther was a failure as a disciplinarian. The bishop would suspend a priest only because of an actual proven offense, whereas from the holiness perspective "a lack of spirituality" was sufficient ground for disciplinary action.[30] From the beginning these idealistic young men were disap-

28. Andrew Porter, "Cambridge, Keswick and Late Nineteenth Century Attitudes to Africa," *Journal of Imperial and Commonwealth History* 5, no. 1 (1976): 5-34; Porter, "Evangelical Enthusiasm, Missionary Motivation, and West Africa in the Late Nineteenth Century: The Career of G. W. Brooke," *Journal of Imperial and Commonwealth History* 6, no. 1 (1977): 23-46.

29. Nothing could be further from the understanding of the power of the Christian gospel in itself, which can be transmitted even by very weak vessels — as portrayed, for example, in Graham Greene's novel *The Power and the Glory.*

30. Porter, "Cambridge," p. 24.

pointed by the African clergy they met and by the appallingly poor spiritual quality, in their eyes, of the African converts on the Niger.

The climax of this conflict between the views of the CMS and the new missionaries on the one hand and Bishop Crowther on the other came in August 1890. Already the original area of the Niger Mission under Crowther had been split into two, the upper Niger section staffed by the newcomers and the southern or lower Niger area staffed by the African clergy under Crowther but advised by a finance committee. This committee was made of the bishop; Archdeacon Dandeson Crowther; another African priest; the European secretary, F. N. Eden; and two missionaries from the Upper Niger Mission. At the meeting of the committee at Onitsha in August 1890, Eden insisted that he had been invested by the CMS parent committee with special authority which allowed him to suspend a number of African clergy, including Archdeacon Dandeson Crowther. That this action was not seen as extraordinary at the time has to be explained, and attributing it to the new personal standards of spirituality that gripped the CMS of this period is not adequate explanation. At this meeting an Anglican priest suspended from their ecclesiastical functions a number of other Anglican priests, including an archdeacon, against the wishes of their bishop. He did this by his authority as a servant of the CMS and secretary of a committee set up supposedly to liberate Bishop Crowther from the burden of worldly affairs.

Could this conceivably have happened if Samuel Crowther had been a European? When one considers that no other African was consecrated as a diocesan bishop in the Anglican communion in West Africa until A. B. Akinyele was consecrated bishop of Lagos in 1951, it is difficult to conclude other than that race was of critical importance in the CMS work in West Africa in this period. Of course, African assistant bishops were appointed in West Africa, two of them immediately after the death of Bishop Crowther; but their status as assistant bishops with no territorial or other autonomy confirms rather than weakens this argument. The result of the whole episode was that for the next fifty years Bishop Crowther was regarded not as the symbol of African success for which Venn had hoped but as the symbol of African inadequacy.[31] The "Niger crisis" was widely seen as a confirmation of all that the race theorists taught.

31. Bengt Sundkler, *The Christian Ministry in Africa* (London, 1960), p. 46.

IV

Stephen Neill has criticized Venn's policy in West Africa, including the way Crowther's episcopate was set up, as if errors of judgment by Venn were the primary problem. Neill insists that Bishop Tucker's East African experience was by contrast a much better example of race partnership in the development of African Christianity.[32] However, when we look carefully at Tucker's work in Uganda, we see again that the racial presuppositions of the English-speaking world of the time profoundly distorted Tucker's intentions.

Bishop A. R. Tucker arrived in Buganda in 1890 and witnessed the last stages of the Christian revolution in that kingdom that left it dominated by Protestant and Catholic laymen of great ability and dedication. After the country became part of the British protectorate of Uganda, both Protestant and Catholic missions received a large influx of European missionaries. The new CMS missionaries saw this "native" church as an infant church, one they were called to lead and guide. Chronologically the Baganda Protestant community was an infant, but in reality it was something very different. It was a church (the state of the Roman Catholic "native church" was similar) that had its martyrs who had been the friends and relatives of the new leaders. These leaders were mostly of the Baganda aristocracy and had led the new church through the fires of persecution, exile, and war. At the time of the new influx of missionaries, these lay leaders were overseeing a massive, enthusiastic evangelistic movement that was spreading the gospel throughout the kingdom of Buganda and well beyond.

This meeting had elements of confrontation within it, between an aristocratic black lay leadership and a growing body of young white missionaries, and has been well described elsewhere.[33] When considering the encounter, however, one also needs to bear in mind that the majority of these CMS missionaries were, like those on the Niger, deeply influenced by the Keswick movement. They faced in Bagandan Christianity a church led by men who were key players in the social and political life of the kingdom of Buganda, a situation where church leadership and political leadership were seen as intimately linked, if not as one. This was a situation, as we have seen, unacceptable to the Keswick distinction between the worldly and the spiritual. The fact that some of these leaders, despite their dedication, heroism, and willingness

32. Stephen Neill, *A History of Christian Missions* (Harmondsworth, 1964), pp. 377, 387.

33. J. V. Taylor, *The Growth of the Church in Buganda* (London, 1958), chaps. 1–4; Adrian Hastings, *The Church in Africa, 1450-1950* (Oxford, 1994), pp. 464-72.

to face exile or even martyrdom for the cause, did not lead the life of high moral purity that Keswick piety saw as the necessary preliminary to effective Christian service only made the situation worse in the eyes of the young enthusiasts.

Bishop Tucker tried to create a constitution for that church in which there would be, to use his phrase, "equality of all workers." This meant that all missionaries should be integrated into the diocesan structure that included an elected Diocesan Council, and that no distinction should be drawn between people of the same ecclesiastical status on the basis of race. He fought for such a constitution for twelve years. As he said of the missionary, "Let him therefore throw in his lot firmly with the natives, identifying himself as far as possible with their life work and organisation. Let him submit himself to the laws and canons of their Church."[34] This was Tucker's version of how to achieve Venn's aim of the "euthanasia of the mission."[35] However, the missionaries consistently opposed him on two fronts. On the first they refused to accept any constitution where there was the possibility of their serving under the authority of an African. Second, they insisted that an exclusively missionary committee should alone deal with all matters relating to their work.

Eventually in 1909 Tucker agreed to a compromise constitution. Within the diocese there was equality of workers, which Neill rightly praises, but in practice therefore no missionary, clerical or lay, was appointed to a task where he or she came under African authority. In effect, as Taylor put it, the missionaries "withdrew upwards." In addition, the situation replicated that on the Niger because, despite all Tucker's efforts, the Missionary Standing Committee retained authority over the work of the missionaries. There were, therefore, as Bishop Willis, Tucker's successor, admitted, two governing bodies in the one diocese, a church in white leading strings.[36] This institutional separation helped develop, again despite Tucker's efforts and his own unambiguous personal witness, a growing gulf between African and European within the church. This appears starkly when we compare the relationship between Baganda and missionary in the early 1890s and that in the 1920s. For example, George Baskerville, who arrived in 1890 with Tucker, always had his house full of Africans day and night. This situation has to be contrasted with that revealed by a letter from the local secretary of the Mission Council to a woman missionary of the CMS in 1925. The letter warned her that "native"

34. Taylor, p. 85.

35. Hastings, p. 294.

36. Taylor, p. 88. Most recently C. Peter Williams, *The Ideal of the Self-Governing Church: A Study in Victorian Missionary Strategy* (Leiden, 1990), chap. 6.

classes must not be held in a house belonging to the CMS, nor must "natives" sleep there except with special permission of the Standing Committee. No wonder an old man told Taylor that people now called the missionaries *bazungu,* but Basika (Baskerville) was not a *muzungu.*[37]

V

In southern Nyasaland the Blantyre Mission of the Church of Scotland went through a similar struggle in the 1890s to that undertaken by Tucker. David Scott, whose words opened this chapter, struggled to create an African church within which Europeans, government officers, and settlers as well as missionaries would find their place. For example, throughout his years in Blantyre, all communion services in Nyanja and English had to be open to Christians of all races. In the fourteen years from his arrival in 1880, Scott was privileged because almost all the mission staff were related to him by kinship or marriage, were his friends, or had been recruited by him. As a result, fulfillment of his vision appeared possible. A beautiful example of his ideal was the marriage of his right-hand man and successor Alexander Hetherwick in 1893. On that day two young African couples were also married, and all three couples presided over a huge open-air marriage feast attended by all their friends, black and white together.

However, by 1893 a group of new missionaries appointed to the mission in 1890 were already unhappy with Scott's leadership and had begun to criticize and oppose him. By 1895 they had all resigned and joined the white settler community. One of them, R. S. Hynde, founded the *Central African Planter,* a white supremacist journal that regularly attacked "the African" as stupid and lazy but most importantly as "an object for contempt from a moral point of view."[38] Tragically the Foreign Mission Committee (FMC) of the Kirk took the complaints from Scottish planters about Scott, together with those of the ex-missionaries, very seriously. The committee was in any case nervous about Scott's theological rhetoric — "the African as the suffering Lamb of God" — and about his plans for the future. He wanted the new church to be nonracial and ruled by a presbytery made up of missionaries and the young African leaders Scott referred to as his deacons. The FMC saw it quite differently: a Kirk session must be set up first, whose only elders should be the white lay missionaries, and the Mission Council (an all-white missionary body, which

37. Taylor, p. 89; *bazungu* (Europeans, plural), *muzungu* (singular).
38. *Central African Planter* 1, no. 8 (April 1896).

Scott had seen as having only one annual advisory meeting) should meet regularly and control policy. The conflict between Scott and Hetherwick in Blantyre and the FMC in Edinburgh was resolved in 1897. A Commission of Enquiry of the FMC investigated the Blantyre Mission, and in its report criticized Scott's general policies, his editorial policies in *Life and Work in British Central Africa,* as well as the content of several of his published sermons.

It was clear that Edinburgh had lost trust in him, and Scott, broken in health, resigned in 1898. Hetherwick tried to continue his old friend's policies. He had something of a victory in that the new Kirk sessions that were set up and united in Blantyre Presbytery had African majorities. However, he had to accept defeat over the Mission Council, whose position and authority was confirmed. This body, made up exclusively of European missionaries, met regularly and exercised a parallel authority to that of the courts of the church. This provides an exact parallel to the situation in both the Anglican Church in Uganda and the United Free Church of Scotland Mission in northern Malawi. So in 1924, when the Blantyre Presbytery joined with the Livingstonia Presbytery to form the Church of Central Africa Presbyterian (CCAP), the missionaries continued their membership of their home churches and the Mission Councils in their respective areas maintained their white existence and authority.

This "whites only" authority was made all the greater when the colonial government began to give grants-in-aid to education and insisted they would pay these only to missions, not to native bodies. The final indignity, from which Uganda was saved by Tucker's constitution, came when the authorities in Scotland accepted the petitions of the settlers, and separate white congregations of the Church of Scotland were set up in both Blantyre and Zomba. These were congregations specifically of the Church of Scotland, not the CCAP. There were now two different Presbyterian churches in Nyasaland, divided by race. This development was paralleled exactly in Kenya, where Church of Scotland congregations were set up distinct and separate from the growing African church coming into being as a result of the work of the Church of Scotland missionaries. The Presbyterian Church in Kenya also suffered, just as the CCAP in Nyasaland and the Anglican Church in Uganda did, from the divide between Mission Council (Missionary Standing Committee in the Uganda case) and indigenous church, the situation summed up by Willis as "two governing bodies in one diocese." This institutional structure, which both Tucker and Scott opposed, was the embodiment of trusteeship, and under a variety of names was universal in Africa where the mainstream British Protestant missions worked. Separate white congregations in Blantyre, Nairobi, or the Copper Belt simply underlined the influence of racial ideas upon British Protestant churches and missionary societies in the first half of the twentieth century.

The turning point for the Church of Scotland can be seen most graphically in the 1895 clash between D. C. Scott and some of the new missionaries. Hetherwick, on leave in Scotland at the time, referred to one of them as "anti-African, anti-mission and anti-Christian." The official response to Hetherwick was a reproof about his intemperate language and an assertion that the missionary in question, though "deficient in sympathy for the African" and who "dwelt on their faults," was still a good Christian and potentially a good missionary![39] In Nyasaland one can draw a contrast between 1890 and the 1920s parallel to that in Buganda. In the 1890s European visitors were taken aback to enter Scott's manse in Blantyre to find a Kololo chief and his retinue or Scott's "deacons" and their wives sipping tea in Mrs. Scott's best china. By 1930 such European visitors were much more at home when they saw venerable African ministers, like any other "boy," standing at the foot of the veranda steps wondering if the "Bwana was in."[40]

VI

Before turning to missionary biographies, we ought to mention briefly the missionary schools created in the nineteenth century. Schools like Lovedale, Fourah Bay Grammar School, Livingstonia, and many others pursued curricula that presumed racial equality. It is striking and in some ways puzzling that the schools kept these curricula throughout the period when "trusteeship" dominated missionary thinking. The maintenance of a curriculum that presumed equality even when some of the teachers using it did not believe in racial equality meant that the church schools were one of the first targets of the 1948 Nationalist government in South Africa. Earlier African pastors, teachers, and parents defended these schools and their curricula when in the 1920s liberal educationalists tried to make their curricula more appropriate to African needs. What could be more ridiculous, reformers said, than Ngoni and Tumbuka youths in Livingstonia learning about Robert Bruce or the Covenanters when they were taught nothing of use in village life? Yet as the late Orton Chirwa, Q.C., gleefully told me, he and his classmates delighted in

39. The whole of this section is based on the writer's *Blantyre Mission and the Making of Modern Malawi* (Bonn, 1996).

40. Oral testimony from Africans and missionaries who worked there in the period, gathered by the writer in the 1960s while researching in preparation for *Blantyre Mission*.

these stories and drew their own conclusions from them about justice and freedom. He also insisted that there was widespread African opposition to the reforms, suggested and partially implemented as a result of the recommendations of the Phelps-Stokes Commission, because people saw them as designed to hold Africans back. Quite different were the reformers who saw themselves not as holding Africans back but as conscientiously trying to give effect to the trusteeship that colonial control of Africa gave them. It is not insignificant that when these educational reforms went through in Blantyre and Livingstonia, they did so when the Mission Councils, not the presbyteries, of the CCAP controlled educational policy.

The last area to be considered, missionary biography, shows the clearest and most unambiguous victory of "trusteeship" in the missionary world. The minor industry that developed around the memory of David Livingstone, when in the first half of the twentieth century almost every child attending a Protestant Sunday school in Britain must have read or received a Livingstone biography, is a classic example of this victory.

Livingstone received a good scientific education at Anderson's College, now Strathclyde University, but in Curtin's terms remained an old-style conversionist. He was a bitter critic of British policy and of the British settlers in the Eastern Cape and a defender of Xhosa rights. This is not treated as of any great significance in any of his biographies until the most recent by Timothy Holmes. Most biographers make play with his clash with the Afrikaners of the Transvaal, a story that conforms to the British stereotype of the Afrikaner being the villain in race relations. What they ignore is that Livingstone went north to central Africa to escape white settlers and white government. Only Holmes considers the stance Livingstone took over the War of 1850-51 as an important element in understanding who Livingstone was. This conflict was between the Cape Colony and the Xhosa of Sandile aided by some Christian "Cape Folk" from the Kat River, tired of their unjust treatment at the hands of the British. Livingstone writes of the end of this conflict: "By the same post I send a letter for my brother containing Sandillah's speech to Renton, to be printed in America. All we learn of the Caffre here is too one-sided. We must hear both sides. It is well that Sandillah speaks out so nobly. Bringing out the converts to assist the English is infamous. We must either preach passive resistance or fighting for one's own countrymen."[41] A little later that same month he wrote again to Thompson in London, saying, "Everywhere there is a strong feeling of independence springing up . . . the de-

41. Livingstone to William Thompson (LMS agent), 6 September 1852, in David Chamberlin, ed., *Some Letters from Livingstone* (London, 1940), p. 177.

struction of my property is a fortunate thing for me. There is not a native in the country but knows for certain whose side I am on."[42] Perhaps even more striking is the omission from all these biographies of any serious discussion of Livingstone's respect for traditional African medicine and traditional African healers so often described by Europeans, even in the last quarter of the twentieth century, totally inaccurately, as "witch doctors." In his instructions to the young Dr. (later Sir) John Kirk at the beginning of the Zambesi expedition, Livingstone wrote,

> One certain means of gaining their favour will be by giving them the benefit of your medical skill and remedial aid. They possess medical men among themselves who are generally the most observant people to be met with; it is desirable to be at all times on good terms with them. In order to this [*sic*] slight complaints, except among the very poor, ought to be referred to their care, and severe cases, before being undertaken, should be enquired with the doctor himself and no disparaging remark ever made on the previous treatment in the presence of the patient.[43]

There are many more examples from Livingstone's books and letters that reveal a man firmly entrenched in the older conversionist mode, though at times, as in his estimate of African medicine, transcending that mode and touching on ideas that are only now becoming accepted.

Yet the Livingstone that appears in the many books produced about him between his death and the Second World War is the pioneer of European imperialism. Even among modern writers, only Jeal and Holmes show unambiguously that his vision was not at all that of the propagandists of empire.[44] In the "scramble for Africa" Livingstone's memory was invoked as a justification for what was being done. The "white man's burden" was being picked up on behalf of the poor Africans in response to Livingstone's appeal. The Livingstone who helped the Tswana get guns to defend themselves against the Transvaalers and who defended the right of the Xhosa to fight for their land did not fit in. It was not that the biographers were deliberate distorters of the truth. For them Livingstone's years in South Africa were a marginal overture to his work in central Africa, and so were passed over rapidly. His language and perceptions they saw through "lenses" shaped by the intellectual climate

42. Livingstone to Thompson, 30 September 1852, in Chamberlin, p. 179.

43. Reginald Foskett, ed., *The Zambesi Journal and Letters of Dr. John Kirk, 1858-63* (Edinburgh, 1965), app. 1, para. 8.

44. Tim Jeal, *Livingstone* (London, 1974), esp. pp. 382-84; Timothy Holmes, *Journey to Livingstone: Exploration of an Imperial Myth* (Edinburgh, 1994), passim.

of their day, which was not the one that had shaped his. They saw him through those racially distorted lenses and propagated the image of a Livingstone that fitted their era.[45] The image in these missionary biographies is normally tailored to fit that associated with the white man's burden, not usually through lies or deliberate distortion but simply as a result of writers understanding people from the past by their own preconceptions. The writers can also be excused because in the early twentieth century many, if not most, missionaries conformed increasingly to that image anyway.

There are, however, examples of genuine distortion that cannot be explained away by reference to the lens through which the observer looked. One particularly blatant case is W. P. Livingstone's biography of Christina Forsyth, which he entitled *Christina Forsyth of Fingoland: The Story of the Loneliest Woman in Africa.* Forsyth lived among the Mfengu of the Xolobe Valley in the Eastern Cape from 1885 until 1916. She was then literally carried out against her will by the mission authorities because of her ill health. The valley elders begged her to return to die and lie among them because "you are not white but one of us." She wanted to do this but was forbidden and invalided back to a Scotland she had not seen since 1884. What an extraordinary title to give a biography of a woman removed against her will from her friends! Some of the gaps in this biographical industry, moreover, appear much more deliberate. John Philip received no late Victorian or Edwardian biography, nor did David Scott.[46] Neither of them could be edited to fit the image, for they were engaged in open and explicit conflict with white supremacy. Livingstone in his South African days was as involved as Philip or Scott, but if one chose to pass over the South African years, the rest of his life could be used in the way it was, as Holmes has pointed out.[47]

From about 1900 to the early 1930s the trusteeship form of race thinking reached the peak of its influence on missionary thinking and practice. The title of a book by the convenor of the FMC of the period, Dr. Ogilvie's *Our Empire's Debt to Missions,* perhaps sums it all up. He does make the point of this chapter even more explicitly in the text where he writes, "Pioneers for Christ

45. See my "Livingstone: The Man behind the Mask," in *The London Missionary Society in Southern Africa,* ed. John de Gruchy (Cape Town, 1999), pp. 37-54.

46. The last years of D. C. Scott's life were spent at Kikuyu, and recent studies have suggested that even he succumbed to a "pro-settler" position; see Hastings, pp. 427, 557. This needs further investigation: against Hastings's interpretation of his work in Kenya we have Mzee Jomo Kenyatta's witness to how he was attracted by Scott to go to learn at Thogoto; see Robert Macpherson, *The Presbyterian Church in Kenya: An Account of the Origins and Growth of the Presbyterian Church of East Africa* (n.p., n.d.), p. 39.

47. Holmes, pp. 64-66.

these missionaries were: pioneers of Empire they became, often not willingly but in the end whole-heartedly and effectively. The record of Empire service is one of the romances alike of modern history and modern Missions."[48] Although in the late 1930s a serious challenge to Ogilvie's ideal began to appear, it was not until the 1950s that British Protestant missionary thinking finally threw off the last institutional forms, such as Mission Councils, of the trustees' perception of race relations. It was with the setting up of the Churches of the Provinces of West and East Africa, and the euthanasia of the Church of Scotland in Zambia, Malawi, and Kenya, that the ideals of Venn, Tucker, and David Scott were finally implemented.

48. James N. Ogilvie, *Our Empire's Debt to Missions* (London, 1924), p. 28.

Missionaries, Science, and the Environment in Nineteenth-Century Africa

JOHN M. MACKENZIE

> In connection with Mlinga, it may be interesting to note that in June 1885 two members of the Mission ascended it and planted a cross on the summit, 3,500 feet above the sea. In February 1897 a party of German surveyors made the ascent with a view to building an observatory on the highest point. Thus Christianity and Science unite in banishing superstition from the mountain.[1]

"Christianity and Commerce" is a celebrated missionary shibboleth (though a contested one) from the nineteenth century. "Christianity and Science" has a less familiar resonance. Yet the above quote from a biography of Bishop Smythies of the Universities' Mission to Central Africa (UMCA) conveys points about both the environment and science that can be found running through the missionary record in the nineteenth century. Mlinga is a mountain in Usambara, northeastern Tanzania, adjacent to the UMCA mission at Magila. The presence of the mission itself made environmental, scientific, and technical points to the local population, but missionaries also had a fascination with mountains. Bishop Smythies was described as finding it difficult to pass a hill or a mountain without climbing it. The symbolic significance of the mountain had distinctly biblical echoes. The mountaintop was a vantage point from which the missionary could take stock, to survey the field and assess present and future endeavor. It offered an opportunity for withdrawal from

1. G[ertrude] W[ard], *The Life of Charles Alan Smythies,* ed. Edward Francis Russell (London, 1899), p. 51.

the world, a withdrawal that nonetheless provided a symbolic position of superiority. In the conditions of the tropics, the mountain symbolized health in its cooler, disease-free heights. It provided recreation, particularly in opportunities for natural history study.[2] And finally, the cross and the putative observatory could make powerful statements to an extensive surrounding region.

With one or two notable exceptions, the relationship between missionaries, science, and the environment has been very little studied. Historians have been much more interested in missionaries' connections with political, economic, and social change; with their diplomatic and cultural relations with Africans; with their significance as ethnographers and philologists; as well as with their success or failure in conversion. Yet conceptualizations of science and the environment are everywhere in the missionary record in the nineteenth and early twentieth centuries. In memoirs and biographies, missionaries constructed the African environment in ways they clearly regarded as central to their religious message. In an age when amateur science was viewed as an educational and recreational adornment at almost all levels of society, they also viewed themselves as both students and bearers of Western science of every sort, including the medical.

David Livingstone remains a titanic figure in all of this. It may well be that many subsequent missionaries followed his example as well as reflecting contemporary norms. Certainly when Livingstone published his great work, *Missionary Travels and Researches in South Africa,* he intended the researches to mark him out as a scientist, as was symbolized by the illustration of a tsetse fly on the title page.[3] Indeed, a very important aspect of his lionization after its publication in 1857 was precisely his reception as a particular type of scientist. As he illustrated in the pages of the book, he corresponded with some of the most notable scientists of the age, Sir Thomas Maclear, astronomer royal at the Cape; Sir Joseph Hooker, director of Kew; Sir Roderick Murchison, geologist and president of the Royal Geographical Society; and later, Sir Richard Owen, director of the British Museum (natural history).

When Livingstone was received with considerable acclaim at Cambridge in December 1857, his hosts made it clear that this was a scientific as well as a religious event. The chairman, William Whewell, master of Trinity, was one of the most distinguished natural philosophers of the age. The cosponsor was

2. Gertrude Ward, p. 9. After an illness, Bishop Hannington described himself as helping his recovery with his "favourite activity of botanising." E. C. Dawson, *James Hannington, First Bishop of Eastern Equatorial Africa, 1847-85* (London, 1887), pp. 285-86. David Livingstone also commented on the health-giving pursuit of natural history: *Missionary Travels and Researches in South Africa* (London, 1857), p. 524.

3. David Livingstone, *Missionary Travels,* title page.

Adam Sedgwick, the venerable professor of geology in the university. In a farewell speech, Sedgwick described Livingstone's visit as the most notable occasion he had witnessed in the Senate House over the past fifty years. (Indeed, Sedgwick's remarks seem to be borne out by the jubilee celebrations held in the Senate House in 1907, surely a unique commemoration.) When the Reverend William Monk came to publish Livingstone's lectures, with an introduction that can only be described as ecstatic, Sedgwick appended a postscript in which he surveyed Livingstone's contribution to the scientific study of Africa in the areas of the vegetable kingdom, meteorology and climate, the animal kingdom, hydrography, physical geography, and geology, with a footnote on linguistics.[4]

Whewell and Sedgwick discovered in Livingstone not only the personification of an extraordinarily successful fusion of religion and natural science, but also a prime practitioner of natural theology. When Monk wrote that Livingstone's message had the capacity "to melt the heart, subdue the being, and enchain the soul" and thereby facilitate "the union of mankind into one common brotherhood of feeling, interest, sentiment and love, despite all differences of race, colour, clime, speech, condition and nationality," he was probably echoing Livingstone's own remarks toward the end of *Missionary Travels.*[5] For Livingstone, the missionary enterprise should be "the means by which God was bringing all His dealings with man to a glorious consummation." Not the least of the workers in this enterprise were "Men of science, searching after hidden truths, which when discovered will, like the electric telegraph, bind men more closely together."[6]

Livingstone's science was profoundly optimistic. This optimism, despite fever, exhaustion, and the loss of journals and notes, permeates his work. For example, he wrote of insects "being brimful of enjoyment," a phrase of which the celebrated natural theologian William Paley would have approved. Livingstone continued: "Indeed the universality of organic life may be called a mantle of happy existence encircling the world and imparts the idea of its being caused by the consciousness of our benignant Father's smile on all the works of His hands."[7] Yet Livingstone was all too well aware of the baleful ef-

4. *Dr. Livingstone's Cambridge Lectures together with a prefatory letter by the Reverend Professor Sedgwick,* edited with an introduction, life of Dr. Livingstone, notes, and appendix by the Reverend William Monk (London and Cambridge, 1858), pp. lxxxvii-xciii.

5. *Dr. Livingstone's Cambridge Lectures,* pp. ii-iii.

6. David Livingstone, *Missionary Travels,* pp. 673-74.

7. David Livingstone, *Missionary Travels,* p. 609. A classic image from Livingstone's natural theology occurs when he sees the "transmutation" of caterpillars into butterflies as equivalent to human resurrection (p. 54).

fects of the tsetse, and he even made a connection between the presence of mosquitoes and malaria.[8] But if his optimism was to wane in his second, Zambezi, expedition and in his last journals, it constitutes an extraordinarily strong thread through his first and greatest work. The exuberance of his descriptions and the minuteness of his observations revealed the manner in which he turned both a microscopic and a telescopic gaze upon Africa. That exuberance is well represented in his extensive passages on ants or in his remarkable descriptions of the Victoria Falls and his celebrated remark about "angels in their flight." *Missionary Travels* was of course a major best-seller, and it is repeatedly acknowledged as an inspiration by travelers, missionaries, hunters, administrators, and even scientists associated with Africa for very nearly a century after its publication. Its influence was profound, and as I have argued elsewhere, it carried sets of pre-Darwinian ideas both on race and on the environment through to a later age.[9]

Livingstone was also hailed as a practical man. Samuel Smiles in *Self-Help* hailed Livingstone's career as "one of the most interesting of all." Smiles admired him as a manual laborer who "dug canals, built houses, cultivated fields, reared cattle and taught the natives how to work as well as to worship."[10] But this is more than a modern echo of *laborare est orare.* The work involved at least some of the scientific knowledge which Sedgwick had acclaimed. Nowhere does Livingstone more reflect his powerful combination of natural theology, science, and approaches to the environment than in his repeated invocation of the garden. And gardens were to be both a practical objective and a powerful environmental metaphor for all subsequent missionaries.

Livingstone learned about the significance of the garden at Kuruman, the station of his father-in-law Robert Moffat. Typically he set about establishing the rate of growth of one of Moffat's trees. Laying out the garden was a vital step in the establishment of each of his own mission stations farther north. Obviously the garden had a severely practical purpose in producing

8. David Livingstone and Charles Livingstone, *Narrative of an Expedition to the Zambezi and its Tributaries and of the Discovery of Lakes Shirwa and Nyassa, 1858-1864* (London, 1865), p. 368.

9. For a survey of such inspirational references, see John M. MacKenzie, "David Livingstone: The Construction of a Myth," in *Sermons and Battle Hymns: Protestant Popular Culture in Modern Scotland,* ed. Graham Walker and Tom Gallagher (Edinburgh, 1990), pp. 24-42; MacKenzie, "The Iconography of the Exemplary Life: The Case of David Livingstone," in *Heroic Reputations and Exemplary Lives,* ed. Geoff Cubitt and Allen Warren (Manchester, 2000), pp. 84-104.

10. Samuel Smiles, *Self-Help,* centennial edition (London, 1959), pp. 244-46. Missionaries in East Africa described themselves as "builders, carpenters, smiths, wheelwrights, sanitary engineers, farmers, gardeners, printers, surgeons, physicians." Dawson, p. 195.

food for subsistence, but it went much further than this. The garden represented geometric order, hydrographic and botanical experimentation, the planting of fruit and other trees (often in avenues) and flowers as well as vegetables and cereals. Its very designation as a garden distinguished its horticultural rather than agricultural intent, its attention to individual plants as to individual souls. On his travels Livingstone occasionally described landscapes as being akin to an eastern garden or to the Garden of Eden, but despite his nomadism he still had a yearning to create gardens. On his first visit to Victoria Falls he set about creating a garden of fruit trees and productive shrubs (peach, apricot, coffee) on the island above the falls.[11] As the parent of all future gardens in the region, as he put it, this would be a symbolic first step to order and enlightened cultivation. He also carved his initials on a tree, symbolically embossing himself upon the environment, although he claimed this was the only time he permitted himself this indulgence. On the Zambezi expedition he left two white sailors at Tete while he traveled west to return the Makololo to their home territory, and encouraged them to make a garden. On this journey he revisited his garden at the Falls. He also saw the garden as the mark of the enlightened African. He visited the irrigated garden of a "superior Barotse." He complimented the people he called the Batoka for their planting of fruit trees. Although he castigated the Portuguese in so many other ways, he was impressed by their gardens in Loanda, as were his Makololo companions.[12]

The garden remained a symbol for most of Livingstone's missionary successors. The gardens at Lovedale on the eastern Cape or of the Scottish missions in Malawi, particularly that of Blantyre, were famous. For Christina Forsyth the mission at Emgwali itself represented a garden, the hand of civilization, "on the rolling expanse of bare country."[13] Robert Laws, according to his biographer, was distinguished as a gardener, in addition to all his other attainments, and taught Africans to grow flowers. So did Mary Slessor in West Africa.[14] Thus the aesthetic qualities of the garden, the emergence from the mere struggle for existence, represented the rediscovery

11. David Livingstone, *Missionary Travels*, pp. 113, 524.

12. Livingstone and Livingstone, pp. 155-56, 336; David Livingstone, *Missionary Travels*, pp. 213, 534-35; Livingstone and Livingstone, 231, 259; David Livingstone, *Missionary Travels*, pp. 379, 389, 401-2, 438-39.

13. W. P. Livingstone, *Christina Forsyth of Fingoland: The Story of the Loneliest Woman in Africa* (London, 1919), p. 43.

14. W. P. Livingstone, *The Hero of the Lake: A Life of Dr. Robert Laws for Boys* (London, 1933), pp. 66 and 132-33. See also Robert Laws, *Reminiscences of Livingstonia* (Edinburgh, 1934), pp. 262-63; W. P. Livingstone, *Mary Slessor of Calabar* (London, 1916), p. 137.

of an Edenic vision. Bishop Hannington gave his name to two plants and greatly admired the garden at Frere Town. For Bishop Smythies the orange avenue at Magila represented both the physical and spiritual beauty of the mission.[15] Magila was almost like a perfect English village, yet was distinctively African. Even at the deserted mission station of Mkomoindo, farther south, the garden represented a continuing hand upon the landscape, more durable than buildings themselves: "The garden is still beautiful — the mango trees imported by the missionaries in full flower — the lemon and citron trees a sight of real beauty, full of great golden fruit, strewing the ground as it falls all around. It is sad in the midst of all this to see the deserted buildings, some of them already tumbling down."[16] Thus even the abandoned garden had the capacity to historicize the landscape, to mark the presence of Livingstone on the Victoria Falls island and the former work of missionaries at Mkomoindo.

Terence Ranger has written of the African environment as a landscape which for the European had to be historicized.[17] While Africans allegedly lived within that landscape without imprinting their history upon it, Europeans saw the historically significant places, structures, and settlements of Europe as the emblems of civilization. W. P. Livingstone, most prolific of missionary biographers, described Africa as "mysterious" and "weird" with "no remembrance of former things."[18] Moreover, governors like Sir Charles Eliot saw environmental taming and training as one of the prime purposes of imperial power.[19] The landscape had to be controlled like a lion in a circus, sent to school and educated to the will of humankind. Just as Eliot argued that African isolation was precisely the result of this lack of environmental control, so did missionaries suggest, following Livingstone, that isolation produced degeneracy. And the marks of that degeneracy lay in the supposed African fear of natural phenomena, the "formidable and unaccountable forces of nature" like disease, lightning, and earthquake, as one missionary put it, which they could only cope with by witch finding and superstition.[20] They were also reflected in their capacity to damage the landscape. Robert Moffat viewed a

15. Dawson, p. 350; Gertrude Ward, p. 28.

16. Gertrude Ward, p. 45.

17. Terence Ranger, "Taking Hold of the Land: Holy Places and Pilgrimages in Twentieth-Century Zimbabwe," *Past and Present* 17 (1987): 158-94.

18. W. P. Livingstone, *Laws of Livingstonia: A Narrative of Missionary Adventure and Achievement* (London, n.d.), p. 1.

19. Sir Charles Eliot, *The East Africa Protectorate* (London, 1905), p. 4.

20. Donald Fraser, *The Autobiography of an African, Daniel Mtusu* (London, 1925), p. 131.

damaged landscape as evidence of a lack of grace.[21] Conversion would put the landscape to rights. Missionaries in northern Nyasaland (Malawi) repeatedly referred to the destructive use of the landscape by the Ngoni, particularly in deforestation and the resulting desiccation.[22] There can be no doubt that missionary heroism was conducted precisely within these contexts of countering the alleged fear of the natural world as well as promoting the historicizing, controlling, and education of the landscape. Their attitudes to that natural world were very much rooted within the revolution in sensibility that had overcome Europe in the romantic period.

Missionary memoirs and biographies abound in descriptions of the landscape. Many of these have an extraordinary positive and mystical quality, with many attempts to create biblical and Scottish referents. Both Lakes Victoria and Nyasa were compared to the Sea of Galilee, with their storms yet their sense of great events.[23] The Universities' Mission bishop, Chauncy Maples, saw the land around Lake Nyasa as a place of pilgrimage, a land "not bounded by earth's limits" where it might be possible to see "far above her mists — the Heavenly strand!" Donald Fraser and W. P. Johnson invested the land with a sense of wonder and mystery, linking it to the romantic images of the past which the Victorians so enjoyed. Johnson's description of "forests in some old fairy-book," "some dark pool near the Lake," clearly had Arthurian resonances.[24] Such historicization was rendered even more explicit by W. A. Elmslie, who saw himself as like Augustine at the court of Ethelbert, or by Johnson, Robert Laws, and Alexander Hetherwick, all of whom cited Columba on Iona as precedent. Alexander Mackay followed Stanley in writing of Uganda as a tropical paradise, while Slessor's biographer wrote of a land which exhibited "exquisite beauty" yet was "formless, mysterious, terrible." The books of Frederick Arnot also abound in ecstatic landscape description. But he made the whole point of this explicit. Where he found a "perfection of beauty," only man, he wrote, "is vile." Mackay also contrasted the

21. Robert Moffat, *Missionary Labours and Scenes in Southern Africa* (London, 1846), p. 66. See also Richard H. Grove, *Ecology, Climate, and Empire: Colonialism and Global Environmental History, 1400-1940* (Cambridge, 1997), pp. 89-91.

22. Laws, p. 186; W. A. Elmslie, *Among the Wild Ngoni* (Edinburgh, 1899), p. 32.

23. *A. M. Mackay, Pioneer Missionary of the Church Missionary Society to Uganda,* by his sister (London, 1893), p. 81 (hereafter *Mackay of Uganda,* as on the spine of the book); J. Cooke Yarborough, ed., *The Diary of a Working Man (William Bellingham) in Central Africa* (London, n.d.), p. 5.

24. Maples, quoted in Ven. William Percival Johnson, *My African Reminiscences, 1875-1895* (London, n.d.), p. 10; Donald Fraser, *The Future of Africa* (London, 1911), p. 3; Johnson, p. 221.

beauty of his surroundings with the "corruption and vice" of the people.[25] The landscape thus becomes at times a paradise, a Garden of Eden, which reflects a perpetual diurnal fall.

As such, it is a landscape that needs to be found and possessed. The graves of missionary pioneers, families, and associates are instructive here. Most missionary travelers in Africa found themselves making pilgrimages to the graves of their predecessors. The graves of Mary Livingstone at Shupanga, of Bishop Mackenzie, Scudamore, Dickinson and Charles Janson of UMCA, or those at the abandoned Cape Maclear by the Free Church became prime religious stations on the water route into central Africa, Henry Drummond's grossly inflated "stupendous natural highway." In Angola and the Congo, Arnot wrote of the chain of graves that marked the route to the interior: his was certainly a mission of notably high mortality.[26] The point was that those graves established moral rights. Cooke Yarborough wrote that Mackenzie's grave, "like the heart of Bruce, lay there, luring on his followers into the thick of battle."[27] In different books the tombs of missionaries were described as milestones for Christianity, for the church militant, stepping-stones and title deeds. Title deeds of course imply ownership: the blood of the heroic martyrs offered rights of occupation. And just as Rhodes aspired to a heroic and holy status through his burial in the Matoppo Hills, so too did James Stewart acquire tutelary deity status by being buried at the top of Sandili's Kop on Christmas Day.[28] His grave soon became a site of pilgrimage, of conventions to plan new educational developments, and of a major monument.

But if environmental control was bound up with heroism and moral power, it could be more practically advanced by science and engineering. These emblematic disciplines of a progressive world were also part of the thrilling incident that placed missionaries so firmly in a late nineteenth-century imperial adventure tradition. James Stewart, whose relations with Livingstone were so famously ambivalent, regarded himself as scientist and practical man, as well as divine and doctor. Not only did he publish botani-

25. Elmslie, p. 134; W. P. Livingstone, *A Prince of Missionaries, the Rev. Alexander Hetherwick* (London, n.d.), p. 173; Laws, p. 65; *Mackay of Uganda,* p. 412; W. P. Livingstone, *Mary Slessor of Calabar,* p. 23; Frederick Stanley Arnot, *Garenganze or Mission Work in Central Africa* (London, n.d.), p. 44; *Mackay of Uganda,* pp. 214-15.

26. Laws, pp. 10, 60; Henry Drummond, *Tropical Africa* (London, 1888), pp. 10, 33, 41, 45, 205, 221; Gertrude Ward, pp. 62, 65; F. S. Arnot, *Missionary Travels in Central Africa* (Glasgow, 1914), p. 106.

27. Cooke Yarborough, pp. 3, 21, 29, 47, 125.

28. Laws, p. 60; Cooke Yarborough, p. 6; James Wells, *Stewart of Lovedale: The Life of James Stewart* (London, 1909), pp. 128, 373-75.

cal works, he also carefully annotated Livingstone's *Missionary Travels and Researches* by drawing up lists of the hero's scientific observations, carefully organized under their different scientific headings. Although his record in central Africa was one of skepticism and disillusion, his biographer portrayed him as following in the Livingstone mold as renaissance man, bringing his command of the whole range of Western disciplines to full fruition at Lovedale.[29] Robert Laws followed in the same tradition, driving Stewart's fascination with the steam engine and the sawmill into a new age by emphasizing the importance of piped water and electricity in creating the appropriate environment for Christian conversion. He had originally trained himself for Africa by working in both a ropewalk and a brickworks, and he continued to see the lake steamer as the prime instrument of conquest by conversion in Africa.[30]

James Stewart's namesake and cousin was an engineer, abandoning a career in the Indian canals system for work in central Africa. As well as helping with the choice and layout of mission sites in Malawi, he worked until his death on the construction of the Stevenson Road. The popular biographer of George Grenfell, the Baptist who worked in the Cameroons and the Congo, described him as fascinated by all mechanical things.[31] He had a love of ships, and his engineering knowledge and mechanical skill were the keys to his missionary exploits. Arnot spent six months at a shipyard near Dundee before leaving for Africa. François Coillard famously turned his practical knowledge of French agriculture to canalization, enthusiastically taken up by Lewanika and at least one Lozi engineer, Mwanangombe.[32] Alexander Mackay, Mackay of Uganda as he was always known in a sub-Henty phrase, was also an engineer, who interestingly shared with the Reverend James Stewart the experience of spending time in Germany, picking up the language and surveying superior German technology. Mackay considered mechanical work "probably as legitimate an aid to missions as medical." Missions, he argued, are more dependent on "the advance the century has made in mechanics than in medicine."[33] This was reflected in the repeated use he made of engineering meta-

29. Wells, pp. 12, 21, and passim.

30. W. P. Livingstone, *Laws of Livingstonia*, pp. 31, 49.

31. Shirley J. Dickins, *Grenfell of the Congo: Pioneer Missionary and Explorer* (London, n.d.), pp. 18, 34, 48.

32. Arnot, *Missionary Travels*, p. x; Gwyn Prins, *The Hidden Hippopotamus* (Cambridge, 1980), pp. 64-68; C. W. Mackintosh, *Coillard of the Zambezi: The Lives of François and Christine Coillard of the Paris Missionary Society in South and Central Africa* (London, 1907), chap. 1.

33. *Mackay of Uganda*, pp. 6, 14; Wells, p. 22; *Mackay of Uganda*, pp. 228 and 250.

phors. Although his time at the courts of Mtesa and his successor Mwanga of Buganda was fraught with alarms and dangers, he never ceased to emphasize the power of his superior engineering and technical knowledge. This could be reflected in the apparently mundane raising of a flagpole, in building and maintaining vessels, in constructing steam engines, in manufacturing coffins for Mtesa and the Queen Mother, in a host of small tasks, or in the rather grander laying out of roads.

African reactions to Mackay's first efforts at road building near the coast in 1877 varied from openmouthed and open-eyed admiration for the *njia kubwa,* or big road of the white man, to an attempt to levy a hundred dollar fine for cutting down trees, to fear that the road meant that "the English are coming to take possession of the country," "an alarm," wrote Mackay, "which I hope will die a natural and speedy death." Mackay had constructed a road broad enough, like the famous streets of Bulawayo, "to allow the largest bullock wagons to pass each other at any point" and no doubt turn round when required. Mackay heard a mixture of environmental, political, and cultural sentiments expressed in an admirably rhyming song sung by his laborers:

> Eh, eh, msungu *mbaya*
> Tu katti miti,
> Tu ende *Ulaya,*

which he paraphrased as "Oh, is not the white man very bad to be cutting down the trees to make a way for Englishmen to come."[34]

Such reactions to the practical efforts at command of the landscape by the white missionary can be found, if less graphically, elsewhere. We are told that the Africans who worked on the construction of mission stations in Nyasaland (Malawi) came to be known as "the bricks."[35] Local people had rightly come to identify the brick as symbolizing much more than simply the building block. The brick was rectangular: it involved the utilization of ant heaps, the ironing out of the structures of the white ant, those omnipresent pimples upon the landscape. It was associated with a new form of kiln. It was a stimulus to basic capitalism, as when the Free Church missionary Elmslie contracted out brick making to an African contractor at the seemingly less than generous price of four shillings per thousand.[36] The brickworks became

34. *Mackay of Uganda,* p. 57.

35. Fraser, *Autobiography of an African,* p. 57; Elmslie, p. 150.

36. John McCracken, *Politics and Christianity in Malawi, 1875-1940* (Cambridge, 1977), p. 98; Elmslie, p. 230.

the sine qua non of the mission station that demonstrated a full command of its environment. And being itself rectangular, it produced rectangular structures. Almost all southern African missionaries, not least those in Nyasaland, reflected on the contrast between the circle and the straight line. Africans built in circles and allegedly found straight lines incomprehensible, pointing to the sun, the moon, and the horizon for their justification. One missionary biographer quoted Ruskin, who had remarked, with a very different intention, that the circle was symbolic of rest.[37] In southern Africa, the writer went on, it is the symbol of laziness. One missionary in his memoir described the patience required to persuade an African bricklayer to lay his bricks in a straight line and to the vertical.[38] Many commented on the sinuousness of African paths, and one traveler was even induced to say that elephants were better engineers than Africans.[39] It is ironic, then, that just as European commentators, following such luminaries as Ruskin and Owen Jones in his celebrated *Grammar of Ornament,* were arguing that architecture and design should seek inspiration from natural forms, missionaries should see the straight line as the means of negating the unbridled circularity of nature. Just as the steam vessel had the power to overcome wind and sea, so had the straight line and its corollaries, the road, the bridge, and the brick building, the power to keep nature at bay, beat back vegetation, conquer streams and rivers, and keep out the animals and insects of Africa as no round hut could do. But straightness went further even than this: it reflected the straight lines of the book, the apparently rational and logical route through Western science and medicine, and the path to the core of a simple and revelatory theology. However much the myth departed from the reality, the missionary hero was straight, as much in his character as in his back.

Geometry, of course, was about straight lines and complex angles, and surveying and astronomical sights were functions of geometry and, in the latter case, of the linearity of time. All were brought to bear upon the selection and layout of the mission station. It is surely no accident that Donald Fraser described his mission at Loudon as shaped like a spade, a symbol both of labor and again of the straight line.[40] In a popular biography we are told that Laws laid out the first Free Church mission at Cape Maclear in the shape of

37. Wells, p. 217. On the circularity of the African approach to building and nature, see, among many references, Drummond, pp. 138-39; H. T. Cousins, *From Kafir Kraal to Pulpit: The Story of Tiyo Soga* (London, 1899), p. 10; Elmslie, p. 33.

38. Fraser, *Autobiography of an African,* p. 80.

39. Drummond, pp. 34-36; Laws, pp. 28-29.

40. Donald Fraser, *African Idylls: Portraits and Impressions of Life on a Central African Mission Station* (London, 1925), p. 18.

the Union Jack.[41] Thus the geometry of the national flag was laid down upon Africa, an interesting assertion of unionism by a Scot. To return to the potent symbolism of gardens, a visitor to the Blantyre Mission marveled at its splendid line of fragrant eucalyptuses.[42] Here the acclimatization of the exotic is itself marshaled into a command of its environment through the straight line of the forester or the creator of the ornamental avenue. The garden at Blantyre, with its three thousand to four thousand plants, many of them exotic, was seen not only as an engine of economic development, through experimentation with coffee, tea, tobacco, and rubber, but also as a means of diversifying and extending the botany of the territory. It stood in the tradition of the great eighteenth-century gardens in the Caribbean, India, and the Indian Ocean, including William Carey's garden at Serampore.[43] It was also part of the major movement for plant acclimatization taking place throughout the British and other empires in the late nineteenth century. This and other mission gardens came to be paradises that were in Africa but not wholly of Africa, part of a biological conquest that could tame the higgledy-piggledy character of African vegetation into the routine and order of the plantation. Not far from the garden, David Clement Scott's elaborate Byzantine church, reflecting its builder's theological and liturgical eccentricities, lay at the center of the radiating system of roads of the mission, the straight lines leading to education, medical care, and both workshops and worship.

When Robert Laws came to lay out his new and controversial Overtoun Institution in northern Nyasaland in the mid-1890s, he clearly thought in terms of the metropolitan estate, with its carefully designed roads and avenues, its areas demarcated for different agricultural and industrial activities, and its buildings ultimately reflecting the variety of their function and the grandeur of their objectives.[44] The illustration (fig. 1) reveals the water supply intake, the sawmill and brickworks, the farms all around the north side, and the arrangement of agriculturalist, medical, workshop, and technical departments, as well as the separation of European and African areas, and those of boys and girls, the latter pushed out toward the edge. The church is not at the symbolic center — that is reserved for a network of roads that seem to imply much future development and population growth — but is toward the edge of the estate and its village. The Europeans are located on the eastern ledge of

41. W. P. Livingstone, *Hero of the Lake,* p. 50; see also the illustration at p. 48 of his *Laws of Livingstonia.*

42. W. P. Livingstone, *Prince of Missionaries,* p. 22.

43. For a popular account of Carey's life, see Edward A. Annett, *William Carey, Pioneer Missionary in India* (London, n.d.). Carey's garden is described on pp. 78 and 140-43.

44. W. P. Livingstone, *Laws of Livingstonia,* illustration, p. 209.

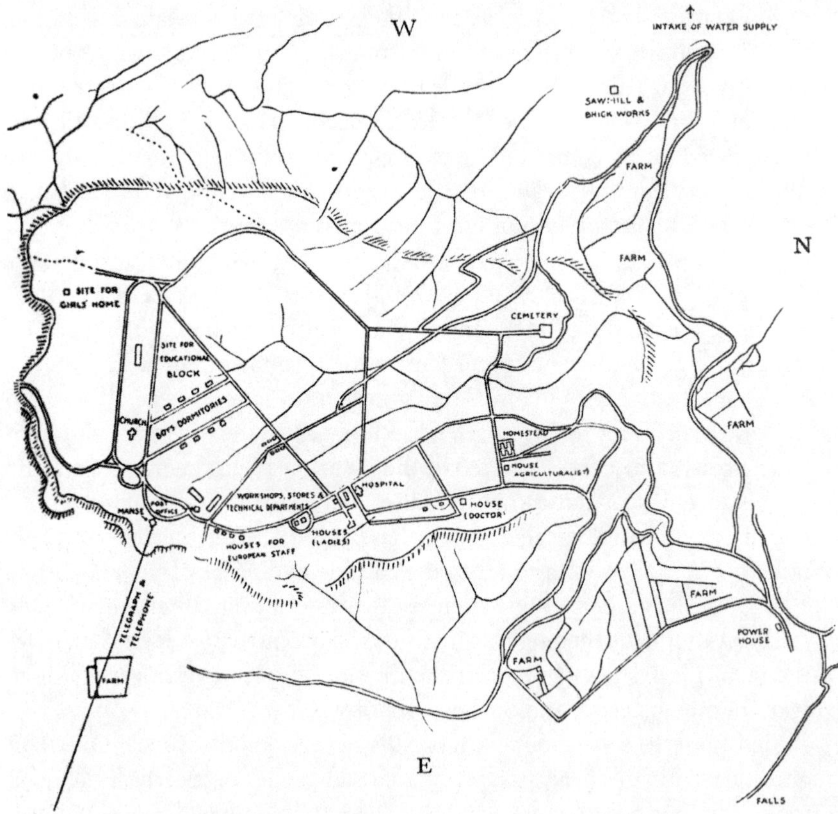

Figure 1. The ambitious plans of Robert Laws for the Livingstonia Mission. From Robert Laws, *Reminiscences of Livingstonia.*

the escarpment looking toward the lake, with the manse perched at the most dramatic corner, the focal point of the incoming, and very straight, telegraph and telephone line. The manse indeed is closer to the post office than the church, an interesting spatial relationship. Laws was proud that the fine general post office, with its dominant tower and large disciplining clock, was built by African schoolboys.[45] As well as the telegraph, for which Laws surveyed the route to the lake, there was a system of heliographic mirrors to signal the lake steamer in Florence Bay. Laws also led his pupils in planting trees, including cedars. As his biographer put it, as the land was "redeemed from

45. The general post office is illustrated in W. P. Livingstone, *Laws of Livingstonia,* p. 257, and *Hero of the Lake,* p. 193.

Figure 2. The general post office at Livingstonia Mission, "built by the schoolboys." From W. P. Livingstone, *Laws of Livingstonia.*

the jungle and the wild beasts, nature would grow kindlier."[46] And just as American schools were financed by large tracts of land, a system which greatly impressed Laws on a visit to the United States, and also just as British cities acquired great estates as part of their search for purer water supplies and healthier arrangements for their citizens, so did Laws want his estate

46. W. P. Livingstone, *Hero of the Lake,* pp. 187-88, 192, 194.

backed by land. After much debate he and the mission acquired more than 45,000 acres, a tract of truly Highland proportions.[47]

Notoriously, Laws's buildings in fact lagged behind for a period, while expenditure was directed toward the other functions of the Overtoun estate. Nevertheless, his fascination with piped water and electricity echoed the municipal socialism of the cities of his Scottish homeland and the ambitions not only of his powerful industrial backers but also of estate owners like Armstrong at Cragside or Fletcher at Rosehaugh. When Laws resolved to pipe water into the mission and build a dynamo at a waterfall, he returned to Scotland to raise the money. Many felt he was "crazy," but he proclaimed, echoing William Carey's famous slogan, that he was "attempting great things for God" and "expected great things from God," and he succeeded, against all expectation, in raising £8,000 from benefactors.[48] As at so many such estates, Fraser at Loudon created an artificial lake by building a dam. Its waters were used for drinking and bathing and its shores for a holiday cottage. But unlike Laws, Fraser never stinted on his buildings. Both he and Elmslie believed the missionary should have an adequate, if not superior, manse as a clear indicator of what the Christian could achieve. (In this they followed Livingstone, who believed the missionary should have a decent house to inspire respect.)[49] Such a building, in the same language as that used to describe the ladies of the mission, had a "refining influence." It should be a noble structure (that adjective was used) in two stories, with fine verandas and good views over the neighboring country, so that the missionary could symbolically scan the horizon and plan further extension. Suitably situated, the mission house could become its own mountaintop. Such a house naturally combined strong horizontal and vertical lines that gave it a dominant position in such an architectural and natural landscape. The other houses in the mission might be called the house of God, the house of education, and the house of medicine. Although conditions often fell far below the ideal, much attention was paid to their relationship and their appearance. They introduced foreign geometry and were alleged to fascinate headmen and others with the glories of Western architecture. Indeed, buildings themselves were described as books, which could convey

47. McCracken, p. 135.

48. W. P. Livingstone, *Hero of the Lake,* pp. 195-97; McCracken (p. 134) indicates that Laws had earlier raised the sum of £9,000 and that it came from his supporters Overtoun and Stevenson.

49. Fraser, *African Idylls,* p. 56; Donald Fraser, *Winning a Primitive People: Ngoni, Senga, Tumbuka* (London, 1914), p. 20, where he suggested that every building was like a book; Elmslie, pp. 210, 213; David Livingstone, *Missionary Travels,* p. 40.

lessons and messages as much as paper and print. And within them were all the emblems of Western command: furniture, pictures, clocks, guns, books, chemicals, crockery, cutlery, and as Fraser put it in a key phrase, "the whitest of table cloths."[50] The white tablecloth symbolized the elevating refinement of the missionary wife, cleanliness, civilized eating, and the sophisticated textile production and bleaching of Western industry.

The siting of churches and missions was also given geographical significance. Famously the UMCA cathedral at Zanzibar was built on the site of the slave market, "raising its silent testimony to the triumph of Christianity over slavery," although we should also remember that, given the circumstances of the time, it was partly built by slave labor.[51] The cathedral on Likoma Island in Lake Nyasa was built on the spot where witches had allegedly been burned.[52] Coillard chose the site of his mission at Sefula partly because it was described as a sorcerers' graveyard.[53] The Paris Missionary Society mission at Lealui was placed on the execution ground.[54] Thus missionaries saw a new moral geography as overlaying another; former dark deeds were expunged by Western engineering and architecture.

While building was itself a literally elevating industrial art, others were taught within the confines of this improving architecture. At Overtoun instruction was given in wireless telegraphy. African students were inducted into the mysteries of electromagnetism to equip them as telegraphists and to contribute to the migration of the Overtoun elite throughout southern Africa. It comes as no surprise to find that Laws, in his memoirs, reflected on the contrast in length of time a message had taken to reach the outside world during his fifty years in central Africa. In the 1870s a letter had taken thirteen months to reach Scotland; by the early 1930s the Livingstonia Mission could communicate with its base in under three hours. Alexander Hetherwick felt that, with the help of Reuters, his mission was the center of the world.[55] Livingstone had transmitted to many of his successors that key relationship between isolation and degeneracy, the notion that commercial and other intercourse contributed to religious elevation. (Bishop Frank Weston of UMCA was a relatively rare exception: he was opposed to both commerce and indus-

50. Fraser, *Winning a Primitive People,* p. 22.

51. Johnson, p. 33; H. Maynard Smith, *Frank, Bishop of Zanzibar: Life of Frank Weston, D.D. 1871-1924* (London, [1926]), p. 73.

52. George Herbert Wilson, *The History of the Universities' Mission to Central Africa* (London, 1936), pp. 126-27.

53. Prins, p. 64.

54. Arnot, *Missionary Travels,* p. 144.

55. Laws, p. vii; W. P. Livingstone, *Prince of Missionaries,* p. 100.

trial training as aspects of missionary activity.)[56] In the dominant Livingstonian paradigm, electricity and the telegraph were the ultimate destroyers of backwardness, the lines that could facilitate Christianity, commerce, and civilization as none others.

If the straight line imposed a certain discipline, so too did the manipulation of time. Missions were run with the discipline of the factories at home from which Livingstone, Mary Slessor, and some of the other missionaries had escaped. The day at Lovedale, Blantyre, and Livingstonia — and no doubt many other places — was carefully broken up into blocks of time, demarcated by the ringing of bells. Thus a form of naval discipline, with the watches divided up into educational, technical, agricultural, and religious blocks of activity, was created. Or to change the simile, the Protestant mission ironically became like the medieval monastery. Blantyre also used a bugle, establishing a military connection as well. Alexander Hetherwick's biographer described the missionary sitting in his manse at the center of the mission hearing the work and worship going on round about him, controlled by bell and bugle. Other musical calls to worship included a whistle, a brass gong, a cornet, and a horn, the latter appropriately instigated by the hunting Fraser, in northern Malawi. Thus both space and time were carefully cut up, establishing a route to redemption through discipline. Yet another means of imposing discipline was through drill and sports. The first was again quasi-military, the second an acknowledgment of rules and control by a referee, reflecting in some respects the rules and natural laws of the environment. Many missionaries, including slightly bizarrely Mary Slessor, extolled the virtues of cricket and football in offering a route to the disciplined and therefore purer life. UMCA missionaries brought up in rather different sporting traditions encouraged football on all their stations. On Zanzibar barefoot African players always beat teams of sailors from the naval ships in the harbor! Through such success Africans demonstrated to the missionaries that they were capable of taking on the disciplines of team sports. As W. P. Johnson of the Universities' Mission put it, the African was not stupid, but ignorant.[57] This approach to race, closely connected as it is to the opportunities provided by Western science, natural rules, and approaches to the environment, reflects another of Livingstone's legacies.

When the Scottish National Memorial to David Livingstone was opened in Blantyre, Lanarkshire, in 1929, the major icons of the Protestant saint were de-

56. Smith, pp. 24, 60.

57. W. P. Livingstone, *Prince of Missionaries,* p. 151; Fraser, *The Future of Africa,* p. 203; W. P. Livingstone, *Mary Slessor of Calabar,* p. 306; Smith, p. 47; Johnson, pp. 135, 162.

Figure 3. "Courage": Armed only with a sextant, Livingstone encounters Nguni warriors. The C. d'O. Pilkington Jackson sculpture at the David Livingstone Centre, Blantyre, reproduced by kind permission of the Centre and of the National Trust for Scotland.

signed to illustrate just such a proposition.[58] Eight statues by the sculptor C. d'O. Pilkington Jackson (with Robert Laws advising on "authenticity") portrayed Livingstone as scientist and teacher. Figure 3 illustrates this well. Livingstone's short stature is emphasized by the headdresses of the presumably Nguni warriors he confronts. If his right hand is raised in blessing, his left clutches a sextant. He is armed not with a gun, but with Western science. His power over both Africans and the surrounding landscape, suggested subtly by some strange vegetation and the canoe, is symbolized by the fact that he knows where he is, or thinks he does, not only in theological but also in spatial terms. As he travels, his sightings with his sextant permit him to place lines and grids upon the map, even if he sometimes gets them wrong. But his right hand raised in benediction and his left clutching the sextant also seems to symbolize his approach to race and the salvability of the African. The Ngoni warriors facing him, despite their history of migration and central organization, are limited not biologically but socially and culturally. Their limitation is reflected not in their genes but in

58. For a description of these sculptures, see James I. Macnair, *The Story of the Scottish National Memorial* (Blantyre, 1929), p. 24.

their shields and arms, in their fierce expressions and their alleged record of cruelty and destruction, including, as we have seen, destruction of the environment. Livingstone himself had doubts about Darwin's *Origin of Species,* which he expressed in a famous letter to Richard Owen. He reflected on biological characteristics that he could not conceive being linked to natural selection and, perhaps surprisingly, proclaimed himself unable to see any struggle for survival in "this wide continent," where "there is room enough and to spare for both man and beast."[59] He had disappeared into Africa on his long final journey and died before the full excesses of social Darwinism could be developed. His legacy and intellectual influence were such that it is difficult to find evidence of a noticeable social Darwinism running through the writings of the missionaries in Africa who were his inheritors. Of course, there are references to Africans being akin to European ancestors. For example, the lake dwellings of the Tonga reminded Laws of the Scottish crannogs he had learned about at university. The art and economy of the Bushmen, inevitably and not entirely inaccurately, were connected to the cave paintings of the hunter-gatherers of a remote European past. But one missionary connected African superstition to the superstitions of fellow countrymen in both the Highlands and Lowlands of Scotland.[60] The full panoply of social Darwinian notions, involving fundamental genetic difference and the inevitability of competition and extinction induced if necessary by war, never appears in missionary writings.[61] Obviously such ideas ran directly counter to the entire missionary enterprise, to the possibility of religious, cultural, and social redemption.

It is noticeable just how much more social Darwinian comment, often accompanied by racial descriptions, appears in the works of secular figures such as Frederick Selous or Henry Drummond. The latter's book of African travels, *Tropical Africa,* so closely associated with missionary enterprise, differs markedly from missionary commentaries. Although missionaries frequently used the contemporary language of race — for example, to Fraser the Tumbuka were "effeminate and leaderless," the Senga "feeble" — Africans differed from Europeans in morals rather than mental capacity.[62] If what mis-

59. A facsimile of this letter appears in John M. MacKenzie, ed., *David Livingstone and the Victorian Encounter with Africa* (London, 1996), p. 98.

60. Laws, p. 43; Fraser, *The Future of Africa,* pp. 106-8; Elmslie, p. 228.

61. For a recent discussion of the absence of social Darwinian ideas, see Paul Crook, "Historical Monkey Business: The Myth of a Darwinized British Imperial Discourse," *History* 84, no. 276 (1999): 633-57.

62. Drummond, *Tropical Africa;* see also Frederick Courteney Selous, *Sunshine and Storm in Rhodesia* (London, 1896), for a strongly social Darwinian approach to Africans; Fraser, *Winning a Primitive People,* pp. 8, 84.

sionaries saw as superstition, sensuality, and obscene play and dance could only be overcome, then rational education, civilization, and Christianity could find a place. To the biographer of Hetherwick, Africans were half awake and bewildered, their minds dormant and without ambition. But as Donald Fraser put it in his biography of Daniel Mtusu, the difference lay in ethics, not in theology.[63] Others, as we have seen in the case of gardens, thought it lay in both aesthetics and ethics.

Perhaps these distinctions are related to the missionaries' avowed conviction in the brotherhood of humankind, bound by chains of steel, as Fraser put it in a notably engineering phrase.[64] In this they seemed to echo Livingstone's views, which may well connect with an earlier intellectual tradition. But they may also be related to the status of so many of them as medical men, again following in the Livingstone tradition. Some missionaries — Elmslie and Donald Fraser are both good examples — had some understanding of the complexities of African medicine and often made distinctions between medicine men or herbalists and the people they characterized as witch doctors.[65] They also often expressed admiration for African veterinary practice. But all saw the new and exciting medical tradition of the nineteenth century as vastly superior, although Livingstone did suggest that the African pharmacopoeia would repay further study.[66] Indeed, the invasive techniques of Western medicine may well have helped to convince them that the difference of color was only skin deep.

Medicine was a central scientific tool of missions. As is well known, even medically unqualified missionaries dabbled in medicine, although their descriptions of their activities in this regard often make them seem more like medicine men than medical men. All were convinced that nothing was more likely to help them ingratiate themselves either with chiefs or with the populace than a modicum of medical skill combined with the compassion that went with it. Even the more highly qualified seem to have operated at a primitive level. McCracken tells us that Laws mainly dispensed Epsom salts and rhubarb pills.[67] Here was another aspect of Western science that facilitated

63. W. P. Livingstone, *Prince of Missionaries,* p. v; Fraser, *Autobiography of an African,* p. 55.

64. Fraser, *African Idylls,* p. 186.

65. Elmslie, p. 66; David Livingstone, *Missionary Travels,* pp. 130-31; Fraser, *The Future of Africa,* p. 153. Livingstone even consulted Sekeletu's doctor over an attack of fever (p. 195). Fraser (*Winning a Primitive People,* p. 141) had considerable respect for African veterinary practices.

66. David Livingstone, *Missionary Travels,* pp. 646-50.

67. McCracken, p. 38.

Christian understanding and redemption, which fitted perfectly with the notion of Christ as the healer of the world.

Yet even though they claimed that Western medicine sought in its rationality to confront alleged superstition and witch finding, missionaries (particularly, perhaps, those who dabbled without training) were very much aware that they set themselves up in a magical tradition. Charles Darwin had himself remarked on the voyage of the *Beagle,* that missionaries were capable of waving an enchanter's wand.[68] Later in the century they were still not averse to securing the plaudits of magic. Much technology was inevitably viewed in this light, particularly that of the great iron canoe and the steam engine. Missionary steamers were also projected to supporters at home as extraordinarily magical intrusions into a primitive landscape. The almost universal printing press offered a near magical route into the worlds of Bible and learning. In memoirs and biographies, missionaries were cheerfully cloaked in the magician's mantle. Bishop Hannington in East Africa was taken to be a magician and linked superstitions and necromancy to his experience of the English West country.[69] (Interestingly, sailors on ships viewed missionaries with superstitious dread, seeing them as Jonahs.)[70]

Mary Slessor, busily knitting or using her sewing machine during palavers, must have given herself a magical air. The organs and harmoniums that seem to have been carried everywhere into Africa had a similar effect. Mackay saw not only the steam engine, but also the turning lathe, the candle mold, and the crude wagon and iron wheelbarrow he used at the southern end of Lake Victoria as offering evidence that white men came from heaven. At the Blantyre Mission, a traction engine was used to frighten off locusts, an intriguing application of steam to the natural world. Meteorological instruments and observations were allegedly credited with the capacity to control the climate. Rain gauges were sometimes seen as creating the very problems they were designed to study.[71]

Astronomical knowledge seems to have offered irresistible opportunities. Donald Fraser was not above using an eclipse of the moon to frighten a chief in a manner which would have done justice to Rider Haggard. The Lozi suspected Coillard of having covered up the sun in the eclipse of August 1886. Using a glass to make fire seldom failed to induce wonder, at least until it be-

68. Wells, pp. 253-54.

69. Dawson, pp. 66-68, 237.

70. Mackintosh, p. 31.

71. W. P. Livingstone, *Mary Slessor of Calabar,* pp. 84, 118-19; *Mackay of Uganda,* p. 72; W. P. Livingstone, *Prince of Missionaries,* p. 117; Livingstone and Livingstone, p. 46; Elmslie, p. 169.

came commonplace. The UMCA missionary artisan William Bellingham discovered that his telescope was treated as a gun.[72] Real guns, particularly recent sporting models, never failed to impress in their range and accuracy. James Stewart, who had shot over his father's small farm in Perthshire as a boy, proclaimed his ambition to move through Africa with a Bible in his pocket and a gun over his shoulder.[73] Like Donald Fraser, he seems to have been a notable sporting shot who kept companions and followers well supplied with game meat. Although Africans complained to the Universities' Mission artisan that white men could make steamers, engines, watches, but not rain, missionaries did indeed often find themselves acting as rainmakers.

Tiyo Soga, the first Gaika minister, educated in Glasgow, ridiculed the reputation of Ross at Pirie beyond the Cape frontier as a rainmaker as early as the 1850s.[74] But later Arnot in Botswana, Elmslie in Ngoniland, even Bishop Weston in East Africa all developed reputations for making rain. When Elmslie struck a fortunate conjunction, his correspondence with fellow missionaries indicated that he was thoroughly embarrassed to discover his new reputation, but in his book for public consumption he put an entirely different spin on his rainmaking success. Arnot tried to enhance his magical power, and incidentally prove the existence of God, by praying for the return of an African's dog.[75] Fortunately for him, he judged its homing instincts correctly.

But other opportunities for magic also presented themselves, including the appropriately named magic lantern, which Livingstone had earlier used to great effect. Recognizing that it was something more than just a projector of pictures, he described it as revealing the oxyhydrogen light of civilization. Arnot discovered that Livingstone's lantern was still well remembered in Barotseland many years after the explorer's visit. Mary Slessor intriguingly used a magic lantern display to add prestige to the funeral of a chief's son and thereby avoid, as she thought, human sacrifice.[76] The magic of the lantern was sometimes used to demonstrate the great power of the white man, as when Livingstonia missionaries showed Ngoni viewers pictures of battles, big guns, regiments, and Mediterranean forts. W. P. Johnson described Archdeacon (later Bishop) Maples as a natural conjurer, who rejoiced in the use of the

72. Fraser, *Winning a Primitive People,* p. 236; Prins, p. 195; Cooke Yarborough, p. 17.

73. Wells, p. 6.

74. Cousins, p. 121.

75. Arnot, *Missionary Travels,* p. 4; Elmslie, p. 176; Smith, p. 79; McCracken, p. 91; Arnot, *Garenganze,* p. 84.

76. The lantern can still be seen at the David Livingstone center, Blantyre: it is illustrated in MacKenzie, *Victorian Encounter,* p. 151; Arnot, *Missionary Travels,* p. 25; W. P. Livingstone, *Mary Slessor of Calabar,* p. 97.

magic lantern. By this time Livingstone had himself become a subject of magic lantern slides.[77] Moreover, by the 1890s photography, aided by the new Kodak cameras and contact film, was itself becoming a common accomplishment of missionaries, helping to supply the illustrations for so many missionary books. Coillard's photographic activities certainly contributed to his magic aura. Soon after the turn of the century the lantern was joined by the gramophone, and not long after that by the cinematograph.[78]

Mention of the cinematograph leads me, finally, to consider the popular cultural representation of missionaries themselves. Perhaps it comes as little surprise to find that popular entertainment has seldom handled them kindly. They have invariably been portrayed either as figures of fun or as people with high ambitions who are frustrated by the overwhelming forces they take on, not least the power of human nature itself. What I find fascinating about this depiction is that it represents almost the precise opposite of their representation of themselves. As we have seen, their self-image was as people who controlled their natural and human environments with the help of technology, science, and Western medicine, as well as through their magical aura, their moral force and state of grace. This reversal is neatly expressed in the music hall and cartoon representation of the culinary encounter between missionary and cannibal, which requires no further comment.

When we turn to film, it is intriguing to discover that Livingstone, as in so many other respects, is left in a class of his own. Just as he, uniquely, was celebrated on the stamps of no fewer than six African countries in the centennial year of 1973, so too does he tend to cut a favorable image in the cinema.[79] In 1925 his story was used by M. A. Wetherell to justify a major location expedition to Africa, including much popular filming of African wildlife, and to elevate the use of film for higher purposes. It seems to have been a reasonably popular production both in the cinema and in church and public halls. In 1939 Cedric Hardwicke and Spencer Tracy, both hopelessly miscast, trans-

77. McCracken, p. 90; Johnson, p. 136; a series of lantern slides on Livingstone's life was produced around the turn of the century by the London Missionary Society. They are now in the collection of the National Portrait Gallery, London, and were projected at the exhibition on Livingstone in London and Edinburgh in 1996.

78. Prins, p. 194. Donald Fraser, among other missionaries, was an enthusiastic photographer (*Winning a Primitive People,* p. 10, and *The Future of Africa,* p. vi), while Laws regarded picture recognition — he often used pages from the *Graphic* — an important part of Western education: Laws, pp. 96-97; Fraser, *The Future of Africa,* p. 78, for the interest in the gramophone; Fraser, *African Idylls,* p. 225, refers to the value of the cinematograph.

79. Peter J. Westwood, *David Livingstone: His Life and Work as Told through the Media of Postage Stamps and Allied Material* (Blantyre, 1986).

formed the Livingstone and Stanley encounter into a timely foretaste of British-American cooperation.[80] Even in the more recent *Mountains of the Moon*, Livingstone is the subject of a favorable cameo. In the 1958 *Inn of the Sixth Happiness*, Gladys Aylward is heroically portrayed, even if the film represents something of the apotheosis of improbable casting with Ingrid Bergman as Aylward and Robert Donat as a Chinese mandarin. In this film, however, the missionary was an obvious vehicle for anti-Communist propaganda.

But for the rest, missionaries in films are all portrayed in an unfavorable light. In Stanley Baker's *Zulu*, the Reverend Otto Witt, faced with the Zulu terror, takes to drink. Almost all other missionary films seem to be about sexual repression. In both Michael Powell's film *Black Narcissus* of 1947 and John Ford's *Seven Women* of 1966, female missionaries are overwhelmed by their surroundings. Exotic circumstances destabilize both their faith and their morality: their eccentricities take the form of sexual disturbance. In the several film versions of Somerset Maugham's *Rain*, of 1928, 1932, and 1957, the missionary is subjected to a sexual conversion by the prostitute he sets out to save. The breaking of the tropical rains represents the releasing of pent-up passions. Other films explore the mutual conversion of missionary and reprobate. In the cinematic versions of Maugham's *Vessel of Wrath* and Forester's *African Queen*, the spinster who has been supposedly dried up by religion discovers love while humanizing and civilizing a male who initially terrifies her by his ungodliness. In each of these, a journey through exotic surroundings produces a transformation in which repressed natural urges find free expression. Instead of offering opportunities for control, the environment becomes the means of release. Where indigenous people appear, they are often caricatures, but of a people who secure the ultimate victory. In the film *Hawaii* of 1966, the missionaries are portrayed as setting out to face down Polynesian sexuality, only to destroy the cohesion of Hawaiian society and achieve a Pyrrhic victory. Audience identification is entirely with the indigenous Hawaiians.[81]

Such a neat reversal of the conquest of both environmental and human nature indicates the manner in which the cultural imperialism of technology, engineering, science, and the landscape encounters the twentieth-century crisis of confidence. When we debate the alleged cultural imperialism of missionaries, we need to move beyond those definitions of Edward Said and the Comaroffs, which Andrew Porter has so penetratingly discussed.[82] We also

80. MacKenzie, "David Livingstone," pp. 38-39.

81. This section on films and missionaries has benefited from discussion with my colleague, Jeffrey Richards.

82. Andrew Porter, "'Cultural Imperialism' and Protestant Missionary Enterprise, 1780-1914," *Journal of Imperial and Commonwealth History* 25, no. 3 (1997): 367-91.

need to consider the imaginative geographies of missionaries and the manner in which these were expressed through the perceived magic of their engineering, surveying, building, medicine, and technologies, large and small. Yet in marshaling their own "magic," they created a paradox. Missionaries also invariably viewed themselves as scientists. Modern, empirical, experimental science was what distinguished their society from that of Africans. As Donald Fraser put it in a dramatic phrase, "Science is our St. George, who fights the dragon Magic most effectively."[83] Science, however, was all-encompassing, embracing all aspects of the mission. When considering with Justin Willis the internal characteristics of missions, we need to look at their layouts, their architecture, trees, and gardens.[84] If Livingstone could be turned into a multi-armed Hindu deity, we would find him bearing not only blessing and sextant but also magic lantern, scalpel, spade, level, brick, and bell.

83. Fraser, *African Idylls,* p. 187.

84. Justin Willis, "The Nature of a Mission Community: The UMCA in Bonde," *Past and Present* 140 (1993): 127-54.

Rethinking Gender Roles: The Field Experience of Women Missionaries in South Africa

DEBORAH GAITSKELL

The twentieth century "has been called the women's century, and undoubtedly it has seen a new era for woman's missionary work begin," proclaimed the Methodist Women's Auxiliary (WA) in 1923.[1] Back in 1911, at the height of the British suffrage struggle, the American Baptist Helen Barrett Montgomery had been sure that "this reaching out of women for fuller freedom and juster opportunities" sprang from a common Christian origin in both West and East.[2] That women outnumbered men on the mission field by the early twentieth century perhaps encouraged such a triumphalist sense of a "new era." Yet the huge increase in female mission recruitment was but one of three new elements to the social revolution of the high imperial era: the "ecclesiastical expansion of England" also drew on far better educated male recruits, while the new faith missions both welcomed men with little training and gave women a special prominence.[3]

This essay explores how far gender roles in the field were actually being rethought — as opposed to the pool of female recruitment simply being enlarged. "As a rule of thumb 'A' for Aylward and 'Z' for Zenana Missions are the two beam ends of an alphabet of women and missionary work,"[4] Byrne sug-

1. Women's Auxiliary of Wesleyan Methodist Missionary Society, *The Story of the Women's Auxiliary, 1858-1922* (London, 1923), p. 31.

2. Helen B. Montgomery, *Western Women in Eastern Lands* (New York, 1911), p. 206, quoted in Lavinia Byrne, *The Hidden Journey: Missionary Heroines in Many Lands* (London, 1993), p. 210.

3. Andrew F. Walls, "British Missions," in *Missionary Ideologies in the Imperialist Era: 1880-1920*, ed. Torben Christensen and William R. Hutchison (Aarhus, 1982), p. 160.

4. Byrne, p. 55.

gests. How far did the representation of women's missionary work, so powerfully shaped by images of China and India, accord with realities on the ground in the very different, and rapidly changing, setting of South Africa? Gauging how far such field changes had an impact on the sending missions and churches themselves is trickier. Whereas British women's history and imperial history are being brought together,[5] the gender-sensitive fusing of mission history and British ecclesiastical history is still awaited.[6] How much did the upsurge of "women's work" for the church at home and abroad contribute to the doctrinal and numerical feminization of British religion?[7] By the 1890s females confirmed in the Church of England well exceeded males, and there were frequent laments that women outnumbered grown men in church.[8] How far were the thousands of Victorian women reading the vast output of printed mission publicity being empowered and strengthened in their faith? "Their pennies and their imaginations were liberated,"[9] certainly, by the novelty of the high-profile work of hundreds of female missionaries, but with what long-term effect? Women's new roles abroad seem hardly to have shifted male clerical dominance at home. Women provided most of the new mission activists from the 1880s, indefatigably organizing and collecting, with what Georgina Gollock called their genius for "concentration of devotion and energy in a restricted sphere," but "greater female subservience to clerical power" in England precluded large, independent female mission societies.[10]

5. Clare Midgley, ed., *Gender and Imperialism* (Manchester, 1998).

6. Brian Heeney, *The Women's Movement in the Church of England: 1850-1930* (Oxford, 1988), pp. 58-65, includes female missionary recruitment and the employment of sisterhoods abroad in his discussion of the "context of subordination," but is completely inadequate (and wrong) on the Society for the Propagation of the Gospel in Foreign Parts (SPG). Sean Gill, *Women and the Church of England from the Eighteenth Century to the Present* (London, 1994), chap. 8, "Women in the Mission Field," raises relevant issues, but most examples are from India. For much-needed analysis of the SPG, and comparison with the Church Missionary Society (CMS), see Steven S. Maughan, "Regions Beyond and the National Church: Domestic Support for the Foreign Missions of the Church of England in the High Imperial Age, 1870-1914" (Ph.D. diss., Harvard University, 1995), esp. chap. 3.

7. Compare B. Welter, "The Feminization of American Religion: 1800-1860," in *Clio's Consciousness Raised: New Perspectives on the History of Women*, ed. M. S. Hartman and L. Banner (New York, 1974).

8. Owen Chadwick, *The Victorian Church*, part II (London, 1970), pp. 222-23.

9. Rhonda Semple, "Women, Gender and Changing Roles in the Missionary Project: The London Missionary Society and the China Inland Mission, 1885-1910," *NAMP Position Paper 39* (Cambridge, 1997), pp. 6, 21.

10. Steven Maughan, "'Mighty England Do Good': The Major English Denominations and Organisation for the Support of Foreign Missions in the Nineteenth Century," in

My analysis offers three concentric circles of increasing specificity. First, developments in women and mission are mapped, with South African illustrations, trying to account for the striking late Victorian shifts in female employment. South Africa is then considered in more depth, to highlight contrasts between 1880 and 1914. Finally, the Transvaal is examined in 1903-14, to see how far the generalizations apply at an individual level. To what extent were women missionaries rethinking their own gender roles and those of African converts, and how far did local clergy and sending mission bodies share their new visions?

Female Missionary Roles before and after 1880

An overview of British missionary women is urgently needed, to complement that of Dana Robert for the USA,[11] although her three-stage depiction of overburdened mission wives, single women teachers and doctors, and Holiness-inspired evangelists obviously has wider currency. The broad generalization holds that, until the separate women's societies got going, deployment of British Protestant women was restricted to missionary wives, "married to the job" and often married for the job. Etherington mischievously comments that the unseemly rush to get early American Board envoys to South Africa suitably married off was "a strange start for a mission that would concentrate so much effort at stamping out 'forced marriages' among the Zulu."[12] Missionary wives' conjugal, domestic, and educational importance was widely recognized in private,[13] if not much publicized until later in the nineteenth century.

Missionary Encounters: Sources and Issues, ed. Robert A. Bickers and Rosemary Seton (Richmond, 1996), pp. 32-34. The female-preaching debate is captured in Jocelyn Murray, "Gender Attitudes and the Contribution of Women to Evangelism and the Ministry in the Nineteenth Century," in *Evangelical Faith and Public Zeal: Evangelicals and Society in Britain, 1780-1980,* ed. John Wolffe (London, 1995), pp. 97-116.

11. Dana Robert, *American Women in Mission: A Social History of Their Thought and Practice* (Macon, Ga., 1996). Welcome meanwhile are Jocelyn Murray, "The Role of Women in the Church Missionary Society, 1799-1917," and Guli Francis-Dehqani, "CMS Women Missionaries in Persia: Perceptions of Muslim Women and Islam, 1884-1934," both in *The Church Mission Society and World Christianity, 1799-1999,* ed. Kevin Ward and Brian Stanley (Grand Rapids and Richmond, Surrey, 2000).

12. Norman Etherington, "Gender Issues in South-East African Missions, 1835-85," in *Missions and Christianity in South African History,* ed. Henry Bredekamp and Robert Ross (Johannesburg, 1995), p. 138.

13. Deborah Kirkwood, "Protestant Missionary Women: Wives and Spinsters," in

It may help to state the obvious at the outset. In several mission society lists men were categorized according to whether or not they were *ordained*, women by whether or not they were *married*. Marriage was a lifelong occupation, a job description and defining status for women in a way not overtly comparable for men. Historians do not write chapters entitled "Protestant Missionary Men: Husbands and Bachelors," to take the corollary of Kirkwood's title. "Lay" or "ordained" were the relevant labels for men, "single" or "married" for women. These assumptions and accompanying material realities (such as lower or nonexistent female salaries) crucially determine the shape of research on women missionaries. Dividing one's analysis accordingly seems inescapable, particularly as the distinction between married and single women, or wives and spinsters, was mapped chronologically onto mission recruitment, with the crucial change of emphasis occurring in the late nineteenth century.

The first missionary wife in South Africa, Eva Kohrhammer, arrived in 1798 with her Moravian husband, as the three bachelors already there for six years felt the need of a "sister" to visit sick Khoi women and provide pastoral counseling.[14] Many more from other societies followed. Piecing together a mosaic of impressions and sources from nineteenth-century South Africa confirms what isolated, often dangerous lives the first rural mission wives led, giving birth to perhaps ten children, far from medical help, feeding and clothing their families (and often a wider household or community too) only through hard, time-consuming effort, and squeezing in domestic and religious instruction for local women and children intermittently and with difficulty — a tale which can be replicated across the mission world.

The letters of Bessie Price, daughter of Robert Moffat of the London Missionary Society (LMS), provide a rich source. Typically her response to the Tswana woman who wanted more teaching was to argue that her work was rather to keep her missionary husband "comfortable & his home civilised & Christian-like & to train my children and servants likewise. I must teach you by setting an example in my home life." She explained to English relatives with customary fervor how difficult it was "to keep up civilization & not to go slip-shod, any way":

Women and Missions: Past and Present: Anthropological and Historical Perceptions, ed. Fiona Bowie, Deborah Kirkwood, and Shirley Ardener (Oxford, 1993), pp. 25-28; Francis-Dehqani, p. 102.

14. Bernhard Kruger, *The Pear Tree Blossoms: A History of the Moravian Mission Stations in South Africa, 1737-1869* (Genadendal, 1966), pp. 81-82. She thus preceded Hannah Marshman — who joined the Baptist Missionary Society (BMS) Serampore mission with her husband Joshua in 1799 — and is dubbed the first of all women missionaries in modern times by Mrs. J. T. Gracey, *Eminent Missionary Women* (New York, 1898), pp. 154-55.

> For myself I find it necessary to be *over* particular rather than *under,* for if one *begins* slipping little duties as of no consequence in such *hard* circumstances — oh how one runs downhill! . . . The wife is indeed the sunshine of her African home. If she is about & bustling, all is cheery & nice — *if* she is laid up the house is a scene of misery in no time. I often feel quite proud of this. . . . Our chief work is to keep the Husbands *up* — up from sinking down down gradually into native style of living — & from losing *hearts & spirits* in that great work in which we but act as organ *blowers* to the musician.

Above all, she aimed to be a cheerful "help-meet" to "poor dear Roger," suppressing her "weak-minded thoughts" and "pent up" emotions. On a practical level, far in the interior of Bechuanaland, the missionary husband was jack-of-all-trades, Bessie noted, with the wife maid of all work. While she made bread, churned butter, and ground coffee, he had to build dwellings and repair wagons. Though she initially managed two afternoons of sewing school a week, later teaching spelling and the alphabet, Mrs. Price only resumed the direct evangelism of her girlhood in 1880, after nearly twenty years of marriage, when an English governess came to help with her children and the school. She also appreciated Tswana warmth and freedom after a long furlough where the unnecessary "strait jacket" of "form & ceremony" marred "the English life to us Africans." She mellowed into a friendlier, gentler gradualism, a new self-awareness of how she "used to be stern & strict and learnt it was a bad plan."[15]

Mrs. Mabille, of the Paris Evangelical Mission, commented in 1888 that those "who imagine that a missionary's wife spends her time in holding meetings and giving lessons in school are greatly mistaken." Her own life was rather "that of a busy farmer," supervising crop cultivation, seeing to cattle, drying fruit, all part of being in charge of supplying and cooking food for over a hundred people every day at the Morija Bible School — students, apprentices, servants, plus her own family — though she was glad she could also share her husband's "more agreeable, higher work." In girlhood in France, she had longed "for an active life in the service of God."[16] Her missionary yearnings, frustrated by gender, had found an outlet through marriage.

15. Una Long, ed., *The Journals of Elizabeth Lees Price* (1956), pp. 216, 104-5 for quotes; 134, 155, 392ff. for mission work; Wendy Urban-Mead, "The 'Civilizing' Mission of Elizabeth Lees Price: Domesticity, Christianity, and Imperialism in Southern Africa, 1854-1883" (master's thesis, State University of New York at Albany, 1995), pp. 59, 74, 102-3.

16. Edwin W. Smith, *The Mabilles of Basutoland* (London, 1939), pp. 355-57, 329-30, 83.

Western clothing displayed missionary "civilisation"; its adoption accompanied African Christian conversion — as well as covering unseemly, immodest nakedness. Pioneer missionary wives endlessly gave sewing instruction and made clothes themselves, "sewing, stitch, stitch, stitch, stitch," as Daniel Lindley described his wife. A diary entry captures her frustration at juggling sewing responsibilities with learning (and yearning) to share the gospel: "Spent the morning in reading and studying Sichuana. Cut a pair of pantaloons for Mr Lindley in the afternoon. Several women came to the door to sell a skin. . . . O how I long to be able to converse with the females about the concerns of their immortal souls!" No wonder a friend's sewing machine, which seemed "to work like magic," evoked heartfelt praise as "a blessing to womankind above all price. May the inventor be saved from all fatigue and from all sorrow of heart!" She did nevertheless manage a daily afternoon school for the children, and later a sewing school welcomed by the Zulu women.[17]

In her first stressful, homesick decade among the Xhosa, when her first three children all died in infancy, Helen Ross of the Glasgow Mission sought perhaps to assuage her misery by literally clothing the unfamiliar. She not only itemized benefactions to converts meticulously — "I gave her 4 frocks, 2 bedgowns, 2 petticoats, 2 shifts & 2 aprons" — but repeatedly and obsessively listed explicit needs for material and clothing in letters home: "6 pairs cotton stockings, 9 yrds bombazet, 7 yrds dark print, 6 white spencers made — 6½ yrds tick (1½ yrds tick cord) 2 yrds white fringe 3 yrds green gauze for the windows 80 yrds strong cotton cloth at 6d. a yard."[18]

The cultured Mrs. Colenso, with older children and closer to Natal urban life, found time to read the *Times, Spectator,* and *Theological Review;* play concerts with her daughters; collect ferns for a friend, and moths and beetles for her sons in England. A description from 1859 conveys her energetic blend of intellectual, aesthetic, and practical activity:

> Mrs Colenso I love very much, she is a thorough lady to begin with, in every thought and feeling, and such a worker, at the same time fancying she does nothing. She is governess to all her own children, and many others who are here, and besides, is constantly overseeing the troop of black girls, and indeed the whole population up here comes to her as

17. Edwin W. Smith, *The Life and Times of Daniel Lindley (1801-80)* (London, 1949), pp. 289, 90, 326, 291, 317.

18. Natasha Erlank, "Missionary Wives and Perceptions of Race in the Early Nineteenth Century Cape Colony" (paper presented to Workshop on Promoting Women's History, Rhodes University, Grahamstown, July 1995), pp. 4, 5.

their Mother, in any kind of sickness and trouble, for she is their doctor as well. She cuts out all the work [to be sewn], looks after the dress of the boys, in fact, I cannot tell you half of what she does, but you may believe it is plenty, being at the head of such an establishment as this; and then, besides all, she is fond of music, drawing, and poetry and flowers, and everything beautiful in nature. Above all she is in love with the [African] people.

Yet on the bishop's death, considering her life had for so many years been "such a mere appendix to his," she despaired of her purpose in life: "My Lord and Master, my superior in every way, morally and intellectually. O, what will become of me now."[19]

Class attitudes came through strongly from two other Anglican wives, irked that "home duties" took up so much of the day "for want of good servants," whose help their higher social group took more for granted than did the Nonconformists. Mrs. Wilkinson, finding her three African servant girls "a dreadful nuisance, so stupid and lazy, so inferior to the boys," reminded herself of her mission to raise such women from a life of drudgery. She nevertheless betrayed her employer expectations by adding, "but when they act as servants one is apt to forget what they are, and to expect more from them." For a while they were "the plague of my life . . . if it were not for their own sakes I would not keep them an hour — I would have boys," but the girls were soon "improving immensely." Mrs. Robertson's assessment was warmer. "Our Kafir 'Boy' and his wife are the greatest comfort. I cannot be thankful enough for such a blessing. We really could not be better cared for by English servants." She pronounced the three girls later working in her house her "greatest help" and "excellent needlewomen."[20]

Sometimes wives did work more like the men's: American Board women helped translate the Bible into Zulu, Mrs. Newton Lindley working on Job and Edward Tyler's mother on Isaiah. Mrs. Mabille, through her decades of widowhood, continued to be concerned for the conversion of the Sotho chiefs and maintained a close relationship with the indigenous pastors. Her

19. Wyn Rees, ed., *Colenso Letters from Natal* (Pietermaritzburg, 1959), pp. 153-56, 314, 208ff., and quotes, pp. 40-41, and 374, 380.

20. *A Lady's Life and Travels in Zululand and the Transvaal during Cetewayo's reign, being the African letters and journals of the late Mrs Wilkinson* (London, 1882; reprint, Pretoria, 1975), pp. 38, 45, 51, 67; *Missionary Life among the Zulu-Kafirs. Memorials of Henrietta Robertson wife of the Rev. R. Robertson. Compiled chiefly from letters and journals written to the Late Bishop Mackenzie and his sisters,* ed. Anne Mackenzie (Cambridge and London, 1866), pp. 25, 5, 59.

decades among the Mpondo empowered the Methodist widow, Mrs. Jenkins, to agitate with officialdom on their behalf in a way that faintly echoes Bishop Colenso.[21] In urban Cape Town, spared the housekeeping challenges of remote rural pioneers, Jane Philip was actually paid as LMS accountant, doing the books from 1826 to 1847, and corresponded exhaustively, even peremptorily, with up to forty-eight missionaries about their finances — "secular business" which she saw as freeing her husband's "more valuable time" for spiritual superintendence. Ever eager for "usefulness," and "much grieved" by missionary wives who required their husbands' "constant attendance," she also took a leading role in founding and running the Ladies' Benevolent Society, the Tract Society, and the first infant schools. Although, as the wife of a powerful man, "her status may have initially rested on his, her contemporaries ultimately came to recognise her for a player in the mission field in her own right."[22]

The general picture is therefore one of missionary wives exercising domestic spiritual influence, by example and intermittent instruction, their role that of "organ blowers to the musician" or "a mere appendix" to the *real* — male — missionary. Considerable obstacles stood in the way of wives providing systematic, sustained religious teaching if they were to fulfill their conjugal and maternal roles properly in difficult, pioneering circumstances — and Christian homes were meant to be part of what the new faith had to offer. Contrary to Dana Robert, home building was more than making a virtue of necessity. Wives used the notion of the home as mission agency to sacralize "the myriad activities that ate up their strength and their days," thereby bringing "order out of the unceasing round of home visitation, sewing lessons, childcare, and prayer meetings."[23]

In fact, partly in an effort to connect with feminist history research elsewhere, domesticity has been a primary concern of recent scholarship about gender roles of women missionaries, to the detriment of inquiries about their more explicitly spiritual encounters with African women — and I include myself in these strictures. Can we make sense of the enthusiastic group prayer and public evangelism of African women that were developing in the second half of the nineteenth century simply in terms of their

21. A. F. Christofersen, *Adventuring with God: The Story of the American Board Mission in Africa,* ed. R. Sales (Durban, [1967]), p. 64; Smith, *The Mabilles of Basutoland,* p. 360; Etherington, pp. 140-41.

22. Natasha Erlank, "Reinterpreting the Writing of Missionary History: The Case of Mrs. Jane Philip (Wife of the More Famous John)" (paper presented at conference on gender and colonialism, University of the Western Cape, January 1997), pp. 10-13, 18.

23. Robert, p. 69.

roots in customary orality and the galvanizing impact of revivalism?[24] We need to know more about the (female?) doctrinal input which made African women both confident that God heard and answered prayer about immediate personal concerns, and eager to urge others publicly to repentance and commitment.

Yet missionary women undeniably brought a spiritualized Victorian domesticity, which had to negotiate with "African notions of space, work, gender and power." Ideologies of domesticity shape notions of labor and time, as well as "architecture and space, consumption and accumulation, body and clothing, and sexuality and gender."[25] Pioneering missionary homes were "emblems of evangelical domesticity" as well as "pulpits and training sites" — having an impact on boys as well as girls, as Nancy Hunt shows for the "intimate evangelism" of Congo mission domesticity. "We have five native teachers in all that love us as tho' we were their parents," wrote the childless Mrs. Allison, after taking up to thirty youths into their home at Edendale in the 1840s for the nucleus of an industrial school. Future African clergy wives (identified and encouraged as such by a spinster missionary matchmaker) furthered their education by accompanying mission families to Scotland on lengthy trips in the 1870s.[26]

The focus on domesticity carried over into more formal schooling, in partial harmony with indigenous priorities of marriage, motherhood, and homemaking — though Victorian mission discourse endlessly argued that field labor and bride wealth made African women in South Africa "beasts of burden" and slaves instead of the companionable "help-meets" to their husbands which Christianity intended — and Lovedale Girls' School, for example, set out to accomplish. The American Board's prestigious Inanda Seminary in Natal, despite its sustained attention to domestic or "industrial" skills, was likewise training housewives (not primarily servants for white settlers) and

24. See Deborah Gaitskell, "'Praying and Preaching': The Distinctive Spirituality of African Women's Church Organizations," in *Missions and Christianity in South African History.*

25. Karen T. Hansen, ed., *African Encounters with Domesticity* (New Brunswick, N.J., 1992), pp. 2, ix.

26. Nancy R. Hunt, "Colonial Fairy-Tales and the Knife and Fork Doctrine in the Heart of Africa," in *African Encounters with Domesticity,* pp. 151, 149; Sheila Meintjes, "Family and Gender in the Christian Community at Edendale, Natal, in Colonial Times," in *Women and Gender in Southern Africa to 1945,* ed. Cherryl Walker (Cape Town and London, 1990), pp. 132-33; Deborah Gaitskell, "At Home with Hegemony? Coercion and Consent in the Education of African Girls for Domesticity in South Africa before 1910," in *Contesting Colonial Hegemony: State and Society in Africa and India,* ed. Dagmar Engels and Shula Marks (London, 1994), p. 126.

women teachers.[27] Not that domesticity should be envisaged as an uncontentious goal. Freely chosen monogamous marriage — perhaps the supreme, irreversible gain that Christianity brought African women[28] — threatened patriarchal power, both of polygamous husbands and bride-wealth-hungry fathers. The spate of runaway girls whose salvaging the Zulu missions trumpeted so jubilantly in the closing decades of the nineteenth century "came to embody competing notions of gender, personhood and domesticity."[29]

The help of missionary daughters may have blunted the urgency of the need for single women who could provide full-time service and continuity. We read of Mrs. Brownlee's daughters helping with the infant school and teaching sewing, and the Mabille girls' aid with housework, the school, Morija Book Depot, and even its post office. All the Lindley children taught in the Sunday school and two daughters in the day school, while one Moffat daughter helped run the home and another the infant school and sewing and Bible classes. The intelligent, competent Colenso daughters had wide responsibilities. At first Harriette taught Sunday school with Fanny, and supervised the housework and linen girls, then started a day school, her mother commenting that "with her ardent disposition she needs some object to expend herself on." In preparing a wronged chief's case, she was "quite her Father's secretary," nicknamed in Zulu his "walking stick"; it was impossible, her mother sighed, "to abstract her from all knowledge of the oppressed and the oppressor." After Colenso's death in 1883, while sister Agnes continued the mission work — supervising the schoolmaster, teaching singing and exercises, and reading *Pilgrim's Progress* to a women's class — Harriette campaigned for years both ecclesiastically on the bishop's behalf and politically for the wronged Zulu royal house.[30]

Other influences perhaps also delayed change. Biographical evidence on fourteen of the first twenty-five American Board wives in supposedly rela-

27. Heather Hughes, "'A Lighthouse for African Womanhood': Inanda Seminary, 1869-1945," in *Women and Gender in Southern Africa to 1945*.

28. Adrian Hastings, "Were Women a Special Case?" in *Women and Missions*, p. 119.

29. Jennifer Seif, "Gender, Tradition and Authority in Nineteenth Century Natal: The Zulu Missions of the American Board" (paper presented to South African Historical Society conference, Grahamstown, July 1995), pp. 49-50.

30. Basil Holt, *Greatheart of the Border* (Kingwilliamstown, 1976), pp. 110-11; Smith, *The Mabilles of Basutoland*, p. 332; Smith, *Daniel Lindley*, p. 291; Mora Dickson, *Beloved Partner: Mary Moffat of Kuruman* (London, 1974), p. 137; Long, p. 9; Rees, pp. 98, 133, 180, 320, 350, 374, 380-81. Also Brenda M. Nicholls, "Harriette Colenso and the Issues of Religion and Politics in Colonial Natal," in *Missions and Christianity in South African History*. On missionary sisters, daughters, and widows, whose respectability could be guaranteed, see Murray, "Role of Women," pp. 72-78, and Maughan, "Regions Beyond," pp. 262-70.

tively healthy South Africa suggests physical and psychological fragility, Etherington accumulating with sardonic relish sundry examples of chronic disease and mental disturbance (from worms and colitis to hypochondria, "brain congestion," and paranoiac insanity).[31] In fact, the mortality rate of young, childbearing wives in Africa made Bishop Hannington write to the CMS in 1885 that he would "welcome a few strapping old maids — send out a dozen to try."[32]

Debate has therefore mounted recently as to why Protestant missionary societies, having employed virtually no single women as teachers anywhere in the middle years of the nineteenth century, moved to their systematic recruitment from the 1860s and 1870s. The Society for the Promotion of Female Education in the East (SPFEE), which in fact sent teachers to South Africa as well as to its prime concerns of China and India, was formed as early as 1834, partly at the instigation of missionary wives who realized their own limitations in sustained educational provision. The SPFEE had sent fifty single women teachers abroad by 1847; their Indian pupils were largely low caste and poor, but when the novelty of female visitation of high-ranking secluded women in the zenanas offered the chance to convert the elite (especially after the 1857 mutiny), the rash of separate women's denominational societies followed, rendering the SPFEE ultimately redundant.[33] The opening of the zenana was like "the discovery of a new continent," resulting in an amazing new orthodoxy: that it was the "plain and manifest duty" of thousands of unmarried Western women to evangelize the women of the East.[34] Most missionaries believed, anyhow, that India's ancient civilizations "demanded the best educated and most obviously able candidates," while "Africa received the leftovers."[35] The fascination and elite female inaccessibility of the East gave it overriding weight in ideology and propaganda — and in female recruitment.

At one level the new female missionary associations were formed to counteract sex discrimination: women could raise funds but not be full members

31. Etherington, pp. 138-39.

32. Quoted in John S. Isherwood, "An Analysis of the Role of Single Women in the Work of the Church Missionary Society, 1804-1904, in West Africa, India and China" (master's thesis, Manchester University, 1979), p. 40.

33. Jane Haggis, "White Women and Colonialism: Towards a Non-recuperative History," in *Gender and Imperialism,* pp. 52-55.

34. Quoted in Rosemary Fitzgerald, "A 'Peculiar and Exceptional Measure': The Call for Women Medical Missionaries for India in the Later Nineteenth Century," in *Missionary Encounters,* pp. 182, 175.

35. Walls, p. 160.

of existing mission societies, and offers from unmarried candidates were generally spurned. The Wesleyan Methodist Missionary Society (WMMS) Ladies' Committee was founded in 1858; the Ladies' Association of the SPG in 1866 — with 186 women missionaries in the field by 1900.[36] Beaver attributes the "dramatic" growth of the female missionary movement to the potency of this enforced separation, while Robert argues that "woman's work for woman" was "one of the major western mission theories of the late nineteenth century" and a dominant force in Protestant missiology until the First World War, legitimating and extending women's special mission work through educational and other social services.[37]

The dimensions of female recruitment are striking — from a negligible percentage of women recruits, by the 1890s the CMS intake (not counting wives) was 51 percent female, the LMS 37 percent, WMMS 28 percent, and the China Inland Mission (CIM) probably over 60 percent. By 1900, of 18,782 missionaries throughout the world, 3,628 were single women and 4,340 wives; by 1929 two-thirds of the mission personnel of six U.S. societies were female.[38] Twin pressures proved decisive: "the needs of missionaries abroad, and the aspirations of women at home." Missions argued that the lack of female appointees had limited their success with indigenous women; it simultaneously became clear that a fair number of women wanted to go and a large number were prepared to form their own women's societies to fund and send them. Hence conservative caution gave way to new assertions that "it was safe for women to be missionaries, that only women could reach women and that the conversion of mothers was a key to greater missionary success."[39]

From midcentury in Britain, women's role in philanthropy and an astonishing range of church work had been expanding, while feminists helped open up new opportunities in girls' education and teaching careers for women. Sarah Potter stresses women's recruitment from these new professions and their channeling into schools, hospitals, and orphanages abroad: for instance, teachers and nurses in the 1890s provided 42 percent of WMMS

36. H. P. Thompson, *Into All Lands: The History of the Society for the Propagation of the Gospel in Foreign Parts, 1701-1950* (London, 1951), p. 235.

37. Robert P. Beaver, *All Loves Excelling: American Protestant Women in World Mission* (Grand Rapids, 1968), p. 86; Robert, p. 137.

38. C. Peter Williams, "'The Missing Link': The Recruitment of Women Missionaries in Some English Evangelical Missionary Societies in the Nineteenth Century," in *Women and Missions*, p. 63; Beaver, pp. 108-9. For detailed tables from 1899, see Maughan, "Regions Beyond," p. 364.

39. C. Peter Williams, "The Recruitment and Training of Overseas Missionaries in England between 1850 and 1900" (M.Litt. thesis, University of Bristol, 1976), pp. 303, 300.

female candidates.[40] Over half the 172 LMS recruits on whom Rosemary Seton had occupational data were teachers, governesses, and nurses — but she underlines the pull of the zenana in their motivation.[41] Missions *did* offer invaluable overseas work opportunities from 1880 to 1900, legitimated by the widespread publicity for zenanas. Hence a quarter of Britain's women medical graduates were working in India at the turn of the century.[42] Female missionaries used Indian women's supposed plight, argues Haggis, to advance themselves professionally in an era of developing capitalism and secular individualism.[43] Williams highlights, by contrast, the spiritually emancipating relevance of new theological insights that led faith and holiness missions to employ larger numbers of women as evangelists.[44]

South Africa, however, provides an underexplored example of the greater deployment of unmarried women in a less emancipatory way, under male clerical leadership in the Anglican High Church tradition. Of course, Bishop Webb's authoritarian attitudes in pioneering large-scale use of women workers did not preclude the unintended consequences of those very women acquiring autonomous power and influence — so that two of his protégées, Sister Henrietta Stockdale and Mother Cecile, have eclipsed his renown.[45] Contradicting the picture some give of sisterhoods as the most "feminist" of the religious options for single women, Webb stressed that women's role was "supplementary . . . to be a 'help-meet' for Man," and that sisterhoods should be under the central control of bishops, "not under the irresponsible rule of any *woman*." But women could do work the clergy could not, using their practical organizational skills and their "womanly intuition" to follow the "lines of action, broad and bold and unhesitating," which originated from men. Women's work was particularly needed in "colonial life" because lack of

40. Sarah C. Potter, "The Social Origins and Recruitment of English Protestant Missionaries in the Nineteenth Century" (Ph.D. diss., University of London, 1975), pp. 218ff., 260-61, 230. She, like C. Peter Williams, considers the CMS, LMS, and WMMS, but adds the BMS where he examines the CIM; both neglect the SPG.

41. Rosemary Seton, "'Open Doors for Female Labourers': Women Candidates of the London Missionary Society, 1875-1914," in *Missionary Encounters*, pp, 61, 57. Also Semple, pp. 10-20.

42. Elizabeth Friend, "Professional Women and the British Empire 1880-1939" (Ph.D. diss., University of Lancaster, 1998), p. 140.

43. Haggis, pp. 66-67, 68.

44. C. Peter Williams, "The Missing Link," p. 47.

45. Cecillie Swaisland, "Wanted — Earnest, Self-Sacrificing Women for Service in South Africa: Nineteenth-Century Recruitment of Single Women to Protestant Missions," in *Women and Missions*, p. 79; and S. Marks, *Divided Sisterhood: Race, Class, and Gender in the South African Nursing Profession* (London, 1994), chap. 1; p. 43.

servants reduced the "supply of disengaged women who have leisure for Church work." While women had been, from the start of his mission in 1863, "helpers from afar, as intercessors, correspondents, secretaries, embroiderers, providers and packers of mission boxes," by the end of the 1870s there were some thirty women on his Bloemfontein staff: one deaconess, various associate workers, and members of his Sisterhood of Saint Michael and All Angels, illustrating the range of female church employment options. Women were teaching white girls as well as African and Colored children, doing hospital and outdoor nursing, visiting and parochial work, and superintending household and laundry arrangements.[46]

Few biographies of spinster missionaries to South Africa exist. A rare example recounts the life of the charming, competent Cecile Isherwood, whom a Webb sermon secured as foundress of the very active Anglican sisterhood, the Community of the Resurrection of Our Lord (Grahamstown). Mother Cecile's strong will and "intense and radiant vitality" proved an inspiration, despite her unadorned assertion that the religious life was "a practical life of self-denial and hard work." The sisters at first worked among whites on lines becoming conventional in England — providing a refuge for unmarried mothers, rescuing destitute children by fitting them for domestic service, and running a teacher training college — but then branched out into mission work among Africans in the 1890s, teaching academic and housecraft subjects at Saint Matthew's Mission at Keiskamahoek.[47] By then such multifaceted teacher-training and boarding institutions in rural African Christian strongholds were probably the most familiar setting for single women missionaries in the Cape and Natal. Mother Cecile's exalted position of authority was highly atypical, as was the lowly isolation of another biographee, a hardy Scottish widow who spent thirty years in a small Mfengu village in an obscure, inaccessible valley.

Christina Forsyth first went to the Transkei in 1879 (at age thirty-five) as a schoolteacher and children's worker. Returning widowed, at forty-one, she revived the church cause at Xolobe — visiting the sick, opening a day school, running a Bible class for African girls, and gathering the people together for services. Her lack of family did not free her from the domesticity which rural survival demanded: plastering walls, scrubbing floors, baking for Christmas,

46. Allan B. Webb, *Sisterhood Life and Woman's Work in the Mission Field of the Church* (London, 1883), pp. 10, 57, 1-2; "The Bishop of Bloemfontein on woman's work in South Africa," *Mission Field*, August-September 1878, pp. 391-92.

47. *Mother Cecile in South Africa, 1883-1906: Foundress of the Community of the Resurrection of Our Lord*, compiled by a sister of the Community (London, 1930), passim and pp. 47-52, 159.

killing sheep, and roasting and grinding coffee. Her church activities illustrate how, in remote spots, women missionaries might perform all the duties of a minister short of administering the sacraments: she ran Sunday services, candidates' classes, Sunday school, a women's Bible class, prayer meetings, and a branch of the Women's Christian Association of the Presbyterian Church of South Africa.[48] Gertrude Hance similarly took such wide-ranging charge of Esidumbeni station for the American Board, in addition to dispensing medicine and settling land disputes.[49] But in both their solitary way of life and their degree of spiritual responsibility, they seem to have been exceptional for their time and place. There is thus something unconvincing in Forsyth's extravagant elevation by the popular mission biographer W. P. Livingstone, during the First World War, partly via that sensationalist subtitle — *The Loneliest Woman in Africa*.[50] It rings hollow when he quotes her minister eulogizing her marginality, disempowerment, and isolation as somehow more spiritually noble and humbly apostolic, compared with the wide responsibilities of great missionary superintendents like himself, riding about "like bishops, ordaining, ordering, giving charges, working late and early." Livingstone seems to relish the very real power male missionaries retained and exercised, whatever the rethinking of gender roles over this period.

The treatment of Mrs. Forsyth may seem patronizing, but it was not confrontational. Rupture could occur when young men in authority tried to boss more forthright, confident women whose skills they found intimidating. Dr. Jane Waterston resigned from Livingstonia Mission in 1880, her faith in God and man shattered, because her pioneering medical qualifications were totally disregarded: "I was judged fit to teach Anatomy in London. I am thought fit for the Alphabet here."[51] The formidable Elizabeth Sturrock started teaching at Peelton in 1864 for the Female Education Society, upholding familiar views of the domestic power of woman, raised by education "to become the companion, not the slave of man," and shaping the nation's future via motherhood because "the cultivation of the heart and the moulding of the will is hers." The black press praised her girls' thorough grounding in both needlework and book work; her LMS superior recognized that she was outstanding

48. W. P. Livingstone, *Christina Forsyth of Fingoland: The Story of the Loneliest Woman in Africa* (London, [1919]), pp. 71-72, 82-85, 111, 114. See Andrew Ross in this volume, p. 104 above.

49. G. R. Hance, *The Zulu Yesterday and To-day* (New York, 1916), pp. 179-80.

50. Livingstone, pp. 228-31.

51. Jane Waterston to Dr. James Stewart, 14 February 1880, in Lucy Bean and Elizabeth Van Heyningen, eds., *The Letters of Jane Elizabeth Waterston, 1866-1905* (Cape Town, 1983), pp. 168, 170.

— yet her last years in South Africa "were embittered by a tragic quarrel" between them, after she shocked him by an impassioned outburst implying "that no mere male could ever teach a girl because he would not be able to understand the windings of a girl's heart."[52] Independent American widows like Katherine Lloyd and Mary Edwards in Natal in the 1860s and 1870s unsettled both home mission authorities and local male colleagues with their caustic criticism and interracial familiarity; a male veteran missionary privately called for what were in effect more unassuming, pliable young female recruits who would not question orders.[53]

Judith Rowbotham suggests that, by contrast with the self-empowering British feminism Antoinette Burton maps out in campaigns for helpless Indian "sisters," mission propaganda "sought actively to divert women from a British feminist agenda by focusing them on work with heathen women abroad." Female self-sacrifice to right the wrongs of others was a far nobler object than the women's rights movement of the 1880s, dismissed in the opening lines of the much quoted poem:

> The rights of women! What are they?
> The right to labour and to pray,

which went on to enumerate female rights to give comfort and love, shed joy, and lead others to God.[54] This alerts us to the complex ambiguity of women's missionary "advance" in this era: as ever, women were both liberated and constrained by Christian faith, inspired to take risks and urged to exercise "womanly" gifts of gentleness and compassion.

Gender Roles in Three South African Missions: Comparing 1880 and 1914

Between the South African (Boer) War and the Second World War, three missions working among Africans dominated the Protestant scene on the

52. Margaret E. Donaldson, "The Invisible Factor — Nineteenth Century Feminist Evangelical Concern for Human Rights," in *Women Hold Up Half the Sky: Women in the Church in Southern Africa,* ed. Denise Ackermann, Jonathan A. Draper, and Emma Mashinini (Pietermaritzburg, 1991), pp. 218, 211-12.

53. Etherington, pp. 141-45.

54. Judith Rowbotham, "'This Is No Romantic Story': Reporting the Work of British Female Missionaries, c. 1850-1910," *North Atlantic Missiology Project* Position Paper 4 (Cambridge, 1996), pp. 29-30.

Witwatersrand (the gold-mining reef east and west of Johannesburg) — the Anglican SPG, the Wesleyan Methodists, and the Congregational American Board of Commissioners for Foreign Missions (ABCFM). Their annual reports for the opening and closing years of our chosen period highlight the contrast between 1880 and 1914 in women's deployment in each mission as a whole, as well as more specifically in South Africa itself, and in the industrializing Transvaal region after 1886. They also illuminate the distinctive ethos and legacy of each mission, while underlining what substantial enterprises missions had become by 1914 — the SPG report that year ran to 260 pages, the ABCFM to 278, with its total receipts exceeding a million dollars.[55]

In 1880 the new importance of single women showed up most clearly in ABCFM statistics and comment. An upbeat address at their annual meeting coupled the welcome increasing facility in native languages and the beginnings of a Christian literature with one last ingredient "needed to complete the preparation for the final victory" — "woman's work for woman." Despite their "sudden rise and growth and success," the woman's boards could not yet cope with the "calls for devoted Christian women to take charge of seminaries, to engage in medical work, and in personal labour with women at their homes, from Japan, China, India, and Turkey." ABCFM women had energetically augmented missionary interest "from Maine to California"; their record financial contribution constituted almost a quarter of total receipts (by 1914 it was nearer a third). The changing gender balance emerges even this early: the ABCFM had added 7 new missionaries and 30 assistant missionaries that year, but women made up 25 of those 37 — 6 wives, 18 single women, and 1 widow. Thus spinsters provided almost half the new missionaries in 1880. For the mission as a whole, female assistants (including wives) were 59 percent of total staff abroad: 246 to the 170 men. The Board's American Zulu Mission (AZM) in South Africa, with 8 married ministers, more than replicated these proportions: their wives and 6 unmarried women (including a widow) made up 64 percent of the total.[56]

Unlike the ABCFM, neither the Anglicans nor the Methodists listed missionary wives (or took them through explicit candidates' procedures). Secondly, both British missions saw their task in South Africa as essentially two-pronged: sustaining a British colonial church as well as reaching the "heathen." Furthermore, the strong strain of clerical celibacy in South Africa's High Anglicanism meant a very considerable dilution of female mission in-

55. *The Annual Report. American Board of Commissioners for Foreign Missions* (hereafter *ABCFM*), *1914* (Boston, 1914), p. 225.

56. *Annual Report ABCFM, 1880* (Boston, 1880), pp. xxxiii-xxxiv, 2-7, 2, 101.

put at this stage. In 1880 the SPG reported 586 missionaries working across the world, the bulk in America and the West Indies (253), followed by Asia with 157, Africa with 121, and Australasia and the Pacific with 54. Of South Africa's seven Anglican dioceses in 1880, four employed unmarried women connected with the SPG Ladies' Association — Cape Town and Saint John's (the Transkei) each had 1, Bloemfontein 2, and Maritzburg (Natal) 3. This total of 7 women compared with 25 priests explicitly identified as "missionaries to the heathen," alongside some 63 other priests also listed as SPG missionaries. (The labor of sisterhoods among noncolonials is unfortunately not traceable by this method.) The only explicit reference to a woman in the actual report from South Africa noted how the Reverend William Greenstock in Springvale was "cast down" by the "sad death" of his wife, whose "activity and devotion" were a loss to the mission. In 1880 the crisis for British imperialism was much more to the fore, in "a story of wars and strife." Mission stations had been destroyed and Christians murdered in various African uprisings, while an insurrection of the Transvaal Boers threatened a restoration of the Dutch Republic (which eventuated in 1881), the beleaguered bishop of Pretoria fearing better-resourced "Romanists and Wesleyans" would steal a march on him.[57]

The Americans, with no patriotic self-interest in British fortunes in the Zulu war, commented tersely on the unfavorable religious impact of "excitements attending the political situation" and "the license that ever attends a time of war."[58] The Methodists, by contrast, wrote at length of Wesleyans in the army and honored the brave fallen of Isandhlwana. While the long South African staff lists for 1880 contained no women's names, the detailed and fulsome Methodist report noted the eager African response to education, mentioning the African girls' schools and the well-attended women's prayer meeting at Healdtown Institution.[59] (This was just the sort of educational growth that necessitated and legitimated single women's recruitment.) India took up two-thirds of the Ladies' Auxiliary's brief report. The half-page on South Africa contained a report from the one single woman sent there of the dozen females dispatched that year (along with 27 male WMMS missionaries).[60] However, once an autonomous South African Methodist Conference was formed in 1883, only the Transvaal stayed under the WMMS. This meant less

57. *Report of the year 1880 of the Society for the Propagation of the Gospel in Foreign Parts* (London, 1881), pp. 14, 51-53, 61, 55.

58. *Annual Report ABCFM, 1880*, p. 12.

59. *The Sixty-sixth Report of the Wesleyan Methodist Missionary Society [1880]*, pp. 142-44, 119, 123, 186-87.

60. *The Sixty-sixth Report of the Wesleyan Methodist Missionary Society [1880]*, p. 19. Ladies Auxiliary Report, pp. 203ff.

attention from the Ladies' Auxiliary than in earlier years, when South Africa had figured more prominently than India, with teachers supported at eight different localities in the Cape and Natal.[61]

In 1914 the numerical importance of American Board women was even more firmly entrenched worldwide, with female staff 65 percent of the total (60 percent in the AZM). Single women constituted just under half of all paid staff (though only a third in the AZM), and a third of the total listed personnel (for the AZM, just under a quarter). Thus single women were rather less prominent in South Africa than in the ABCFM as a whole, perhaps because the board's main areas of work were not in Africa but in Turkey, India, China, and Japan, where single women had long been prioritized.

Missionary Staff Employed by ABCFM, 1913-14

	Total	Zulu Mission
Ordained men	172	9
Men not ordained	52	3
Single women	209	7
Wives	205	11

Nearly two-thirds of the 1914 new appointments were female: 14 couples, 11 men, and 28 single women (including 4 widows). "All honor to the Woman's Boards!" was the effusive tribute, especially for more record fund-raising, ensuring "flourishing" female institutions and lines of activity despite the outbreak of the world war and trouble with the "ultra-independent spirit" of some leading churches in Johannesburg. Although recording laundry work and sewing by the 132 girls at Inanda and the 86 scholars at the Umzumbe Home, other details suggested that mission education had moved on from pioneering Victorian domesticity. Nearly three-quarters of Inanda girls came from mission stations (generally from Christian homes); the AZM could not fully accommodate female demand for schooling; and 85 girls were receiving teacher training at Amanzimtoti.[62]

By 1914 South African Methodists outside the Transvaal had been beyond WMMS direction for three decades, receiving a mere £900 [900 pounds sterling] in grants that year for their church of 126,000 members and 280 ministers. The Transvaal itself had experienced a "stormy year" of "grave industrial and social disturbances," but Methodism appeared well established, with some 26 white and 37 African ministers shepherding African and Colored

61. Women's Auxiliary of Wesleyan Methodist Missionary Society, p. 11.

62. *Annual Report ABCFM, 1914*, pp. 224, 23, 17-18, 39-40, 52-55.

congregations; the huge Witwatersrand Methodist Mission boasted 70 churches and 160 preaching places. Women got only a minor mention — on the staff of the Pretoria Girls' Training Institution were Mrs. Bradfield (matron) and Miss Lilian Burnet (daughter of the chairman of the district). Completely unacknowledged in any formal sense — yet vital on the ground, as the ensuing section will show — was the involvement of the wives of white ministers working among Africans. South Africa still did not really capture the imagination or the purse of the WA, despite hopes of finally attending to Africa's "very just and extremely urgent" pressing new claims.

The WA triumphantly enumerated its 93 British women at work in 1913, the 40 orphanages and boarding schools it funded or helped, 370 day schools reaching nearly 20,000 girls, plus 22 medical centers helping 3,662 inpatients and 221,835 at dispensaries. Individual generosity was even more meticulously itemized and publicized in the full WA report. The legacy of zenana obsession comes through in the list of workers' locations, with 64 based in India, 22 in Ceylon, 17 in China, 2 in Burma, 1 in Spain, and 2 still in South Africa, Miss Caley at Healdtown and Mrs. Hobden at Shawbury Training Institution. Rev. W. Mears praised Shawbury's successes in the Pupil Teachers' Exam, and claimed the 103 pupils in the Normal Department were the "largest numbers of women [teacher training] students in any native institution throughout the country." The wider imperial crisis vied with vistas of female opportunity in the overall message of the WA. The "Women's Movement spreading rapidly in Eastern lands" needed "above all things Christian leadership," while the new value set on women's education constituted "a missionary call of peculiar urgency." They were therefore pledged to an Advance Movement, which war had not managed to cripple.[63]

Whereas the ABCFM complement of single women had stayed much the same in South Africa — 6 in 1880, 7 in 1914 — the Anglicans showed astonishing growth. The High Church elevation of (often celibate) priesthood was far more noticeably coupled with extensive use of unmarried female labor. Again with sisterhoods absent from the equation (except for Sister Bertha in Bloemfontein), SPG women workers — totaling a mere 7 back in 1880 — in 1914 numbered 32. Of the nine dioceses, only George and Kimberley had none; Natal and Pretoria had most (8 each), with 7 in Bloemfontein (which included Basutoland), 4 in Saint John's Kaffraria, 2 each in Cape Town and

63. *The One Hundredth Report of the Wesleyan Methodist Missionary Society* (London, 1914), pp. 26, 144-45, 233; *Report of the Women's Auxiliary of the Wesleyan Methodist Missionary Society for the Year Ending December 31st, 1914* (London, 1915), pp. 76, 7-13, 43, 48, 14-15. Subscriptions and donations run from p. 70 to p. 183!

Zululand, and 1 in Grahamstown. White priests identified as SPG "missionaries to the heathen" numbered at least 84 — but again brotherhoods are underrepresented, such as the Society for Saint John the Evangelist (SSJE) working among Africans in Cape Town.

The SPG as a whole had 1,366 missionaries on its list for 1914, including 343 women, of whom 58 were non-European. It sent 43 men to work abroad that year, and 18 women (whereas 25 had gone in 1913). Strikingly, only 1 of those, a teacher, went to South Africa — 6 teachers, 4 nurses, and 7 general workers went East, mostly to India. They were the responsibility of the substantial Committee of Women's Work (CWW), with its fifty vice presidents (including two viscountesses and seven "Ladies"), an elected committee of twenty, and a Work and Clothing Committee of twelve. The CWW employed a secretary (Miss B. Gurney) and five (single women) assistant secretaries — for candidates, foreign work, home work, finance, and travel — as well as four honorary consulting physicians and one woman doctor. The CWW's size confirms the transformation of the SPG since 1902. Previously "the least progressive and coldest of the English missionary societies," its Ladies' Association in its unproductive first thirty-five years was, Maughan suggests, "a place for women to harmlessly dissipate their energies while producing some extra income for the Society." But the SPG had completely reorganized its women's work once Bishop Montgomery became secretary, making "such great strides . . . that it surpassed CMS in levels of independence and responsibility given to women workers."[64]

Hence women's work was very much more to the fore in the South African section of the 1914 SPG report than had been the case in 1880, despite the extensive coverage of the war effort. The Community of the Resurrection (CR) sisters had left Saint Matthew's Keiskamahoek after eighteen years, to be succeeded at the Girls' Hostel by Miss Wright and Miss Klamborowski (previously at Queen Margaret School, Scarborough, perhaps suggesting that professionalization was ousting religious sisterhoods). Girls' education remained a staple concern: welcome new buildings at Saint Hilda's, with its eighty boarders; difficulties with the industrial school in Maseru; enrollments expanded from nineteen to fifty at Saint Agnes in Johannesburg. The new fervent solidarity of adult African churchwomen was also notable. In the Transkei Mrs. Waters described an evangelistic mission to a chief by 30 women, and Deaconess Catherine a two-day conference of "native women workers," while mission services at Mafeteng in Basutoland mustered up to

64. On reform of the SPG, see Maughan in this volume, pp. 32-57 above, and his "Regions Beyond," pp. 327-57; quotes from pp. 343, 328, 327.

130 zealous women. The Pretoria diocesan report provides the natural bridge to the final section of this chapter, alerting us to the very different urban, industrialized context of some in the second- or third-generation Christian mission community, for example by its portrayal of the highly Europeanized lifestyle of Potchefstroom Africans in well-equipped cottages; the hostels set up in both Johannesburg and Pretoria for African girls who were being assisted to find domestic service jobs; and evangelism and church building via female visits to urban "slumyards" and locations.[65]

Women Missionaries in Johannesburg, 1903-14

Since women missionaries "were perforce civilizing agents more than evangelists," scholars have observed, "their increased participation augmented both the healthier and the more dubious elements in a broadly cultural imperialism."[66] However, more careful periodization of both female mission "civilizing" and evangelism in South Africa prompts a reconsideration. Victorian rural mission households (and even rural female boarding schools as surrogate families) aimed to Christianize and civilize African life by personal contact and example. Mission families in early twentieth-century urban Johannesburg, by contrast, lived very different lives, more physically secure, with far fewer children (even one or none), in an increasingly racially segregated city where Western clothing and houses were taken for granted, not seen as badges of a new spiritual allegiance. Domestic instruction was no longer an all-encompassing, semispiritual task. The work of female missionaries, whether single or married, was largely based outside their homes. Apart from two girls' boarding schools and the supervision of day-school sewing, girls' education was outside their remit and in the hands of African teachers under male mission authority. So the civilizing element was far less overt.

By contrast, even if more rarely encountering the completely unevangelized, Anglican women especially were endlessly giving church teaching to groups of women and children in preparation for baptism and confirmation, and in weekly female devotional meetings. The African women's organizations established in all three churches — Anglican, Methodist, and Congregational — before the First World War were themselves keenly evangelistic, something women missionaries welcomed and supervised with general en-

65. *214th Annual Report of the Society for the Propagation of the Gospel in Foreign Parts for the Year 1914* (London, 1915), pp. 208-20, 30-31, 14-15, 110-20.

66. Christensen and Hutchison, introduction, p. 9.

thusiasm. Hence "evangelism" has to be seen as more central than Christensen and Hutchison imply, not least because of its potential for forging partnership between indigenous and Western women.[67]

It is true that after the First World War female missionary social and philanthropic work had an increasingly prominent place,[68] and that British Methodist and American missionary wives also regained "some of the status . . . lost in the late nineteenth-century emphasis on single missionaries."[69] But in the prewar situation of inadequate American female leadership and limited Methodist wives' involvement with African prayer women in the Transvaal, the work (and therefore the sources) of Anglican women missionaries was comparatively rich, and their numbers unmatched — a dozen or so worked in Johannesburg from 1907 to 1914. Even that brief period illustrates a diversity of gender roles and women's relative weakness. After the South African War, celibate men from the (Mirfield) CR pioneered Anglican mission work in the newly British Transvaal. Their appeal for female help elicited a high-profile response in late 1907 from Deaconess Julia Gilpin, warden of the SPG hostel for training women missionaries, who had also worked in Delhi.[70] The house she and two younger colleagues shared in downtown Johannesburg adjoined and took its spiritual rhythm from the CR fathers' abode, where African ordinands were being trained (to whom Julia gave some lectures). The women developed a routine of regular church classes in existing African Christian congregations up and down the Reef. By 1913 Deaconess Julia had initiated three ventures of lasting importance — a women's devotional society; a girls' industrial school, Saint Agnes, Rosettenville, opened in 1909; and a hostel for the safe accommodation of African women they hoped to help place in domestic service.

Frank interview notes and training home comments on candidates from this prewar batch underline the expectation that women had to be able to live together harmoniously. Excessively strong-minded, self-confident individuals were suspect: "It is a curious mind — cocksure in many ways, ready for any

67. Robert, p. 169.

68. Deborah Gaitskell, "'Getting Close to the Hearts of Mothers': Medical Missionaries among African Women and Children in Johannesburg between the Wars," in *Women and Children First: International Maternal and Infant Welfare, 1870-1945*, ed. Valerie Fildes, Lara Marks, and Hilary Marland (London, 1992); Gaitskell, "Upward All and Play the Game: The Girl Wayfarers' Association in the Transvaal 1925-1975," in *Apartheid and Education: The Education of Black South Africans*, ed. Peter Kallaway (Johannesburg, 1984).

69. Robert, pp. 219, 123.

70. See *SWM [Society of Women Missionaries] Journal*, April 1944, p. 12; November 1945, p. 2.

difficulties . . . perilously near to self-satisfaction," was the comment on one, while of others it was written, "chief fault undue self-confidence" or "too self-centred and introspective . . . wounds and aggravates others — emotional and sentimental, with no real love. Wants to be first and to manage." Another's reports chart her progressive subjugation: "slightly less assertive. . . . Needs much self-discipline. . . . Quieter in manner and trying hard to improve."[71] It was both fitting and necessary for women to be able to cooperate and follow rather than strive to lead. In the field they would have to take orders from priests or established women leaders.

Deaconess Julia's age (forty-six in 1907), experience, and lifelong ordained status certainly gave her authority with male priestly superiors and evoked deference from female colleagues — Marion Trist, her devoted friend, always called her "Deaconess" in letters home. Other spinsters were more dependent on the approval of superiors, and vulnerable to abrupt termination of employment. Rowena Oslar was backed by the CR when she dismissed the exceptionally gifted needleworker Georgina Sibley from Saint Agnes for opposing the endless machining of "*very rough* garments such as the natives wear," but later priests made it clear Oslar herself would not be welcome back after her first furlough: she was deaf, in a "jumpy" state, and had proved too authoritarian. However, the devoted Amy Kent enlisted other CR help to get Oslar back to the Reef — contributing to the ousting of another missionary, the aggrieved Theodora Williams.[72]

These women seem more insecure and put-upon in their gender-segregated church work than priests, with a lifetime consecration. A perennial anxiety about "nerves" was perhaps not entirely misplaced. "I think women feel the altitude and the strain of the work even more than men and once they begin to go to pieces, their progress in that direction becomes rather rapid," argued Bishop Furse, favoring more frequent female furloughs. Amy Kent considered the stresses of the difficult work aggravated by isolation from their own "race." Regarding salaries, Furse robustly declared, "At present I think that we starve them all," a view endorsed by the forthright Theodora Williams: "no raw Kaffir 'piccanin' would come as 'house boy' for the salary we get." Sewing was, ironically, still of great importance, with single women pressed into "always making or mending" for the CR fathers, as well as sup-

71. Rhodes House Oxford, USPG Archives, Candidates' Dossiers, 2491, G. Sibley; Committee of Women's Work (CWW) 79, A. M. Young, 23 July 1904; CWW 89, A. E. Bridge, E. Williams.

72. USPG, CWW Letters, R. Oslar to Miss Gurney, 14 April 1912, G. Sibley to Miss Harris, 24 February 1912; E. T. Williams to Miss Saunders, 27 July 1915, 8 and 11 October 1915, 3 January 1916.

plying school sewing classes by making "little garments" to sell, buying "materials, thimbles cotton etc, out of the small profits," then "perpetually making cassocks & surplices for native men & boys, & altar frontals & curtains for the little churches," with "at least 40 churches & over 100 catechists to be supplied." The CWW considered these demands "quite impossible." Pronouncing the women anemic-looking and their house "squalid, and unrestful," CWW threatened to send no more candidates unless these quarters were improved — which was done. Nevertheless, Bishop Talbot after the war still had a feeling that the women missionaries had "been looked upon a little bit as 'Poor relations,' in the Diocese."[73]

This contrasts markedly with the relative lack of austerity — financial, cultural, and social — in Dorothy Maud's Sophiatown settlement. It also shows how the situation in the field fell far short of Minna Gollock's 1912 aspiration (in an article expressing her frustration at the lack of meaningful decision-making power for women in missions):

> It seems only good that the natives should see the Christian women missionaries not segregated, not treated as if they must by reason of sex be kept out of authority and responsibility, always subordinate, even the wisest and ablest, to the most callow and tactless young man; but treated by fellow missionaries as honoured and trusted fellow workers, fellow-thinkers — able to serve with self-control and with a sacred sense of responsibility which comes not from the commands of man, but the consecration of the Christian to the service of the Master.[74]

In the interwar period, Anglican single women missionaries achieved greater solidarity and vocal assertiveness with their regular conferences and modest publication, *SWM Journal*, plus 147 members by 1939.[75] In 1914, however, the Johannesburg few come across as a small, somewhat divided and occasionally dispirited group. Although Bishop Furse glimpsed the potential importance and scope of the female mission contribution to African church work, his commitment to the ensuing war effort made his grandiose vision of overall

73. USPG, CWW, Furse to Bp Montgomery, 13 February 1913; A. Kent to Miss Saunders, 14 July 1919; T. Williams to Miss Saunders, 15 December 1912; Miss Phillimore to Miss Gurney, 21 March 1913; Furse to Miss Saunders, 17 September 1913; Bp Talbot to Miss Saunders, 24 November 1920.

74. Minna C. Gollock, "The Share of Women in the Administration of Missions," *International Review of Missions* 1, no. 4 (1912): 684, quoted in C. Peter Williams, "The Missing Link," p. 66.

75. See *SWM Journal*, April 1939, pp. 27-32.

coordination completely unrealizable. With provocative joviality, he proposed as essential "one woman worker capable of being a sort of 'Archdeaconess' for Women's work!" Furse thought Deaconess Julia would do admirably.[76] In the event, Julia left for a lower altitude for her health — later working in the dioceses of Cape Town and George until her death in 1948 at age eighty-seven. She never became an archdeaconess for women's work, and it was Furse's charismatic niece, Dorothy Maud, who finally made Johannesburg Anglican female mission activism a substantial force in the 1930s.

Conclusion

Brian Stanley's history of the BMS suggests that the plight of the secluded zenana women provided "the motivation for a movement which was to give women an assured (though still subordinate) place" in the overall missionary endeavor "and sow the seeds of an eventual challenge to the assumptions of exclusively male control." Yet that very creation of a separate female mission sphere from 1867, "if anything, made it even harder for single women to secure a recognized autonomous role within the BMS itself," so that right up to 1914 "the BMS remained a predominantly male society, staffed and controlled almost entirely by men." This was also true of other societies: the very separation which helped mobilize women to support societies they felt they "owned" meant that real partnership of men and women in missionary societies remained unachieved. The stopgap response to the Edinburgh 1910 pressure to end division — by incorporating women's organizations within the main mission body — was being increasingly adopted toward 1914. In that year the Baptist Zenana Mission, for instance, was incorporated within the BMS as its Women's Missionary Association, its structures intact and with no guarantee that any women other than the thirty elected by the Women's Missionary Association would serve on the General Committee.[77]

Women missionaries in South Africa before 1914, in a society without the elite female seclusion of the East, nevertheless worked in a separate female sphere, directing spiritual and social efforts almost entirely toward women and children, under male clerical direction and in support of male-dominated Sunday worship services. Not surprisingly, few questioned the

76. CWW Letters Received (Originals) Africa, 1913 and 1914, Furse to Bp Montgomery, 13 February 1913.

77. Brian Stanley, *The History of the Baptist Missionary Society, 1792-1992* (Edinburgh, 1992), pp. 228, 232, 374.

theological validity or social appropriateness of such arrangements. While changing models of Christian motherhood remained influential, by 1914 African women were consolidating their own fervent corporate spirituality. Though their vocal "praying and preaching" challenged mission assumptions, they too had to accommodate their gendered solidarity to established patterns, creating in time a powerful parallel female church world, with clergy wives virtually "ordained" group leaders, and Thursday the women's day just as Sunday was the preacher's. Dana Robert suggests that the dismantling of the women's missionary movement, which they were powerless to stop as they had no voice in church councils and could not be ordained, "shocked mainline women into fighting for the laity rights and then clergy rights of women," with some of the first to seek orders being women missionaries.[78] Research on British Protestantism and its South African offshoots still needs to explore whether this American pattern has wider validity for the period after 1914.

78. Robert, p. 304.

British Missions and Indian Nationalism, 1880-1908: Imitation and Autonomy in Calcutta and Madras

CHANDRA MALLAMPALLI

In October 1909 the English writer G. K. Chesterton argued that the "art of politics is not managing a machine, but managing a personality." By this he meant that political life ought to give expression to the distinctive cultural ethos of a people. Applying this thesis to India, Chesterton wrote, "The principal weakness of Indian Nationalism seems to be that it is not very Indian and not very national. It is all about Herbert Spencer and Heaven knows what. . . . When all is said, there is a national distinction between a people asking for its own ancient life and a people asking for things that have been wholly invented by somebody else. There is a difference between a conquered people demanding its own institutions and the same people demanding the institutions of the conqueror."[1] In making such bold assertions, Chesterton was probably unaware that by the end of the nineteenth century Indian nationalists were far along in their quest for a distinctly Indian concept of nationhood.[2] They had expanded the scope of nationalism from a purely politi-

1. G. K. Chesterton, "The Indian Nationalist Movement," *Illustrated London News,* 2 October 1909 (American edition). A word of thanks is owed to Vishal Mangalwadi for making this article available to me. Special thanks, as well, to Christi-An Bennett, Alan Guenther, and Dorothea Woll Rice for their helpful critiques of an earlier draft.

2. Here the term "nation" refers to a group that has the *sense* of its own peoplehood based on claims to a common past, destiny, ethnicity, religion, or ideology. This is to be distinguished from a "state," which is a governing apparatus whose administration and control over a population is prescribed by specified territorial boundaries. "Nationalism" is that

Research for this article was made possible by a grant from the Research Enablement Program of the Pew Charitable Trusts.

cal project of securing rights within the British Empire to a cultural project of defending "Hindu society" and "Hinduism" against the culture and religion of the conqueror.[3] Often Indian nationalists defended Hinduism against the influence of British missionaries who embodied, in their minds, the soul or conscience of the European standing in judgment on their way of life. Whether such defenses actually constituted an outcry for indigenous institutions or amounted to an imitative reaction against the "Christian nation" is a question that warrants further inquiry.

Much of the writing on Indian nationalism presents the nationalist encounter with Christian missionaries as a contest for religious allegiance, one that ends either in "conversion" to the "foreign religion" or in effective "Hindu resistance."[4] My central aim in this essay is to show that by the end of the nineteenth century, missionaries and Indian nationalists were engaged in a contest not so much over conversion, but over the cultural personality or imagining of the Indian nation. Rather than competing for the "souls of Indians," they competed for the "soul of India." Missionaries supported Indian nationalism when, even in its most Hindu colors, it manifested signs of "the Christian impact" on India. Conversely, Indian nationalism achieved its greatest autonomy from missionary influence when it ceased to allow Christian religious or societal norms to measure its own legitimacy. This dialectical quest for agency and autonomy within nationalist consciousness can be viewed with greater clarity by applying theoretical tools found in some of the more recent studies on nationalism to the specific urban contexts of Calcutta and Madras from 1880 to 1908.

The Construction of Religious Difference

According to Liah Greenfeld, nationalism originates in unconscious feelings of *ressentiment* or envy toward another culture or civilization, which lead one

process whereby the claims to nationhood are generated and the specific entitlements of the nation (e.g., "home rule," or statehood) are pursued. This process contains both "cultural" and "political" elements.

3. The term "Hinduism" here encompasses a wide array of devotional sects, philosophical schools, deities, and local traditions, predominantly Sanskrit based and native to India. Nineteenth-century apologists of Hinduism attempted to synthesize this plethora of "smaller" traditions into a single monolithic religion, which could compete with Islam and Christianity in the competitive market of religions. "Hindu society," in this essay, refers primarily to the traditional customs, practices, and institutions of the twice-born castes of India.

4. The theme of conversion versus resistance is a fundamental trope not only of "missionary histories" but also of Indian nationalist historiography.

group to define its identity in distinction to the values and beliefs professed by the other. Particularly significant is Greenfeld's discussion of how the one who envies, in the very act of rejecting or denigrating the values of the rival civilization, unconsciously borrows or mirrors those values, in her words "borrowing with an opposite sign."[5] This notion of *ressentiment* seems applicable to how, for example, the Hindu Tract Society (HTS) in Madras tried to defeat missionaries at their own game by preaching the "superiority of Hinduism." However, to apply the concept of *ressentiment* to Hindu-Christian dynamics in India requires not only that we treat "religions" as "nations," but also that we do so within a colonial context.[6] This transition to the analysis of Hinduism as an expression of "anticolonial nationalism" is facilitated by Partha Chatterjee's discussion of the "spiritual" and "material" domains of Indian nationalist thought.

Chatterjee, while agreeing with Benedict Anderson's insights concerning the "imagined" character of nations, objects to Anderson's claim that the historical experiences of western Europe, the Americas, and Russia have provided the modular forms of nationalism for the rest of the world.[7] If colonial subjects of the Third World had simply adopted hook, line, and sinker the forms of nationality derived from the West, there would have been nothing left, in Chatterjee's view, for them to imagine. Anticolonial nationalists of the Third World, he contends, set themselves apart from Western forms of nationalism by preserving the distinctiveness of their "spiritual culture" before they "politically" contested colonial rule.[8] Though Bengali nationalists, according to Chatterjee, conceded superiority to the West in the domain of the "outside," which includes economy, statecraft, science, and technology, they established sovereignty in an inner, "spiritual" domain in which the "essential marks" of cultural identity were "insulated from colonial intrusion."[9]

While Chatterjee's analysis offers insights on how the Indian nationalist mind organized its world, his analysis raises other questions about the religious component of nationalism. If Indian nationalism was "posited not on identity but on *difference*" from the West, to what extent was the positing of difference governed by the dynamics of *ressentiment*? By about 1900 numer-

5. Liah Greenfeld, *Nationalism: Five Roads to Modernity* (Cambridge, 1992), p. 16.

6. By the end of the nineteenth century, Western-educated Hindu publicists, Theosophists, and more radical members of the Indian National Congress (INC) all had made some facet of Hinduism central to their nationalist politics.

7. Partha Chatterjee, *The Nation and Its Fragments* (New Delhi, 1993), pp. 4-5.

8. Chatterjee defines the "spiritual" broadly to include many aspects of cultural activity — e.g., mother tongue, art, novel, drama, and family.

9. Chatterjee, p. 6.

ous societies were formed to defend the "inner domain of culture" in terms of a *religious* nationalism, that is, a monolithic "Hindu religion" upon which Indian identity must be based. If this defense of the Hindu religion essentially borrows the modular form of "the Christian religion" and simply gives it "an opposite [Hindu] sign," how can the inner domain of Indian nationalism be said to evade the universal history Chatterjee decries? To address this question, it is necessary to gauge the extent to which the Hinduism espoused by nationalists was either grounded in the institutions of local society or constructed as a reaction to Christian influence.

The following section on Bengal addresses this issue by comparing the outlook of Bhudev Mukhopadhyay with that of Bankimchandra Chattopadyay. The section on Madras approaches the same issue by analyzing the rhetoric of the Hindu Tract and Theosophical Societies. By such examples, it will be shown how some expressions of nationalist sentiments are reflective of Christian influence while others seem far removed from any molding by Christianity. In each case it is necessary to determine whether nationalist responses betray either imitation or autonomy.

Defenses of Hinduism in Bengal

Toward the turn of the century, upper-caste, English-educated Bengalis (known as *bhadrolok*, or "respectable people") rigorously defended Hindu culture and religion against different aspects of Western influence. When responding to Christian interlocutors, Hindu apologists such as Swami Vivekenanda stridently defended the superiority of Hinduism as the religion best suited to guide India's national regeneration. Such ethical claims for Hinduism, as missionaries themselves observed, often implied that Hindus were adopting, however unconsciously, Christian notions of what a religion ought to look like.[10]

10. This refashioning of Hinduism relates not only to its presentation as a monolithic religion, but also to the recasting of traditional symbols and doctrines to give them a more activist or ethical character. See Indira Chowdhury-Sengupta, "Reconstructing Spiritual Heroism: The Evolution of the Swadeshi Sannyasi in Bengal," in *Myth and Mythmaking*, ed. Julia Leslie (Richmond, 1996), pp. 124-42. Also, Sumit Sarkar, "Indian Nationalism and the Politics of Hindutva," in *Making India Hindu: Religion, Community, and the Politics of Democracy in India*, ed. David Ludden (New Delhi, 1996), pp. 270-94; Robert E. Frykenberg, "The Emergence of Modern Hinduism as a Concept and as an Institution," in *Hinduism Reconsidered*, ed. Gunther D. Sontheimer and Hermann Kulke (New Delhi, 1989).

Other Hindus, suspicious of this resemblance, defended not a religion but a traditional way of life, grounded in caste, against any and all forms of "servile imitation" of Western culture and religion. During the Swadeshi movement (1903-8), nationalists sought to "reclaim" traditional practices and institutions of Hindu society (e.g., caste, the joint family, image worship, and child marriage) that had been attacked by missionaries, Indian reformers, and British officials. The traditionalist approach was less imitative than defenses of modern Hinduism, but also less able, because of its adherence to caste, to encompass all segments of the Indian population.

These different responses to Western influence are well illustrated in Tapan Raychauduri's account of the lives of two Calcutta Brahmans, Bhudev Mukhopadhyay (1827-94) and Bankimchandra Chattopadyay (1838-94). Their experiences, inside and outside their families, offer critical insights into why they defended Hinduism as they did. In the following discussion I argue that while Bhudev's defense of Hinduism was rooted in his total commitment to his family's caste traditions, Bankim's defense was more severed from those familial roots, and hence more *de-cultured.* This rupture between Bankim's immediate, familial experience of Hindu tradition and his ideological formation contributed to a more reactionary construction of Hinduism.

Well situated in the social world of a Bengali Brahman, Bhudev only once questioned the values of his upbringing. During his college years he experienced a crisis of faith when, under the influence of missionaries, he disavowed idol worship and refused to participate in household rituals to various deities.[11] Under the patient and caring tutelage of his father, who explained to him the symbolic meaning of idol worship, Bhudev eventually resumed his belief in every aspect of his ancestral faith. His father's influence convinced him to preserve his orthodox Brahmanical identity against the fashionable departures from Hindu tradition encouraged by his Western education. Bhudev grew up deeply admiring his father and, following the crisis over idol worship, remained intensely committed to the ritual observances of a Brahmanical home. The strong sense of religiosity he developed early in life led him to become formally initiated into the Hindu Tantric tradition.[12]

The satisfaction Bhudev derived from following the strict injunctions of his religion and caste, however, was accompanied by frustration over the "servile imitation of the ruling race" he saw in his friends.[13] Throughout his writings he

11. Tapan Raychauduri, *Europe Reconsidered* (New Delhi, 1988), p. 28.

12. Raychauduri, p. 30.

13. Bhudev was deeply hurt by the conversion to Christianity of one of his most admired friends, Madhusudan Dutt, as well as by other conversions by students of Henry Derozier. Raychauduri, pp. 30-31.

affirms and defends Hindu Brahmanical values, which he regards as the core of Indian identity that was under siege by Western cultural influence.[14] He believed Indians had nothing to learn from the West regarding familial and social ethics. The norms of Indian society, he contended, which emphasized the "selfless," corporate values inherent in the joint family system, are superior to the egalitarian ideals of Europe.[15] His defense of Indian society against Western critiques led him to defend even the most contentious practices of the day. "Those who are alive only to the evils of early marriage," he wrote, "and are blind to its advantages, may be safely described as constantly striving to ape the English."[16] Bhudev also attributed the harsh treatment of household servants by their Indian masters to the imitation of patterns set by British officials in India: "I am afraid the disease of beating one's servant is getting contagious with us. That is the effect of undue imitation. English masters beat their native servants. They also beat their servants who look admiringly on all actions of Englishmen."[17] Bhudev's unwavering defense of things Indian must not be seen as a crude variety of indigeneism. His critique of the West derived from his adherence to his caste identity, coupled with a careful study of a wide range of Western philosophical ideas. Bhudev was acutely aware of the potential for reactionary behavior, even in the way Hinduism would be defended against missionary critiques. Not fooled by what he regarded as the Westernized Hinduism espoused by an Indian Theosophist, Rajnarayan Basu, Bhudev asked, "In what way has the author proved the superiority of Hinduism? He has only shown that it is similar to the Englishman's religion. In the author's mind, the English are the measure of all things."[18] Though he engaged the developments of science and social philosophy from the West, Bhudev made it a priority to remain answerable to the authority of his Brahmanical heritage.

In contrast to Bhudev's unyielding acceptance of Brahmanical tradition, Bankim's personality is defined, in Raychauduri's account, by his ongoing "conflict" with European attitudes as well as his own Hindu tradition.[19] Bankim's writings carry a recurring theme of Indian humiliation at the hands of Englishmen. He often referred to himself and others who worked for the government as "petty servants" of the ruling race. Some of his closest friends

14. Raychauduri, p. 58.

15. Raychauduri, p. 91.

16. Priyaranjan Sen, *Western Influence in Bengali Literature* (Calcutta, 1966), p. 245; from Bhudev Mukhopadhyay, *Paribarik Prabandha, First Essay* (1882; 11th ed., Chinsurah, 1939), p. 1.

17. Sen, p. 244.

18. Raychauduri, p. 35.

19. Raychauduri, pp. 104-6.

and relatives were deeply immersed in this bureaucracy and its values. Bankim himself worked as a deputy magistrate, moving to a "First Class" ranking in salary and status. Yet, even as so-called petty servants of the European, "Bankim's family with its five Deputy Magistrates in two generations achieved a status in the new colonial context higher than the one they enjoyed in traditional Brahman society."[20] The investment of Bankim and his family in the status and security of government positions contributed to their compromise of traditional, Brahmanical practices (including ritual and dietary observances and adherence to hereditary professions).

Internal factors also confused Bankim's attitudes toward Hindu tradition. His great-grandfather's marriage to a woman from a considerably lower caste background and the consequent loss of ritual status may have diluted the "Brahmanical glue" within his family.[21] As an oldest son who had acquired public acclaim for his writings, Bankim shouldered the burdens of huge financial debts from his father and a younger brother who constantly needed money. These pressures, according to Raychauduri, influenced Bankim's movement toward values of self-reliance and individualism early in his writing career.[22] In contrast to Bhudev, who deeply admired his father, Bankim found himself torn between "deference, a sense of duty, impatience and resentment."[23] Though he strained to display filial piety toward his father, he maintained inner feelings of resentment. Such incongruity permeated his attitudes toward Hindu tradition as a whole.

Because of these ruptures in his personal world and his ambiguous relationship to Hindu tradition, Bankim was able to experiment, more freely than Bhudev, with elements of Western thought. For a time the positivism of Comte as well as the utilitarianism of Bentham and Mill profoundly influenced him. This secular, philosophical influence from the West led him to become a passionate skeptic of all religion, while retaining some appreciation for the logic and rationalism to be found in the *samkhya* and *nyaya* schools of Hindu thought. From Comte and Mill he derived tools of social analysis to diagnose various illnesses within Hindu society such as apathy, idleness, superstition, and inequality. By 1917 he had reached the conclusion that Hindu philosophy in its entirety was "a great mass of errors," but only a year later he criticized the "slavish imitation" of Western ways.[24]

20. Raychauduri, p. 106.

21. His father's grandfather married into a wealthy family of considerably lower caste status, probably for material reasons. Raychauduri, pp. 105-6.

22. Raychauduri, pp. 110, 105-6.

23. Raychauduri, p. 108.

24. Raychauduri, pp. 138, 145.

A decade later Bankim shifted from being a harsh critic of Hindu thought to being an ardent defender. This abrupt shift in his thinking coincided with a heated confrontation in the columns of the Calcutta *Statesman* (September to October 1882) between himself (writing under the pseudonym Ram Chandra) and the Reverend William Hastie, principal of the General Assembly's Institution of the Church of Scotland. Bankim's debate with Hastie is significant for two reasons: First, it was during this debate that he made his "first, uncompromising avowal of faith in Hinduism."[25] Second, the debate illustrates a shift in the response of nationalists to their European interlocutors. Rather than measuring the worth of Hindu society according to the external criteria of Western culture, nationalists such as Bankim sought, as Chatterjee suggests, complete sovereignty over the intimate domain of culture and religion. A summary of the exchange will help illustrate both points.

The controversy ignited when news broke that some of Calcutta's most prominent Hindu citizens, known for their stand against image worship, had attended a funeral ceremony at the famous Sobha Bazar Raj house in Calcutta, in which an idol of Krishna (worshiped as Gopinath, lord of the milkmaids) was venerated. In the first of his six letters to the *Statesman,* Hastie, shocked by this news, criticizes the learned Hindus for sending the message to their unenlightened countrymen that they approved of "idolatry." He explained: "But it is just because I know that they are *not* inwardly sincere or true to themselves in any of their forms of idolatrous worship, and because I believe that this practical insincerity or unreality of theirs is sucking the lifeblood out of the very hope of their community, that I venture to touch however slightly, upon this delicate subject."[26] Regardless of how aware he claimed to be of the "delicate" nature of the subject, Hastie's tone was triumphalistic. Discoursing on idolatry with pompous alliteration and assorted polemical quips, he offered "a god-send to any satirist."[27] He followed up his initial courtesies with blaring condemnation of the "Shiva temple that makes one shudder," the "elephant-headed and huge-paunched Ganapati," and the "merry music and mincing movements" of sensuality underlying Krishna worship.[28]

Hastie's tone makes him seem either unaware of or indifferent to the rising Hindu nationalist sentiments of this period, his polemics echoing the

25. Raychauduri, p. 146.

26. *Statesman,* 23 September 1882. All the articles from the *Statesman* are printed in Shri Jogesh Chandra Bagal, ed., *Bankim Rachanavali* (Calcutta, 1969), hereafter *BR.*

27. Raychauduri, p. 122.

28. *Statesman,* 23 September 1882; *BR,* p. 187.

anti-Hinduism of early nineteenth-century evangelicals.[29] His rhetorical strategy, first, isolates the educated, "enlightened" Hindus of Calcutta from their countrymen who continue *sincerely* to worship idols; second, amplifies the dissonance that he reads into their participation in Hindu ceremonies; and third, exhorts them to use their status as cultural leaders to dissuade others from worshiping idols.[30] The goal of this strategy was not to convert learned Hindus, but to make them fellow crusaders against idolatry, the single greatest source, according to Hastie, of Indian degeneracy.[31]

In his third letter, Hastie shifted from idolatry to an assault on the "higher" philosophy of Brahmanism. Here he cited European scholars such as Monier Williams as authorities on the meaning of Hindu scriptures.[32] He went so far as to say that "both Sanskrit language and the Sanskrit literature are much better understood at this moment in Europe and America than they are in India."[33] Yet, in Hastie's mind, the dissemination of this knowledge in the West only served to display to all the error of Hinduism. It was to such claims that Bankim took the most serious objection.

The central theme of Bankim's replies to Hastie was the distinction between, first, the "husk" or nonessential, surface characteristics of Hinduism that preoccupy and inform European scholarly interest and, second, the essentials, or "kernel," of Hinduism. Bankim's rhetorical strategy appealed to an authentic and intimate knowledge of Indian religion to be derived from vernacular traditions. He challenged Hastie to learn about Hinduism by studying the original Sanskrit scriptures under Hindus who actually *believe* in them, not by reading European translations or commentaries.[34] While acknowledging the contributions of European scholarship, Bankim distin-

29. See David Kopf, *British Orientalism and the Bengal Renaissance* (Berkeley, 1969). Hastie argues against the claims that idolatry (1) is necessary for those who cannot conceptualize a formless God; (2) is a step along an evolutionary ladder toward higher forms of spirituality; and (3) is no more harmful than the adoration of dolls by children in the West: 23 and 26 September 1882 to the *Statesman.*

30. *Statesman,* 26 September 1882; *BR,* pp. 191-94.

31. This shift in missionary emphasis from religious conversion to a cultural conversion to be led by Western-educated Hindus increasingly shaped the ethos of educational branches of missionary societies during the late nineteenth century. His alarmist rhetoric notwithstanding, Hastie's letters can in fact be situated within this ethos. For a detailed description of this change in missionary strategy, see A. Mathew, *Christian Missions, Education, and Nationalism: From Dominance to Compromise, 1870-1930* (New Delhi, 1988), pp. 50-93.

32. Hastie begins his 26 September 1882 letter to the *Statesman* defending European Sanskritists; see also *BR,* p. 191.

33. *Statesman,* 7 October 1882; *BR,* p. 201.

34. *Statesman,* 6 October 1882; *BR,* p. 200.

guished a "scholarly" understanding of Hinduism from the understanding that comes from true belief, the use of vernacular languages, and oral traditions. Translation dilutes the meaning of the original text because of the inability of the new language to adequately capture ideas foreign to it: "Now, a people so thoroughly unconnected with England or Germany as the old Sanskrit-speaking people of India . . . had necessarily a vast store of ideas and conceptions utterly foreign to the Englishman or the German, just as the Englishman or the German boasts a still vaster number of ideas utterly foreign to the Hindu. These, which form the spirit and the matter of religious and philosophical treatises, are entirely distorted and, as a matter of necessity, misrepresented in every translation — even in the best."[35] In addition to distortion through translation, Bankim called attention to the "vast mass of [traditional] and unwritten knowledge in India, used to supplement, illustrate, or explain the written literature."[36] These oral traditions, maintained by generations of learned pandits, form the "flesh and blood to the dry bones of the written literature," and were wholly inaccessible to the European scholar.[37] Bankim also refers to Tantric literature, about which the European knows nothing, as having powerfully influenced the fate of "some of the Indian people."[38] Hence, rather than engaging Hastie on his terms, Bankim redefines the rules of the game by invoking an intimate domain of cultural knowledge outside Hastie's reach.

Attacking Hastie's original criticism of those attending the Calcutta funeral, Bankim wrote,

> Mr. Hastie attacks, without any provocation, the proceedings, in a solemn mourning ceremony held in the private dwelling-house of one of the most respectable Hindu families in the country; attacks all the most respected members of native society; attacks their religion; attacks the religion of the nation. And all this without the slightest provocation. . . . And then, when a humble individual of the nation whose religion he tramples upon, ventures upon a single retort, Mr. Hastie's temper is on fire and it explodes. The combatant who loses his temper in fight is rarely believed to be on the winning side. . . . If this is the attitude which

35. *Statesman*, 16 October 1882; *BR*, p. 204.

36. *Statesman*, 28 October 1882; *BR*, p. 211.

37. *Statesman*, 28 October 1882; *BR*, p. 211.

38. *Statesman*, 28 October 1882; *BR*, p. 212. The Tantras are texts which set forth esoteric practices by which the mother goddess Shakti and its host of lesser female divinities are to be worshiped.

> the Christian missionary of the present day thinks it proper to assume towards Hinduism, Hinduism has nothing to fear from his labors.[39]

Bankim's statements are significant not only because he designated Hinduism the religion of "the nation," but also because he located himself within that nation and, by implication, within Hinduism. Casting aside his earlier ambivalence regarding Hindu philosophy and traditions, Bankim rose to defend the religion of his nation against the onslaught of the verbose Scotsman.

While the impact of the Sobha Bazar controversy on Bankim's thinking must not be exaggerated, the much stronger Hindu emphasis in his writing from 1882 on is noteworthy. This emphasis along with the fact that Bankim's responses to Hastie contain his "first, uncompromising avowal of faith in Hinduism" suggest that a degree of *ressentiment,* of "borrowing with an opposite sign," now governed his outlook. In response to Hastie's Christian polemics, Bankim reified a brand of Hinduism that previously he was reluctant to embrace. His sudden, self-conscious return to Hinduism was not to orthodox caste observances nor to its rationalist traditions, but to its theistic, devotional expression.[40] In the years following Hastie's attack on Hindu gods, Bankim extolled the path of bhakti (devotion or love of God) in praise of the mother goddess, worshiped as Shakti (power incarnate). In so doing, he constructed a feminine object of national devotion directly antithetical to Hastie's masculine, Christian nationalism. His famous hymn, "Bande Mataram," personified the Hindu nation as a Mother whose weapons in her ten arms represented an image of great power. By 1905 *Bande Mataram* (which means "Hail Motherland") became the chief slogan and symbol of militant, defiant, "Hindu" nationalism.

By refusing debate on another's terms, Bankim was able to assert an imagined Hinduism impervious to European learning and criticism. This strategy of disengaging the foreign interlocutor, far from being confined to the realm of religious polemics, became a crucial, defining feature of the new forms of political agitation during the late nineteenth and early twentieth centuries. Nationalist politics of this period disengaged the British parliamentary process and asserted "Hinduness" as a means of furthering national objectives. During the Swadeshi movement (1903-8), leaders such as Lal Lajpat Rai, Bipan Chandra Pal, and Sri Aurobindo Ghose abandoned the "moderate," constitutional methods of the early congress and advocated the more "ex-

39. *Statesman,* 16 October 1882; *BR,* p. 203.
40. Raychauduri, pp. 137, 145.

tremist" politics of boycott, civil disobedience, and the politicization of Hindu festivals and slogans.[41]

The aim of the Swadeshi movement was to force the government to reverse Lord Curzon's decision of 1903 to divide the province of Bengal into two administrative units. The Partition most adversely affected the Hindu *bhadrolok* of East Bengal,[42] and as a means of protest, Hindu leaders called for the large-scale boycott of all foreign *(bideshi)* goods, especially British-made goods, and promoted the purchase of indigenous *(swadeshi)* goods. This economic strategy had a very strong cultural component as well. The Swadeshi emphasis on "self-reliance" *(atmasakti)* not only entailed support of indigenous products, but also a comprehensive defense of Hindu society against the ideals of liberal, Christian society.

In pushing for cultural self-reliance, Swadeshi advocates reasserted features of traditional Hindu society previously attacked by missionaries and Indian reformers. They replaced the coldly rational petitions of congressmen with an unprecedented evocation of vernacular songs, slogans, drama, and popular Hindu festivals aimed at awakening the masses to Swadeshi ideals.[43] Bal Gangadhar Tilak, who used both the Shivaji and Ganesha (the elephant god) processions as tools for political mobilization in the Bombay Presidency, captured the revivalist sentiments of the day when he declared in a Bengalese newspaper, "We are all idolaters and I am not ashamed of the fact."[44] Following Tilak's example, agitators in Bengal used the Shivaji festival to fire nationalist sentiments at the popular level.

In addition to the politicization of popular, devotional symbols, Swadeshi advocates in Bengal sought to apply the norms of caste discipline at a more collective, societal level.[45] They imposed a "social boycott" or caste sanction against anyone exposed even indirectly to foreign goods. The boycott included "withdrawal of ritual services, refusal of inter-dining, boycott of wedding receptions and funeral ceremonies and other pressures amounting to partial or total ostracism of those considered guilty of deviation from *swadeshi* norms."[46]

This unmitigated defense of traditional Hindu society and rejection of ev-

41. Sumit Sarkar, *The Swadeshi Movement in Bengal: 1903-1908* (New Delhi, 1973).

42. Gordon Johnson, "Partition, Agitation and Congress: Bengal, 1904 to 1908," in *Locality, Province, and Nation,* ed. Gallagher, Johnson, and Seal (Cambridge, 1973), p. 240.

43. Sarkar, *The Swadeshi Movement,* p. 254.

44. Sarkar, *The Swadeshi Movement,* p. 422. Taken from *Bengalee,* 6 June 1906.

45. They did this by ascribing "impurity" to foreign products and to those who trafficked in them. "Purity and pollution" are, according to Louis Dumont, the organizing principles of Hindu caste hierarchy.

46. Sarkar, *The Swadeshi Movement,* p. 5.

erything "foreign" brought Swadeshi advocates into direct conflict with more progressive, reform-minded Hindus.[47] The tension that developed was not simply between tradition and reform, but between different notions of what it meant to nationalize Hindu tradition. Should Hindus project all aspects of their local cultural experience — including caste hierarchy — onto their emerging concept of nationhood? Or should they selectively appropriate aspects of Western culture toward the construction of a more progressive and dynamic Hindu nationalist identity?[48] Ranajit Guha describes the tension as one between caste and nation: "Heedless of what a maturing nationhood could do, in theory, to undermine primordial caste formations, social boycott thus went ahead to serve the interests of the big society that was the nation by insisting on procedures used by the little society of castes to resist innovation and change."[49] This move from caste, or *jati,* to nation, or *mahajati,* most closely resembles the outlook of Bhudev Mukhopadyay, who shunned all imitation of the West and presented Brahmanical leadership as the key to India's advancement. In line with the nationalist vision of Bhudev, the Swadeshi movement, by its use of caste sanctions, gave the Brahman new, national prominence as the priest, warden, and mentor of Hindu society.[50]

This reification of Hindu culture as national culture alienated Muslims as well as Christians. In one sense the status of Christians became even more marginal than that of Muslims. Unlike Muslims, who stood at the center of the politics surrounding the Partition, Bengal's Christians made little political contribution. While both Muslims and Christians were inevitably alienated by Hinduized politics, the inclusion of Muslims was nevertheless an essential aspect of the nationalist ideal during this period, at least at the level of rhetoric. The same cannot be said for Christians. The *swadeshi* ideology of self-reliance, when extended from the economic to the cultural domain, reified Christianity, as never before, as a "foreign religion."[51] While missionaries themselves were infrequent targets of *swadeshi* rhetoric, some complained that loud and deliberate chanting of the slogan *Bande Mataram* interrupted their open-air meetings.[52]

47. Sarkar, *The Swadeshi Movement,* p. 60.

48. Cf. Chatterjee, pp. 34-37.

49. Ranajit Guha, *A Disciplinary Aspect of Indian Nationalism* (Santa Cruz, Calif., 1989), p. 11.

50. Guha, p. 16.

51. "Spirit of Unrest," *Harvest Field,* April 1908. See also Vincent Kumaradoss, "The Attitude of Protestant Missionaries in South India towards Indian Nationalism with Special Reference to Tamil Nadu, 1900-1907," *Indo-British Review* 15, no. 1 (1988): 134.

52. "Spirit of Unrest."

The "Hindu Public" of Madras

Throughout much of the nineteenth century, an educated, professional class of Hindus shaped public opinion in Madras in a manner similar to the *bhadrolok* of Calcutta. Like the *bhadrolok*, Madras Hindus used their status as cultural leaders to advance Hindu revivalist causes.[53] In contrast to the *bhadrolok*, who opposed policies that empowered Muslims, Madras Hindus opposed evangelical influence upon government policy and tried to check conversions to Christianity.[54] It should be noted, however, that the revivalist interests of Madras Hindus did not influence the politics of southern nationalism to the degree that Hindu revivalism influenced nationalism in Bengal and north India. This is not to suggest that Tamil and Telugu districts within the presidency were not deeply Hindu. Richly endowed temple establishments, *maths* or religious schools, pilgrimage sites, festivals and ceremonies of Brahmans and other high-caste Hindu communities all flourished under the Madras government. Yet these expressions of Hindu vitality did not form the brick and mortar of an anticolonial "cultural nationalism" as this developed in Bengal.

This disparity between Bengal and Madras stems from a number of factors: the highly segmented social terrain of the presidency, the rise of Tamil and Telugu linguistic nationalisms, which resisted the hegemony of Sanskritic culture, and the emergence of non-Brahman caste politics.[55] Nevertheless, a self-conscious Hindu public did arise to defend Hinduism against missionary influence. Members of this public founded new societies during the 1880s whose principal aim was to defend Hinduism and undermine the public legitimacy of Christianity. Among these societies were the Hindu Sabha, the Aryan Forefathers' Society, and the HTS.

These "countermovements" show the clearest signs of imitative, reactionary tendencies. Although their nationalist rhetoric is predicated on the theme of religious *difference* from the West, it borrows the modular form of a religion from Christianity while invoking the ideas of European radicals in its assault against missionaries. To use the language of the last section, these societies demonstrate the *ressentiment* of Hindu elites against the Christian

53. See D. Sadasivan, *The Growth of Public Opinion in the Madras Presidency* (Madras, 1974).

54. Robert E. Frykenberg, "On Roads and Riots in Tinnevelly: Radical Change and Ideology in Madras Presidency during the Nineteenth Century," *South Asia*, n.s., 4, no. 2 (December 1981): 46.

55. Eugene Irschick, *Politics and Social Conflict in South India* (Berkeley, 1969); also David Arnold, *The Congress in Tamilnad* (New Delhi, 1977), pp. 16-17.

religion. What made the pro-Hindu rhetoric of these societies reactionary was its absence of grounding in institutions and categories of thought germane to the religious landscape of south India.

The impetus for the founding of various Hindu societies came from Western-educated publicists backed financially by Hindu merchants. Under the influence of the Theosophical Society, which by 1879 had established offices in major Indian cities, these publicists borrowed radical, secularist ideas from Europe and deployed them in their campaign against Christianity in India. This strategy simply countered the rhetoric of Christian missionaries who denounced "Hindu superstition" with rationalist arguments.[56] Under such rationalist influences, Madras Hindus discarded the orthodox arguments that had been used to denounce Christianity by Tamil, Shaivite groups (which invoked the authority of the Vedas and the concepts of orthodox, Shaivite tradition) in the earlier part of the century.[57] They replaced orthodox arguments with rhetoric that emphasizes the radical inclusiveness or tolerance of the Hindu religion. This profession of "Hindu tolerance" was almost invariably pitted against the intolerance and sectarianism of Christian missionaries.[58]

While borrowing the modular form of a religion from missionaries, modern Hindus attacked the doctrinal substance of Christianity.[59] Some, either under the influence of the Brahmo Samaj or Theosophy, pointed to the decline of Christian influence in the West as they sold Hinduism as the religion best suited for the modern world. The fundamental doctrines of Christianity, they noted, were breaking down under the stress of modern science and biblical criticism: "[Christianity] is losing its hold on the cultured minds of the West as unhistorical and unethical. . . . There seems to be no limit to this process of expurgation and elimination. It is impossible to say what will remain

56. Ironically, both "modern" Hindus and evangelicals staged their contest for public legitimacy within the ideological framework of the European Enlightenment. For western India, see Rosalind O'Hanlon, *Caste, Conflict, and Ideology: Mahatma Jotirao Phule and Low Caste Protest in Nineteenth-Century Western India* (Cambridge, 1985).

57. Dennis Hudson, "Arumuga Navalar and the Hindu Renaissance among Tamils," in *Religious Controversy in British India,* ed. Kenneth Jones (Albany, N.Y., 1992), or Richard Fox Young and S. Jabanesan, *The Bible Trembled* (Vienna, 1995).

58. The themes of sectarianism and tolerance were not only prominent in the writings of Vivekenanda, but also in the literature of the Theosophical Society. See "Religion and Sectarianism," *Theosophist* 27, no. 1 (October 1905), and "Is the Moral Supremacy of Christendom in Danger?" *Theosophist* 27, no. 5 (February 1906).

59. Brahmo Samajists were among the first to observe declining relevance for the distinctive doctrines of Christianity while upholding its moral and spiritual significance. See "Interview with Mr. Sibanath Sastri," *Harvest Field,* March 1889, p. 315.

of Christianity in years to come. In those circumstances, it is extremely unlikely that the philosophical mind of India will cut itself adrift from its ancient moorings and turn to Christ for its spiritual sustenance."[60] Other modern Hindu apologists made no issue of Christian decline in the West, but directly attacked Christian doctrine. Their offensive, however, did not rest on the unadulterated doctrines of the Vedas, but on the ideas of Robert Ingersoll, Charles Bradlaugh, and Thomas Paine, as well as "facts" derived from biblical higher criticism. Missionaries keenly observed the influence of Western anticlerical thought on Hindu nationalist ideology in Madras, an influence they attributed to the charismatic Theosophist Annie Besant.[61]

Besant embodied the curious romance between the Western ideologies of secularism and "free thought," and the new apologetic of Hinduism. Many critics, mystified by the so-called nine lives of Annie Besant, describe her journey from Christianity to revivalist Hinduism in terms of radical breaks and discontinuities.[62] Yet her intellectual itinerary epitomizes the ongoing symbiosis between a Europe that was becoming increasingly "post-Christian" and a class of Indians deeply flattered by foreigners' romanticization of Hinduism. While other nationalists, Justice Party members, and orthodox Hindus had their differences with Besant,[63] few modern Hindus could resist her praise of Hinduism and her conviction that Indian nationality must be based on its free thought and catholicity. Yet, few could have been aware of how Besant's pro-Hindu hymnody appropriated India to the patterns of European secularism: "Hinduism, beyond all other faiths, has encouraged intellectual effort, intellectual research, and intellectual freedom. The only authority recognized by it is the authority of Wisdom, and that convinces the reason, it does not trample on it. The six Darashanas are the proofs of Hinduism's intellectual liberty."[64] Besant's Orientalism made Brahmanical leadership and

60. G. Venkataranga Row, "A Christian View of Hinduism," *Indian Review*, January 1913, p. 22.

61. According to T. E. Slater, the names of Bradlaugh and Ingersoll had already become "household words." See *Report of the Third Decennial Missionary Conference held at Bombay, 1892-3* (Bombay, 1893), 1:277. See also Rev. E. W. Thompson, "Movements of Hinduism in South India," in *Fourth Decennial Missionary Conference Held at Madras, 1902* (London, 1902), pp. 292-311.

62. Bipin Chandra Pal, *Mrs. Annie Besant: A Psychological Study* (Madras, 1917), pp. 69-72.

63. Besant was convinced of the intellectual "superiority" of Brahmans over other castes, views which elicited heated responses from Tamil anti-Brahmanical movements. V. Geetha and S. V. Rajadurai, "One Hundred Years of Brahminitude: Arrival of Annie Besant," *Economic and Political Weekly* 30, no. 28 (15 July 1995): 1768-73.

64. Annie Besant, "Hinduism and Nationality," *New India*, 9 January 1915.

Hindu revival centerpieces in the struggle for home rule. Her personal charisma, vision for social reform, and outspoken criticisms of British rule eventually earned her the presidency of the Home Rule League and the Indian National Congress. Besant shared the convictions of many nationalists that India's growth and freedom had to be argued for along Hindu lines. "Hinduism," she said, "is peculiarly fitted to shape and color the National future, for it is non-aggressive as regards to other religions: it makes no converts, it assails no beliefs, it is as tolerant as the earth itself."[65]

In describing Hinduism in this manner, Besant may or may not have had in mind the various organizations that had been formed within the Madras Presidency to defend Hinduism and counter the influences of Christian missionaries. Among these were the Hindu Sabha (1880); the Aryan Forefathers' Society, founded in Tinnevelly (with many members who were Theosophists); the Bellary Sanmarga Samaj; and the Association for the Propagation of the Aryan Vedic Religion, founded by Ragunatha Rao (who also became a Theosophist) in 1886.[66]

Shortly following the formation of Rao's society, the HTS was formed in 1887 primarily with the goal of countering Christian missionary activity. The Tract Society's campaigns involved the distribution of both Tamil and English tracts along with public preaching and lectures.[67] Far from displaying yogic indifference to Christianity, the society published numerous tracts that vented its outrage over the inferiorization of Hinduism. Tracts such as *The Absurdity of Christianity* or *Is Jesus God?* attacked Christian morality, theological claims, and the Bible while defending the legitimacy of Hinduism, largely with scientific or rationalist arguments.[68]

This assault upon Christianity by the HTS was accompanied by the adoption of many Christian techniques for the propagation of Hinduism. Religious newspapers, public lectures and "sermons," "catechisms" for Hindu children, and street preachers were all employed by Hindus. From 1888 to

65. Besant, "Hinduism and Nationality."

66. Geoffrey Oddie, "Anti-missionary Feeling and Hindu Revivalism in Madras: The Hindu Preaching and Tract Societies, 1886-1891," in *Images of Man: Religious and Historical Process in South Asia,* ed. Fred W. Clothey (Madras, 1982), pp. 217-42.

67. Vincent Kumaradoss identifies these defenses of Hinduism in Madras with nationalism, in "Christianity and Hindu Nationalism: A Reassessment of the Hindu Tract Society, 1887-1891" (paper delivered at the meeting of the Church History Association of India, Mangalore, Karnataka, 16-18 October 1998), p. 4.

68. Kumaradoss, "Christianity and Hindu Nationalism." Some Christians even believed that in denouncing Christianity, the HTS was disseminating some truths about Jesus Christ. S. V. Thomas, "The Hindu Tract Society," *Madras Christian College Magazine,* April 1889.

1889 alone, the Tract Society had twenty-six affiliated branches, twenty-one in Tamil districts and five in Telugu districts. According to Geoffrey Oddie, the imitation of Christian methods was taken to extreme measures. The Madurai branch is said to have sent out "Bible women" to distribute tracts and other materials, which, according to the *Missionary Herald*, were often "filled with low jokes" against Christianity "from Ingersoll and Bradlaugh."[69]

This borrowing of Christian apologetic forms was labeled by the editor of the *Harvest Field* a purely reactionary development, orchestrated by Annie Besant. The editor reviewed the content of the *Sanatana Dharma Catechism, a Catechism for boys and girls in Hindu Religion and Morals*, a work issued by the English Board of Trustees of the Central Hindu College in Benares in hopes of teaching children the basics of the Hindu religion.[70] He then questioned the whole project of turning Hinduism into "a religion of the book." Citing first the challenges in store for those who wished to homogenize Hindu religion into a single entity (e.g., caste inclusiveness), the editor moved on to identify theological themes in the catechism resembling Christian belief such as faith in a personal God, and concepts of sin and righteousness. Besant he labeled "a Westerner who came to employ the methods of the West to teach the wisdom of the East."[71]

Such borrowing shows that Hindu tractarians in Madras were answerable to two starkly contrasting sets of interlocutors: to missionaries, against whom they posited a more tolerant and enlightened Hindu religion, and to radical secularists to whom they presented a rational, nonsectarian ideology.[72] Hindu nationalist imagination permitted ample room for the borrowing of religious form and content from the West while maintaining a sense of its own historical agency in the process. Regarding Christian conversion, however, the nationalist mind immediately assigns agency to the "foreign power," to the "colonizer" who induces conversion by his superiority in the "outer," material domain. Ironically, Hindu nationalism, though *consciously* attempting to "decolonize" the inner domain of culture by opposing Christianity, was unconsciously being fashioned by the organizing forms and dialectics of so-called Christian society.

Because it accepted so many "foreign" criteria for legitimacy, it is difficult

69. Oddie, p. 229, from *Missionary Herald* 84 (October 1888): 439.

70. "Two Catechisms," *Harvest Field* 13, no. 7 (July 1902): 250-51. According to this report, another catechism was written and published in Kanarese by an orthodox Brahman.

71. "Two Catechisms," p. 251.

72. This concurs with O'Hanlon, pp. 52-55. Lesslie Newbigin (drawing on sociologist Peter Berger) argued that missionaries and modern Hindus often accepted the same "plausibility structure" within which beliefs derived legitimacy: see his *Foolishness to the Greeks: The Gospel and Western Culture* (London, 1991).

to regard public defenses of Hinduism in Madras as a "powerful, creative, and historically significant project," as Chatterjee describes nationalism.[73] Such defenses of Hinduism might alternately be viewed as the fulfillment of a very foreign agenda — either as Europe's own project of secularization re-creating itself in the ethos of "Hindu tolerance" or as Hinduism climbing the evolutionary ladder of religion toward its ultimate "fulfillment in Christ."[74] Missionaries themselves debated these issues in the face of nationalist "unrest."[75] Their critiques of Indian nationalism toward the turn of the century were part of the larger discussion of missionary policy toward the educated classes.

A New Missionary Policy

The development of missionary ideology toward the end of the nineteenth century paralleled developments within Indian nationalist thought in a way that made it difficult to determine who was reacting to whom. As Hindu leadership sought to transform nationalist rhetoric from an elitist discourse to a more popular one, evangelical missionaries urged their mission societies to redirect missionary resources away from education and toward the evangelization of the masses.[76]

By the 1890s educational missionaries had to respond to evangelicals who cited the low numbers of conversions along with the rising nationalist sentiments among educated Indians (who were often hostile toward missions) as evidence of a failed policy. As a corrective measure, evangelicals urged their societies to devote more resources to popular preaching. The response of educational missionaries, by contrast, was to redefine missionary objectives from religious conversion to cultural conversion.[77] According to this new

73. Chatterjee, p. 6.

74. For a recent study of conversion, belief, and cultural crosscurrents between Europe and India, see Gauri Viswanathan, *Outside the Fold: Conversion, Modernity, and Belief* (Princeton, 1998).

75. "Restlessness," "unrest," and "awakening" had become terms most often used by missionaries in reference to rising nationalist consciousness. See "Restless India," *Harvest Field*, September 1896, pp. 327-37; J. A. Bourdillon, "Opportunity of the Unrest in India," *Church Missionary Review*, August 1909, pp. 449-57.

76. See "Education and Mass Movements in India: Report and Resolutions Adopted by the General Committee of March 12, 1912," *Church Missionary Review*, April 1912, pp. 247-49.

77. This redefinition of missionary goals is outlined in Eric J. Sharpe, *Not to Destroy but to Fulfil* (Uppsala, 1965), and in A. Mathew, *Christian Missions, Education, and Nationalism.*

logic, even nationalism in its most Hindu and anti-Christian expressions was the work of God in India. By way of fulfillment theology, educational missionaries such as T. E. Slater, J. N. Farquhar, and W. H. Findlay identified missionary agency or influence upon nationalist consciousness, not formal conversion or baptism, as the crux of their mission to India.

In 1889 a heated controversy within the ranks of the Wesleyan Methodist Missionary Society (WMMS) revealed growing concerns over the relationship between nationalist sentiments, Christian education, and missionary lifestyle. The controversy erupted when the *Methodist Times* ran a series of anonymous articles that attacked missionary adherence to Alexander Duff's educational policies along with the "luxury" of the missionary lifestyle.[78] Henry S. Lunn, a medical missionary to Madras, wrote the articles, but Hugh Price Hughes, the *Methodist Times* editor and a close friend of Lunn, assumed responsibility for the views expressed in the articles before Lunn's identity eventually was disclosed. The articles not only decry the "failures" of missionary education, but also speak of the separation of WMMS missionaries from "natives" caused by the more extravagant lifestyle of the former and the inferior status given to Indian Christians in the Society's official functions.[79]

Lunn's articles evoked caustic responses from other WMMS missionaries in the columns of the *Harvest Field,* and even prompted the WMMS to appoint a subcommittee to review his claims. The subcommittee's report "completely exonerated" the missionaries from all of Lunn's charges regarding their lifestyle and relation to the indigenous population.[80]

Lunn's first article criticized the initial Duff strategy, of attacking Hinduism by converting Brahmans through the English medium of Christian education. With rash, apocalyptic boldness Lunn condemned the Duff policy as a "disastrous failure" because of how it equipped Brahmans to "dominate" the nationalist movement.

> Instead of an explosion within the citadel of Brahminism, as the result of missionary work, we witness the walls of that citadel crumbling beneath the influence of the "Zeit Geist," built up again in a new form and with a new strength by the young Brahmans educated in our missionary colleges. . . . [The policy of educating Brahmans] has produced a

78. Excerpts were eventually published as *The Missionary Controversy: Discussion, Evidence and Report, 1890* (London, 1890).

79. These criticisms are summarized in Hughes and Lunn's *Summary Statement of the Facts and Arguments upon which the "New Missionary Policy" is Based* (n.p.: Wesleyan Methodist Missionary Society, 1890).

80. See *Harvest Field,* August 1890, p. 78.

> haughty and exclusive caste to substitute an intellectual ascendancy for the spiritual supremacy possessed by their fathers. There is no greater danger to the National Movement in India, than that it should be dominated by a Brahminical caucus, and if that result ever does ensue it will be due to the carrying out of the policy of Alexander Duff.[81]

Lunn also claimed that missionaries spent a "startling proportion" of their total budget on Brahman education, and committed "at least three-fourths of the ablest men sent out by all the Protestant Missionary Societies" to educating Brahmans, who constituted a mere 4 percent of India's total population.[82]

As sweeping as Lunn's claims were perceived to be, they revealed certain assumptions central to missionary debates over nationalism. For instance, Lunn contended that the spirit of nationalism was serving the redemptive project of eroding Brahmanical orthodoxy. However, instead of demolishing the "citadels of Brahminism," missionary schools raised Brahmans to be national leaders with an anti-Christian bias. While Lunn assigned agency to missionary schools in furthering Brahmanical ascendancy, he said very little about the origins of nationalist consciousness itself. It was precisely this question of agency that educational missionaries addressed in their responses to Lunn.

One of the most distinguished was William Miller, principal of Madras Christian College, who argued that Brahmans would have been just as educated and had just as much "intellectual ascendancy" even without Christian schools. If some of them have become openly critical of Christianity, this merely shows that they are at least not ignorant of Christian claims. As for the nationalist movement, Miller applauded the Brahman leadership within the congress. "It is a strange use of words," he retorted, "to speak of the 'danger' of a movement coming to be 'dominated' by those who originated it and have all along taken the leading part in it."[83]

In response to the charge that graduates of missionary schools were promoting an "anti-Christian renaissance" of Hindu thought, Miller, drawing from his experience at Madras Christian College, stated that he did not know of even one student to whom the charge applied. Even if true, Miller explained that it would be no cause for alarm, since there had always been resistance to Christianity among those who "know the truth." Such resistance never provided grounds to cease efforts to "inculcate truth."[84] This was not to

81. *The Missionary Controversy,* p. 2.
82. *The Missionary Controversy,* p. 4.
83. *Harvest Field,* June 1889, p. 404.
84. *Harvest Field,* June 1889, p. 403.

deny, however, that an "awakening" was indeed occurring among those educated in Christian schools (one-fifth of the total number of educated Indians). According to Miller, this awakening and the reactions it elicited from the uneducated, orthodox Hindus was in fact the "explosion" within Hinduism to which Duff had referred. Far from being a cause for alarm, Hindu revival, opposition, and antagonism were necessary steps in India's "movement Christward."[85]

Miller is one of several "fulfillment theorists" who, in essence, validated the flourishing of modern Hinduism by locating it within their own theological framework. Other fulfillment theorists included G. M. Cobb and F. W. Kellett of the WMMS, and T. E. Slater and J. N. Farquhar of the London Missionary Society. Against evangelical charges that they were diluting the gospel and ignoring the masses by working with the educated classes, such thinkers defended their more irenic posture toward Hinduism along with the enterprise of Christian education by contending that Hindu nationalism was a movement toward Christian ends.[86] In contrast to evangelicals who measured the success of missions primarily by conversions, fulfillment theorists celebrated Hindu revival insofar as it signified the creation of another religion in "the image of Christianity."[87]

Among the various responses to Lunn's rousing articles, W. H. Findlay's most outspokenly advanced a fulfillment position. To him the very construction of modern Hinduism provided grounds for believing that Christian educational policy was a glorious success. The main task of missions in India, he argued, was not to "wean the people from a religion to which they are passionately devoted," but to "teach the value and nature of religion to a people wholly indifferent to it."[88] The "coma" from which the Indian people had to be awakened was the superstitions, ceremonies, and "meals offered to stone

85. Miller's view of Hindu revival and national awakening as the realization, not the failure, of Christian educational policy derives from his own idea of the purpose of Christian education. The aim of the Chistian college is not to convert, but to spread or diffuse Christian thought and Christian influence throughout non-Christian India. Sharpe, *Not to Destroy,* p. 83. For an excellent discussion of the secularization of education in India, see Rudolph Heredia, "Education and Mission: School as Agent of Evangelization," *Economic and Political Weekly,* 16 September 1995, pp. 2332-40.

86. For example, A. G. Hogg, cited in Eric Sharpe, *The Theology of A. G. Hogg* (Madras, 1971), pp. 51-52.

87. G. Studdert-Kennedy, *British Missions, Indian Nationalists, and the Raj* (New Delhi, 1991), and *Providence and the Raj: Imperial Mission and Missionary Imperialism* (New Delhi and London, 1998) place these theological developments amidst other Christian imperialist influences upon the policies of the Raj.

88. *Harvest Field,* June 1889, p. 422.

idols in temples." The construction of Hinduism, by contrast, represented something new, and something very much derived from Christianity:

> [The revivers of Hinduism] are not supporting Hinduism as their fathers believed it or as we describe it; they are trying to *imagine* it to be, or to frame out of it, a worthy rival of Christianity, worthy when measured by the highest spiritual standards. *I do not say they are consciously doing this.* So ignorant have Hindus, in general, been in the past, of what their conglomerate religion is, that they can easily persuade themselves that what they now call Hinduism is the old genuine belief of their fathers, which in our descriptions we grossly malign. . . . *Our triumph is that the Hindus who have, at last, begun to value religion, have a high, a Christian ideal of what a religion should be.*[89]

Findlay, as if acquainted with the latest, "postmodern" theories of identity formation, identified and celebrated something very Christian in the construction of a "sanitized" Hinduism. Like Miller and others, he spotted the triumphs of a Christian historical project even in a movement aimed at checking conversion to Christianity! Though the fulfillment theorists disagreed with evangelicals on the significance of baptism and conversion, and on the methods of evangelism, they agreed on one point. History moved from the Protestant missionary movement outward. Like the cue ball on a billiards table, *they* were the impetus behind the changing face of Hinduism.

Summary and Concluding Remarks

The previous sections described, in line with Partha Chatterjee, how nationalists in Calcutta and Madras were not engaged in a purely political project of contesting imperial policies. Nationalists also engaged in the cultural project of asserting their difference from the West by publicly defending and celebrating social, philosophical, and popular aspects of Hinduism. The cases of Bhudev, Bankim, and other advocates of "cultural self-reliance," however, show that autonomy over nationalist imagination requires something beyond the mere construction of an oppositional Hinduism.

True autonomy requires that the very idea of the nation be grounded in the concrete, local reality of indigenous institutions such as lineage *(vamsha)* or caste *(jati)*. Without such grounding, nationalism ultimately derives its

89. *Harvest Field*, June 1889, p. 423.

modular form and public legitimacy from the rival nation. This factor makes Bhudev's nationalism, grounded in his adherence to his own Brahmanical tradition, more autonomous and authentic than Bankim's nationalism, which was much more a case of *ressentiment* — of "borrowing with an opposite sign." The Swadeshi movement's call for cultural self-reliance combined the outlooks of both Bhudev and Bankim. In its effort, however, to project the symbols and discipline of the "little society" of castes onto the "big society" of the nation, the Swadeshi movement's Hindu, Brahmanical orientation inevitably alienated the non-Hindu segments of Bengali society.

Defenses of Hinduism in Madras show the clearest signs of reactionary behavior, a development that was evident to the missionaries themselves. Hindu tractarians and Theosophists borrowed the form of a religion from Christianity while using the ideas of European religious radicals to counter missionary influence. But rather than regarding "the missionary" and "the freethinker" as two distinct interlocutors, it can be argued that Christianity was the primary interlocutor of the new Hindu organizations in Madras.[90] When Madras Hindus invoked the tolerance and universality of Hinduism while assaulting the sectarianism of Christian missionaries, they were only reenacting episodes of Western history. Such rhetoric reveals the imitative tendencies of Hindu organizations, not the creative agency of nationalism that Chatterjee describes.

Finally, as objects of *ressentiment*, missionaries themselves did not avoid reactionary behavior. What explains, after all, the call to redirect missionary efforts away from the Brahmans and toward the masses? Many of these calls, including Lunn's articles to the *Methodist Times*, were framed in such a way as to suggest that popular preaching was not central to missionary endeavors throughout the nineteenth century. It was. The call to redirect attention toward the masses, then, derived from the alarm within Christian circles over the rising revivalist sentiments of the educated classes, which signaled a "failed" Duffian policy.

As calm, collected, and theologically equipped as Miller, Findlay, Slater, and other fulfillment theorists were in interpreting Hindu nationalism, their attitudes were far more paternalistic than evangelicals, who measured success strictly by conversions.[91] Unlike evangelicals, who at least recognized Hindu nationalists as the agents of their own actions, fulfillment theorists saw their

90. Free thought and secularism, after all, were ideologies of modernity, which challenged Christian influence in the West: Owen Chadwick, *The Secularization of the European Mind in the Nineteenth Century* (Cambridge, 1975).

91. Studdert-Kennedy explores this new paternalism in *British Missions, Indian Nationalists, and the Raj.*

own "Christian" agency behind the Hindu face of nationalism. Such paternalism, however, evaded the scrutiny of nationalists who continued to identify the colonialist threat to Hinduism with conversion. Unlike Findlay, who saw in the birth of modern Hinduism the triumph of a Christian project, Hindu revivalists were unaware that the borrowing implied in their very defense of Hinduism preempted the workings of their own imagination.

Rethinking Mission in China: James Hudson Taylor and Timothy Richard

LAUREN F. PFISTER

Reevaluation of the influences on Chinese mission strategies stimulated by these two great British Protestant missionaries to China is long overdue. The last straightforward comparison of their efforts dates from the 1950s,[1] since when much has changed regarding the study of missions and mission theology, and in our understanding of the nature of nineteenth-century China. There is also a need to readdress some rather weighty questions related to their involvement in the broader project of British imperialism. The questions are weighty because the linkage of their missionary activities with specific British political interests is difficult to identify: they often joined other missionaries in criticizing British involvement in the opium trade and sometimes during their long years of missionary activity made a point of avoiding involvement with British officials residing in mainland China. On the other hand, Chinese Marxist critics regularly associate some of their missionary activities with spying and, in the case of Timothy Richard, decry his outright attempts to influence the attitudes of Qing dynasty officials as part of a larger imperialist agenda. Furthermore, being men of their age, they employed images and statistics both about Chinese people and their British homeland in their influential publications in ways that revealed variously their own particular religious sentiments, some unusual cultural interests, and certain political preferences.

This essay considers first why the images of these two men need to be reconsidered, focusing primarily on their roles as missionaries in China. It then

1. Paul A. Cohen, "Missionary Approaches: Hudson Taylor and Timothy Richard," in *Papers on China: Volume 11* (Cambridge, Mass.: Harvard University Press, 1957), pp. 29-62.

provides a general evaluation of how they presented the peoples of Qing China to their various audiences, illustrating these claims with specific examples from throughout their long careers of the ways they reiterated and reconceived the images of China and Chinese people during the late nineteenth century. Finally, it analyzes the correctives they made to their own missionary strategies and institutions in China in response to the rapidly changing conditions of the late Qing empire. This is done by focusing on the differences in their theological interpretations and practical mission strategies.

Ambiguous Images: Taylor and Richard as "Prototypes" of Late Nineteenth-Century Protestant Missions in China

In creating and reflecting images of the vast Manchurian empire of the Qing dynasty (1644-1911) and its peoples, James Hudson Taylor (Dai Desheng, 1832-1905) and Timothy Richard (Li Timotai, 1845-1919) were master image-makers. Their audiences, however, were often very different, almost as sharply distinct as the personalities they created for themselves within their respective literatures.

Taylor's emphatic interest in his missionary publications was twofold. The first was to reach the English-speaking world with updated information on the cultural complexities and religious openness of Chinese and other peoples within the Qing dynasty. Then, and largely on the basis of the "needs" of "one quarter of the world's population" in Qing China, he sought to awaken British Christianity to its own complacency and mediocrity in light of the standards of an evangelical faith. His form of Christian spirituality catalyzed immense transformations among missionary-minded English-speaking Christians in the 1880s and 1890s, forming patterns still visible in many missionary societies and in Chinese Protestant traditions to this day.[2]

2. A. J. Broomhall, *Hudson Taylor and China's Open Century,* 7 vols. (London, 1985-89), hereafter *HTCOC,* emphasizes this self-conscious two-pronged mission in Taylor's life and writings. For Taylor's wider impact outside China, see J. Herbert Kane, "J. Hudson Taylor, 1832-1905: Founder of the China Inland Mission," in *Mission Legacies: Biographical Studies of Leaders of the Modern Missionary Movement,* ed. Gerald Anderson et al. (Maryknoll, N.Y., 1994), esp. pp. 198-99. Chan Kim-kwong, a noted scholar of contemporary Chinese Christianity, recently stated that Taylor is "not well remembered" in China today, and rightly claims that the "average people of China" have little awareness of the history of Christian missions. However, outside mainland China among Chinese Christians, Taylor and the China Inland Mission (CIM) are almost always immediately recognized. Contemporary Christian bookstores in Hong Kong, Singapore, and Taiwan carry Chinese translations of several of Taylor's biographies and his early autobiography. Consult "The Miracles

Much of the literature Timothy Richard produced or helped to publish, especially while secretary of the Society for the Diffusion of Christian and General Knowledge *(Guangxue hui)* in Shanghai (1891-1916), was in Chinese for elite Chinese audiences so that they could understand more completely the multiformity and global "benefits" of "true Christianity and true Christian civilization."[3] Nevertheless, Richard did publish over forty articles in English in the influential missionary journal, the *Chinese Recorder.* In addition, he also produced unusual English translations of popular and scriptural Chinese Buddhist literature, reflecting an important missiological interest, which will be discussed later.[4] Armed with an engaging intellect, clever rhetorical strategies, a practical spiritual vision, and a will to communicate with the highest ranks of officialdom in the Qing empire, Richard was an unusual avant-garde missionary figure. While he lived as a traditional missionary for over twenty years, he left his greatest impressions not among Christians in China or overseas, but on the political and cultural landscapes of the Manchurian empire, which struggled with debilitating foreign militarism and ultimately fatal internal rebellions. Convinced of the strategic importance of the support of the Manchurian and Chinese hierarchy, he broadened his missiological practice to include anything that would positively influence them toward Christianity and its representatives in China and abroad.[5]

---

after Missions: An Interview with Kim-Kwong Chan," *Christian History* 15, no. 4, issue 52 (1996): 42-44, a special issue devoted to "Hudson Taylor and Missions to China." See also Dai Desheng [James Hudson Taylor], *Xianshen Zhonghua* (Sacrificing life for China) (Edmonton, 1986).

3. Quoted from Timothy Richard's "Scheme for the general enlightenment of China," published in the *Chinese Recorder* (hereafter *CR*) for all Chinese missionaries, introducing the new plans of the SDCGK, or *Guangxue hui: CR* 23 (1892): 131-32.

4. These articles in *CR* extend the whole length of Richard's career, the first published in 1876 and the last appearing in 1915, whereas Taylor only published two independent articles in *CR* throughout his long career. This difference must be considered in the light of Richard's long-standing concern for missionary literature and Taylor's weighty administrative responsibilities as director of the CIM.

5. E. W. Price Evans, *Timothy Richard: A Narrative of Christian Enterprise and Statesmanship in China* (London, 1945); Paul Richard Bohr, *Famine in China and the Missionary: Timothy Richard as Relief Administrator and Advocate of National Reform, 1876-1884* (Cambridge, Mass., 1972), esp. pp. 129-83. For an assessment of Richard's involvement and literary activities during the rise of the reform movement in China, see Wu Huili, "Zhongwen jizai zhong suo jian Wiexin yundong qijian Li Timotai de huodong" (Timothy Richard in Chinese literature, 1895-1898) (M.Phil. thesis, Chinese University of Hong Kong, 1974); Yuan Weishi, *Wan Qing dabianju zhong de sichao yu renwu* (Ideological trends and people during the great changes within the last years of the Qing dynasty) (Shenzen, 1992), pp. 150-200.

Both Taylor and Richard have attracted academic attention as prototypes of nineteenth-century foreign missionaries of Protestant Christian persuasion. The Marxist critique of religions in contemporary China places most nineteenth-century missionary activities into politicized frames of reference, and so understandably in the standard Chinese text *Missionaries and Modern China,* there is relatively little about Taylor but much comment on Richard's activities.[6] In English language media these two missionaries have since the 1950s had their strategies placed in relative opposition, generally portraying Taylor as the "conservative" and Richard as the "liberal." Despite occasional qualifications, the general effect has been to portray them as representing nearly diametrically opposed positions within Chinese missionary circles.[7] This picture requires significant revision for both its theological suggestions and its general understanding of both late nineteenth-century Chinese missions and the nature of the Qing dynasty.

Though certain important theological differences are manifest in their approaches to Christian mission in the Qing empire, Taylor and Richard were both committed Nonconformist "evangelicals." Both perceived their missionary task as having an ultimate goal in the eternal salvation made possible through the death and resurrection of Christ for all peoples, including Qing citizens of all kinds.[8] Their separate kinds of Nonconformist orientations tended to make them less doctrinaire in theology and more ecumenical in practice, though Taylor was more attracted than Richard to the unashamed biblicism of the famous Baptist preacher Charles Haddon Spurgeon.[9] Differ-

6. See Gu Changsheng, *Chuanjiaoshi yu jindai Zhongguo* (Missionaries and modern China) (Shanghai: People's Press, 1981).

7. Cohen, "Missionary Approaches"; C. William Mensendick, "The Protestant Missionary Understanding of the Chinese Situation and the Christian Task from 1890 to 1911" (Ph.D. diss., Columbia University, 1958).

8. The evangelical voice of Taylor is consistent throughout his writings, while in Richard's Chinese works there was often an indirect affirmation. This has caused some confusion, because in his English articles statements confirming his evangelical commitments are not hard to locate. In fact, his evangelicalism cannot be questioned. In developing new approaches Richard often applied a larger intellectual scaffolding than most missionaries, regularly drawing from contemporary explorations in comparative religious studies, but his underlying theological commitments remained the same.

9. Richard's resistance to dogmatic insistence on certain creeds was typical of the more radical kinds of evangelical "Independency": see Rita Therese Johnson, "Timothy Richard's Theory of Christian Missions to the Non-Christian World" (Ph.D. diss., Saint John's University, 1966), pp. 63-68. Spurgeon's sermons appeared early in *China's Millions,* and numbers of the earliest CIM missionaries were sent out from his church, the Metropolitan Tabernacle. It is significant that Spurgeon's death in 1892 was also recorded in *China's Millions,* something usually reserved only for missionaries and the closest supporters.

ences in their approaches related more to theological reflections on the exigencies of the larger Chinese Empire at the end of the nineteenth century than to fundamentally distinct theological orientations. Although they differed in eschatological emphasis, something explored below, nevertheless the existential realities of Manchurian despotism in a period of foreign "semicolonial" impositions[10] were at least as important as a stimulus for theological reflection as the differences in theological emphasis between the Baptist, Methodist, and Brethren traditions.[11]

As to their distinctive missiological tendencies, it is more accurate to describe both men's positions as correctives to the broader assumptions behind missionary institutions in the 1870s and 1880s. Although in another context their standpoints might appear directly opposed, these two missionaries decided on approaches to certain sectors of Qing society that for various reasons were being avoided by most other missionary societies. This owes much to both the more conservative tendencies of Sino-British foreign policy during the 1870s and the reactionary entrenchment of the Qing Foreign Affairs Bureau, the *Zongli yamen,* as a consequence of the complications caused by many "religious cases" *(jiao'an).*

Viewed from the angle of their target audiences in China, Taylor's and Richard's missionary strategies appeared simultaneously as correctives focusing on different spheres of Qing society rather than contradictory methods. Taylor confronted the restrictive tendencies of the *Zongli yamen* and British "minister plenipotentiary," insisting that his missionary colleagues pursue active itinerancy across the entire Qing empire. By this means Taylor sought to counteract the natural inclination of most mission societies to withdraw into what he considered premature stages of institutionalization in their primary

10. The ideological term "semicolonial" *(ban zhimindi de)* has been one of those used by Chinese Marxists to designate the state of affairs in the later nineteenth century in the Qing empire.

11. Richard's heritage in Baptist institutions is historically uncontroversial, but described only briefly in all the major accounts of his early life, and so should be more thoroughly researched. According to his own account, his earliest education was taken in a Congregational school, but his formative years were spent under the influences of Baptist ministers and teachers. Most accounts rely on Richard's own bald characterizations of his training at Haverfordwest Theological College in Pembrokeshire (1865-69): *Forty-Five Years in China: Reminiscences by Timothy Richard* (New York, 1916), pp. 22-28. Taylor's influences are a little more complex. Nurtured in a Methodist home, he was influenced greatly by certain Brethren communities in England during his first furlough. Earlier misunderstandings, particularly by scholars associating Taylor with the dispensational theology promoted by J. N. Darby, have been corrected by Broomhall, *HTCOC,* 3:447-53.

stations on mainland China's eastern coastline.[12] Richard chose to counteract the assumption of many foreigners that Qing imperial officialdom was to a man antiforeign and unresponsive to any Christian work, an image largely supported by increased persecutions occurring during this period.[13] While most Protestant missionaries pursued converts among the tens of millions of peasants, Richard focused on the religious leaders as well as the social elites, adjusting his literature and methods to match their interests and concerns. This, Richard believed, would ultimately replace inimical attitudes with amicable appreciation, leading ultimately to greater religious freedom and to many more conversions from all sectors of Qing society.[14]

Complicating accounts of missionary activity during this period is a new recognition that the form of Manchurian despotism was more complex than some accounts have made it out to be. New research into Manchurian language sources confirms now that the Qing empire was a multiethnic and expanding entity, even though it was brought to its knees by the militaristic imposition of foreign mercantile and cultural interests during the middle and late nineteenth century. Although at least 90 percent of the population of the Qing empire was of Han ethnic origin, other peoples were recognized and left un-Sinicized by the Manchurian leadership, including the Tibetans, the Mongolians, various Muslim ethnic groups, and many Western minorities particularly in Sichuan and Yunnan.[15] It was this diversity of peoples that members of Taylor's China Inland Mission (CIM) *(Nei di hui)* met face-to-face in their extensive penetration of the Chinese hinterland, an ethnic diversity that shaped the CIM's missiological strategies and linguistic preparation, as well as the public images missionaries presented of them in the CIM's organ, *China's Millions and Our Work among Them.*[16] Because Richard became strategically involved with broad ranges of Qing officialdom, he also could not

12. This is effectively described by Broomhall, *HTCOC,* vol. 6.

13. Richard wrote about these matters in a startlingly direct manner, as in "Christian persecutions in China — their nature, causes, remedies," *CR* 15 (1884): 237-48.

14. Bohr argues that Richard became completely convinced of this strategy after working with city, district, and provincial officials during famine relief operations in Shanxi. See Bohr, pp. 129-70, and a collection of Richard's essays supporting this missiological claim, *Conversion by the Million in China,* 2 vols. (Shanghai, 1907).

15. This is hotly debated: Evelyn S. Rawski, "Reenvisioning the Qing: The Significance of the Qing Period in Chinese History," *Journal of Asian Studies* 55 (1996): 829-50; Ping-ti Ho, "In Defense of Sinicization: A Rebuttal of Evelyn Rawski's 'Reenvisioning the Qing,'" *Journal of Asian Studies* 57 (1998): 123-55.

16. This was the title for the first year; it was then shortened by Taylor's decision simply to *China's Millions:* Broomhall, *HTCOC,* 6:45. We use its more popular and shorter title.

avoid the differences between Manchurian, Han, and Muslim leaders he met. Although the vast majority, if not all, of his literary efforts and interviews with them were carried on in Chinese, Richard engaged these political figures just as ethnic tensions were being politicized. His insight into these higher levels of Qing society affected not only his own strategies but his reports to the larger missionary communities within China and his representation of China to the English-speaking world. On the basis of these revised assumptions regarding Taylor's and Richard's foundational theological commitments, their differing roles as missionary leaders, and the newly recognized complexities of a multiethnic Qing empire facing unprecedented political threats from both foreign and internal opposition, a fuller and more precise evaluation of the missiological changes they brought about can be made.

Correctives to the Standard Assumptions of Missionary Bodies in the Late Qing Period

Both Taylor and Richard assumed traditional missionary roles as professional evangelists in Qing China, but faced somewhat different social conditions. Their responses to the Qing environments they encountered involved reshaping their own missionary roles as well as the institutions they helped create and develop — the CIM for Taylor, and for Richard the Society for the Diffusion of Christian and General Knowledge among the Chinese (SDCGK) and the innovative Shanxi University (1901-10).[17]

Taylor landed in Shanghai as part of the third generation of Protestant missionaries in the early 1850s, during the more active years of the Taiping insurgency (*Taiping Tianguo*, 1851-64). Threats to invade Shanghai by Taiping troops caused instability in many areas, and at times persistent antiforeign attitudes due to the insurgents' partial reliance on Protestant precedents in their religious literature and forms of worship. This limited the extent of itineration by even the boldest missionaries during this period, limits Taylor stretched as far as possible following the example of one of his earlier missionary heroes — the controversial Prussian missionary Karl Gützlaff (1803-51). In the early 1830s Gützlaff traveled along the eastern coastline on opium boats, exploring the feasibility of missionary activities in areas closed to for-

17. The common abbreviation for Richard's Society in the contemporary literature was shortened even further to the SDK, but the emphasis we will place here on the differences between "Christian and General" knowledge as Richard developed them warrants the longer abbreviation.

eigners by the conservative Qing imperial policies.[18] These restrictions had been loosened slightly under the Nanjing treaty of 1842, after the First Opium War, and were to be practically overruled by the controversial provisions of the Tianjin treaty of 1858. Certainly these special conditions for missionaries and Chinese Christians embedded in the details of military treaties related to British imperial interests were seen as perennial proof of British missionaries' "guilt by association" by many Chinese officials. Yet it was under these conditions that Taylor in the mid-1860s developed his vision for the CIM, and pressed the boldest of his missionary "agents" forward across the entire Qing empire to scout out possibilities for establishing indigenous churches and missionary stations in the vast hinterland.

Suffering from the incompetent administration of his sending mission during the mid-1850s, Taylor developed his own style of indigenizing "faith" mission strategy independent of their directions, ultimately leaving them to pursue his form of missionary life in 1858.[19] Leaving China in 1860, just before the military conclusion of the Second Opium War was highlighted by Lord Elgin's infamous burning of the imperial Summer Palace, Taylor spent five years away in Britain.[20] There he regained his failing health, strengthened and updated his professional skills as a medical doctor, and ultimately created the CIM. Under these conditions, we should emphasize, the CIM was consciously established as an alternative to the standard foreign mission structures of the day.[21] Taylor himself worked as the CIM's general director until his partial retirement in 1900, leaving it completely in the hands of the next general secretary (Dixon Hoste, 1861-1946) in 1904, a year before he died.

Thirteen years younger than Taylor, Timothy Richard did not arrive and settle into his initial mission station in the city of Zhifu (Chefoo) in Shandong province until 1870, part of the fourth generation of Chinese missionaries. By this time the *Zongli yamen* had been working for a full decade under the new Tianjin treaty of 1858, and the problems of "religious cases" involving Catholic and Protestant missionaries had become an irritating inter-

18. For the general significance of Gützlaff's exploits and their important influence on the young Taylor, see Broomhall, *HTCOC*, vol. 1, esp. pp. 209-10, 227-28, 349-50. I am indebted to R. Gary Tiedemann for emphasizing this point.

19. See his autobiographical reflections published first in *China's Millions* as a series of articles entitled "A Retrospect" during 1886-88, and later republished in various forms.

20. Broomhall, *HTCOC*, 3:214-22.

21. Among the important differences of the CIM administrative structure was the requirement that the director of the mission live in China and direct operations from there as much as possible. As we shall see below, administrative changes occurred in the mid-1880s as the CIM grew in extent and complexity.

national reality. British foreign policy in Beijing (Peking) had already become less responsive to missionary requests for help in resolving conflicts with Qing citizens, particularly because of the knotty political problems they regularly engendered.[22] By 1870 British foreign policy in Beijing had reverted to a defense of mercantile interests, and was once more less concerned with the "missionary question," while the *Zongli yamen* also began a long-term ideological campaign against missionaries as part of the broader "barbarian question." Ultimately a "Missionary Memorandum" written by representative Chinese missionaries was sent in 1869 to the British Parliament to counter biased political criticisms, but the missionary troubles of the 1860s left a negative legacy that deeply affected British and Qing foreign policy for the rest of the century.[23] Consequently Richard faced opposition from Shandong officials immediately upon arrival, and so sought to develop means to regain their confidence so they would not hinder normal missionary work, either directly or indirectly. His own changed attitude toward the professional production of Chinese newspapers and translated literature in the late 1880s arose directly from these conditions. On the basis of his practical successes and the persuasiveness of his public arguments about these problems, Richard was invited to become the second secretary of the SDCGK in Shanghai in 1891. By this means he gained a position of immense influence within both Chinese missionary communities and the official structures of the Qing Chinese empire that lasted for the next twenty-five years.[24]

Correctives to "Standard" Images of Qing China and Her Citizens

To interpret the influence of these two prolific and unusual writers on the public images of Qing China is a daunting task, owing to the amount and variety of literature involved. The public images necessarily include those writ-

22. Among the most outstanding of these conflicts were riots in Yangzhou, Jiangsu province, in August 1868 that directly involved Taylor himself. For accounts of the period from the angle of both Roman Catholic and Protestant missionaries, as well as British and Qing foreign policy, see Broomhall, *HTCOC*, 4:376-402 and 5:77-226.

23. See "Missionary Memorandum," *Parliamentary Papers* (1870) LXIX, China No. 9, pp. 4-12, selectively reprinted in Broomhall, *HTCOC*, 5:458-62. The standard study of the first decade of these "religious cases" from the perspective of missionary–*Zongli yamen* interaction is Paul A. Cohen, *China and Christianity: The Missionary Movement and the Growth of Chinese Antiforeignism, 1860-1870* (Cambridge, Mass., 1963).

24. *Forty-Five Years in China*, passim.

ten in Chinese literature — this being a very significant dimension of Richard's work — making the task even more complex.[25] As a consequence, what is offered below is only an initial attempt to grapple with the multidimensional character of these influences, in the hope that it will stimulate further interpretative study. Through the extremely influential missionary organ of the CIM, the monthly *China's Millions,* a kaleidoscope of Chinese scenes and cameos of other ethnic groups paraded into the homes and churches of an increasingly large international readership. It commenced publication in 1875 under Taylor's firm editorship, remaining one of his major projects as the CIM's general director until 1895.[26] Besides the extensive work of *China's Millions,* Taylor produced several other books in English seminally formative of the missionary portrayal of Qing China. *China's Spiritual Need and Claims,* first published in 1865, reached its ninth edition in 1890. Further missiological reflections on the CIM's "occupation" of China were captured in *After Thirty Years* (1895), while more personal angles on this mission society's early efforts can be drawn from Taylor's autobiography, *A Retrospect.* Here attention will focus on the content of *China's Millions.*

Although *China's Millions* was not the first missionary magazine to publish lithographs and drawings reflecting aspects of China and Chinese people, it represented an enormous advance in technical quality and diversity of images.[27] Because it commenced publication in 1875, the CIM staff were able to enhance the realism of their images owing to recent technological advances and the gradual development of techniques of photographic reproduction in

25. As far as I can discover, Taylor himself did not produce any manuscript or leaflet written in Chinese and published as a public document. That he spoke and even taught Chinese language to missionary candidates is well documented.

26. Taylor made all the final editorial decisions and contributed substantially to content and layout. He was also dependent on help in Britain, from his second wife, "Jennie" (Jane Elizabeth Taylor, 1843-1904), but especially the general secretary of the CIM in London, Benjamin Broomhall (1829-1911, general secretary 1878-95). This study refers only to the British edition, but a North American edition was also established in the 1890s that impacted that part of the English-speaking world. Broomhall, *HTCOC,* vol. 6.

27. Broomhall suggests that *China's Millions* was the first missionary magazine to employ steel engravings of images already published in the secular media, but this would be misleading if it meant there had been no previous pictorial representations in earlier missionary organs. For example, lithographic productions and sketches of China appeared in the *Evangelical Magazine and Missionary Chronicle* in the 1840s, and in the *Chinese Repository* (1832-51). The former was edited by John Morison (ca. 1785-1858), Congregational minister, a director of the London Missionary Society (LMS), and father-in-law of Chinese missionary–sinologist James Legge (1815-97). The latter was edited for the longest time by the American missionary Elijah C. Bridgman (1801-61), a resident of Guangzhou (Canton). See Broomhall, *HTCOC,* 6:45.

print.[28] These pictures included common street scenes, Chinese people in still and active poses, various places throughout the Qing empire encountered in missionary travels, and the more unusual images of tribal peoples in their normal and "Christian" attire. The pictures ranged across social classes, with images of common peasants, city dwellers, religious figures, and Qing officials. Nevertheless, these attempts to "mirror" reality were obviously limited by the preference of the artists and technicians for "still" images over those involving some form of action. Another dimension of technical "error" is evident to anyone who actually reads Chinese. The symbols mimicking Chinese characters on street signs and in temples were almost always completely illegible and incoherent; when intelligible, they were not always interpreted correctly (see fig. 4).

Images in the early volumes were sometimes drawn from the secular presses, particularly from the *Graphic* magazine, which reinforced Orientalized images of the "penurious" Chinese male and the enticingly attractive and submissive Chinese female (see fig. 5). Another source of images was John Thomson's collage of Chinese pictures, first published in the early 1870s, including panoramas of cities, rivers, mountains, and numerous kinds of people.[29] At some point these borrowed images were replaced by what we assume were the CIM's own productions, tending toward "more realistic" portrayals of Qing citizens, male and female, of many ages and ethnic backgrounds. For a British public that had developed a taste for "up-to-date information" and "facts," these pictures corrected many previously stereotyped (and less humane) caricatures of Chinese persons and others from the ethnic minorities. Details about the ethnic groups besides the majority Han people were new, and revealed the political complexities of the Qing empire as well as some of its underlying social tensions.[30] Regu-

28. So, for example, there appeared in the 1877 volume (only the second annual volume in the series) a photograph of the "Members of the First General Conference of Missionaries in China" held in Shanghai in 1877. Under the picture was a graphic image numbering each of the missionaries in the photograph, Taylor being identified as #41. Richard was unable to attend, and so does not appear there. Only in the 1890s was it apparently more feasible technically and financially to reproduce the photographs in the regular issues of *China's Millions.*

29. See John Thomson, *China and Its People in Early Photographs* (New York, 1982), a republication of his work of the early 1870s. Vol. I, pl. XIV shows a set of Qing soldiers that can also be found in *China's Millions.*

30. Specific articles catalogued under "Tribes" and dealing with the Miao, Lolo, and "Kahchen" people groups appeared already in 1878, while later on in 1881 and 1885 articles on "Thibet" appeared occasionally as CIM "agents" initiated contacts with these people and prepared strategies for maintaining a mission station among them. Fairly quickly these highlighted items were submerged into the regular correspondence published from the writings of specific missionaries.

Figure 4. Chinese punishments — the pillory and the wooden collar. Here the scratchings that "represent" Chinese characters are in fact completely illegible, a few of the simplest among them being actually the reverse (written backwards!) of some characters. To an informed reader this can only manifest that the artist and the editors were unable (or unwilling) to render anything authentically Chinese on the signs decking the criminals. From *China's Millions,* 1886 annual edition, p. 27.

Figure 5. A street fortune-teller. This is only one of a number of sketches taken from the *Graphic* and published in early issues of *China's Millions*. Most continued this stereotypical representation of the Chinese male as a "stingy" person and the Chinese female as a "submissive beauty." From *China's Millions*, 1877, p. 25.

lar additions included maps of continental China, often including the routes of their young missionaries' most extensive itineraries, all of which ultimately benefited the CIM's public image.

From the start, *China's Millions* frequently contained specific articles designated "For the Young," discussing daily life from the angle of a Chinese child growing up in Qing society.[31] While explanations of the standards of Chinese filial piety *(xiao)* appeared very early as positive examples of Chinese life, these discussions necessarily raised the more controversial problems associated with ancestral reverence and its associated familial rituals.[32] Subsequently, more extensive and diverse discussions of Chinese habits and customs probably had an even larger influence on young readers.[33] These articles included descriptions of the ubiquitous beggars, dogs, and other less appealing features of contemporary life in China, as well as details about the significance of different hair dressings worn by young children.[34] These were presented in an attempt to reinforce the practical realities faced by missionaries and the common folk who were their neighbors. Sometimes the mundane was juxtaposed with the morose, for example, illustrations of baby girls' hairstyles with discussions of infanticide.[35] A detailed and systematic analysis of all the articles and missionary correspondence would certainly make possible a far more accurate assessment of the interplay of images, "factual" information, and the subjective interpretations of missionaries in differing circumstances.[36]

Generally speaking, these CIM presentations of the lives and activities of Chinese and other people in the nineteenth century achieved two basic aims. First, the more human and culturally intelligible sides of Qing life were made accessible to non-Chinese readers. Additionally, and overlapping the descriptive elements of this literature, their "spiritual needs" were constantly underscored. For example, descriptions of opium users led quickly to questions about British mercantile involvement in the Indian and Chinese opium trade, the capitalistic evil it produced inside and outside China, the fatalities accompanying addiction, and the desperation of those who sought relief from

31. Such articles for "younger minds" ceased altogether from 1891.

32. For examples of filial piety, see *China's Millions,* 1879, p. 22; 1882, p. 60.

33. *China's Millions,* 1879, pp. 12, 157; 1882, p. 10.

34. Illustrated article by "Miss Johnston," *China's Millions,* 1889, p. 177.

35. Marie Guex, "Our poor little sisters in China," *China's Millions,* 1892, p. 12.

36. Cf. Kathleen L. Lodwick, *The Chinese Recorder Index: A Guide to Christian Missions in Asia, 1867-1941,* 2 vols. (Wilmington, Del., 1986). Such a tool for the CIM, the largest Protestant missionary society, would be of great value to scholars including historians, missiologists, and sinologists.

opium's consequences.[37] Pastor Xi Shengmo ("Pastor Hsi," 1830-96) of Shanxi province was a prime example of the educated and successful scholar who became an opium addict and then needed spiritual liberation in order to overcome his terrible predicament.[38]

In his English-language publications, Timothy Richard's imaging of Chinese people and officials in the imperial bureaucracy was in some ways radically different from Taylor's in *China's Millions.* Although never denying the importance of normal missionary activities and itinerancy (which he also performed during his first twenty years in China), Richard was preoccupied with indigenous Chinese religious traditions, the problems of Christian persecution, and the use of translated literature as a means for breaking through the ingrained antiforeignism of many Qing bureaucrats, especially from 1890 to 1910.

Richard was open to religious dialogue in China across all traditional boundaries, and many of his most startling works related to his unusual views of Mahayana Buddhism *(Dacheng Fojiao).* His early interest in this area was underscored by his translation into English of the popular Buddhist novel *Xiyou ji* (lit. "Records of a Western Journey"), which he rendered *A Mission to Heaven.* More significant was his "Christian" translation of Ashvagosha's *Dacheng qixin lun* (The Mahayana Buddhist tradition's doctrine on the awakening of faith), which he claimed first to have read in 1884, and then translated with the help of a Chinese convert to Buddhism, Mr. Yang Wenhui.[39] Following contemporary comparative religion theories, Richard argued that the essential doctrines and principles of this form of Buddhism with its Babylonian roots were consonant with Christian teachings and worth further exploration.[40] Hoping his studies might lead to a quicker evangelization of

37. The opium question was regularly featured in *China's Millions.* Benjamin Broomhall, on the editorial staff, was an outstanding public critic of British complicity in the trade.

38. Mrs. Howard Taylor, *Pastor Hsi: Confucian Scholar and Christian* (London, 1900). "Pastor Hsi" became a famous example of the broader implications of Christian missionary activity in China. After overcoming his addiction and devoting himself to Christian ministry, Xi changed his name to Shengmo (lit. "victory over the Devil") and became an indefatigable advocate of Christian opium refuges.

39. *Forty-Five Years in China,* pp. 334-35; Timothy Richard, ed., *The Awakening of Faith in the Mahayana Doctrine — the New Buddhism* (Shanghai, 1907), introduction.

40. This strange and short-lived form of sinological Orientalism was also promoted by Joseph Edkins of the LMS and originated with the eccentric scholarship of Terrien de Lacouperie. A sinological Buddhologist and self-proclaimed classical expert in London, Lacouperie produced a journal on Babylonian and Oriental themes, trying to link differing religious groups by philological connections.

Buddhists, Richard persisted in spite of public criticism by other missionaries, producing not only translations but also late in his life an evangelical appeal to Buddhists.[41]

When city riots and troubles encountered on missionary itineraries featured as "news" in *China's Millions,* Taylor simply and earnestly requested prayer from interested Christian readers. Richard, however, worked on practical, preventive measures in addition to prayer.[42] Among the chief causes of these terrible problems, Richard claimed, was genuine ignorance of "the true history of Christianity" among the elite, who often associated Protestant Christianity with the Taiping rebellion and assumed it would encourage similar insurrectionist movements.[43] These fears were not allayed by missionary rhetoric that referred metaphorically to the missionary enterprise as "revolutionary." This language was explicit in the 1869 "Missionary Memorandum," and was reiterated by representative British missionary figures in subsequent decades.[44]

These troubles were also greatly exacerbated by missionaries' general unwillingness to appeal to the British consulate for help, notwithstanding the treaty conditions. This owed as much to their Nonconformist attitudes toward government intervention in religious life, and to the protests by the *Zongli yamen* against Catholic and Protestant aggression, as it did to strategies to maintain their evangelistic tours inside China. Nevertheless, the avoidance of contact with British officials adds to the complexities in evaluating the "imperialistic complicity" of these missionaries. While Richard explained how this political quiescence caused suffering Chinese Christians great perplexity (when they sought their missionaries' support and received only theological instruction to endure in love), he did not mention the inherent politi-

41. For a strong criticism raised by Bishop Handley Moule about Richard's exegetical rendering of *The Awakening of Faith* and his more general thesis, "New Testament of Higher Buddhism," followed by Richard's response, see *CR* 42 (1911): 350-54. Related works written or translated by Richard are: as translator, *Guide to Buddhahood, Being a Standard Manual of Chinese Buddhism* (Shanghai, 1907); as author, *The New Testament of Higher Buddhism* (Edinburgh, 1910) and *An Epistle to All Buddhists throughout the World,* with Chinese translation by Min Houshao (n.p., 1916). For a modern appraisal, see Yoshito S. Hakeda, trans. and comm., *The Awakening of Faith Attributed to Asvaghosha* (New York, 1967), p. 17.

42. Richard, "Christian persecutions," pp. 237-48.

43. Richard, "Christian persecutions," pp. 242, 245. Richard had already initiated discussion in the late 1870s about these matters in the Chinese-language Christian magazine *Wanguo gongbao.*

44. See n. 23 above. Another significant example of "revolutionary" missionary rhetoric is seen in James Legge, *Confucianism in Relation to Christianity* (London, 1877).

cal dilemma it involved. Missionaries who reported these matters to foreign officials often brought about, in the end, greater political restrictions by the British government on its citizens resident in China. For those like the CIM director who were intent on itineration, this was a political control they did not want.[45] For his part, Richard by the mid-1880s became a determined advocate of the rule of law, promoting the development of better treaty laws, and in later years he urged governments to consider the establishment of an international standard of law, replacing previous precedents made inherently weak through aggressive militarism.[46]

Richard's promotion of greater direct engagement with the "fickle" Qing officials by the general body of missionaries met widespread open criticism. He himself admitted that the process would take time, but many including Taylor and his CIM staff felt that time was against "China's millions" who faced personal destinies of "eternal condemnation" without the knowledge of the Christian gospel.[47] This salvific concern, rooted in expectations of the imminent and physical return of Christ to rule on earth, imparted a particular urgency to Taylor's missiology. Its special eschatological drive put Taylor's theology in tension with most "culturally adaptive" approaches, which required more time and institutional stability for their success. This appeal was broadly accepted in Taylor's own day, stimulating a large response even from previously unenthusiastic university students, the most famous among these being the so-called Cambridge Seven.[48]

When opposition grew to Richard's basic approach (including, for instance, his support for Western-style universities built upon Christian foundations), and it was rejected even by some of his younger Baptist colleagues in

45. While CIM members could approach local mandarins, Taylor forbade them to appeal to British officials in their areas, lest the latter resort to "gunboat" diplomacy: Broomhall, *HTCOC,* vol. 6.

46. For his own account of his connections with the peace movement, see *Forty-Five Years in China,* pp. 367-76.

47. Taylor saw in the issues raised by Richard the "Shansi (i.e., Shanxi) spirit," defined by Broomhall as "a spirit of complaint and loss of conviction and purpose." Ultimately, however, the two men's attitudes were less conflicting than complementary. Until the First World War, it was Taylor's emphatic commitment to evangelize that swayed most China missionaries, and it was Richard's strategic corrective in dealing straightforwardly with Qing officials that provided new impetus for Christian missions in the first decade of the twentieth century.

48. This premillennial eschatology is unduly downplayed by Broomhall, *HTCOC.* Cf. letters from Joseph S. Adams, an American Baptist missionary who initially joined the CIM, which point to this motivation as a primary reason for Taylor's emphasis on itinerant missionary work. See n. 55 below.

1888-89, he and his family moved away to Tianjin. While retaining his ties to the Baptist Missionary Society, he began a very different career in newspaper publications, devoting most of his time to communicating with public officials about the broadest aspects of "true Christian civilization."[49] This was done in a distinctive manner, using graphs and statistical charts, which captured the imagination of the younger reformist-minded Confucian (Ruist) scholars of his day. Before their eyes Richard paraded "the facts" about the world in which they were inextricably involved. He employed many other literary images, but these charts became particularly famous and effective in promoting a critical approach to conditions in the Qing empire. On the basis of the essays he wrote to accompany these charts, Timothy Richard's strange-sounding foreign name, *Li Timotai*, became a Chinese household word.[50]

Though these statistical charts may appear primitive now, at the time they provided revolutionary information for the normal Chinese reader. *Zhongguo*, the "Middle Country" non-Chinese have called China, was no longer in the "middle" of the world, a fact Matteo Ricci had also tried to convey to the Wanli emperor in the early 1600s. Yet while Ricci kept the name and position of China distinctly present on the world map, Richard in the 1890s left China as only part of Asia *(Yazhou)*, one of the six continents in the "round earth" *(di qiu)*.[51] Further shocks awaited any parochially minded reader in maps and charts displaying the comparative enlargement of Chinese, Russian, and British dominions (see fig. 6, map 3) and the number of people belonging to each "country" (*guo*, see fig. 7). China is presented as having the largest population (380 million), "England" (Britain) being second with 256 million (patently false, since this number included the populations of all British colonial possessions), followed by Russia, the United States, France, and Germany.

Christianity's advantage was presented in a comparative chart relating the number of persons associated with each major religious tradition or "teaching" *(jiao)*. "Christianity," used as a general term to encompass all the branches of religious tradition associated with Jesus Christ, is presented in

49. For this transition, see *Forty-Five Years in China*, pp. 203-8, 253-68, 299-310, and Brian Stanley, *The History of the Baptist Missionary Society, 1792-1992* (Edinburgh, 1992), pp. 180-97, 200-207, 303-7.

50. So popular were these charts that Richard published them independently, along with their original articles, in a separate Chinese edition: *Shishi xinlun* (New essays on the affairs of these days), 3 vols. (Shanghai, 1894).

51. This is notably the first map in the whole series of forty-five maps and statistical charts presented in Richard's *Shishi xinlun*. An original version of Ricci's map mentioned above is displayed in the Museum on Christianity at Soongsil University in Seoul, Korea.

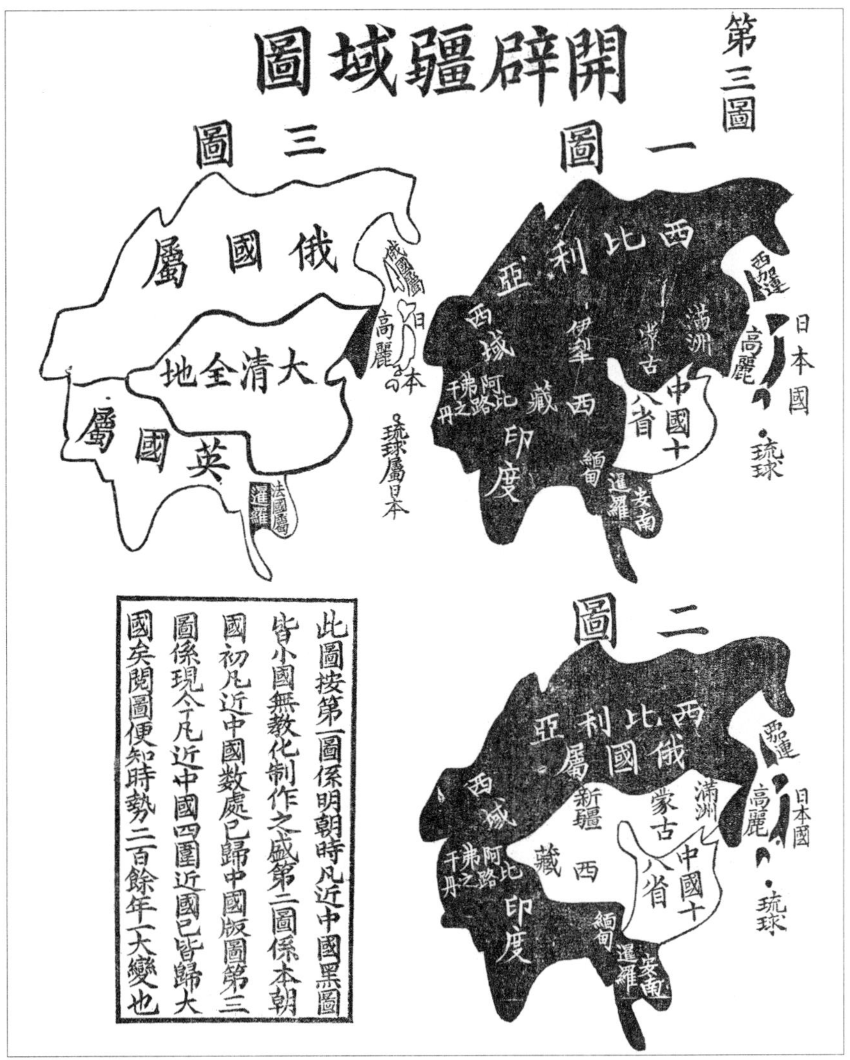

Figure 6. Timothy Richard's three maps of China and surrounding nations at various periods. The first map (upper right) shows (in white) the landmass of Ming dynasty China (fifteenth to mid–seventeenth century). The second (lower right) shows the increase in possessions by the Qing Manchurian rulers around 1650, mentioning besides the "18 provinces of China," from *r.* to *l.*, Manchuria, Mongolia, Xinjiang ("New Boundary Lands"), and Tibet. The third map is intended to represent the situation at the end of the nineteenth century, giving prominence to "Russian possessions" to the north of the "Great Qing" lands, and "English possessions" to the south.

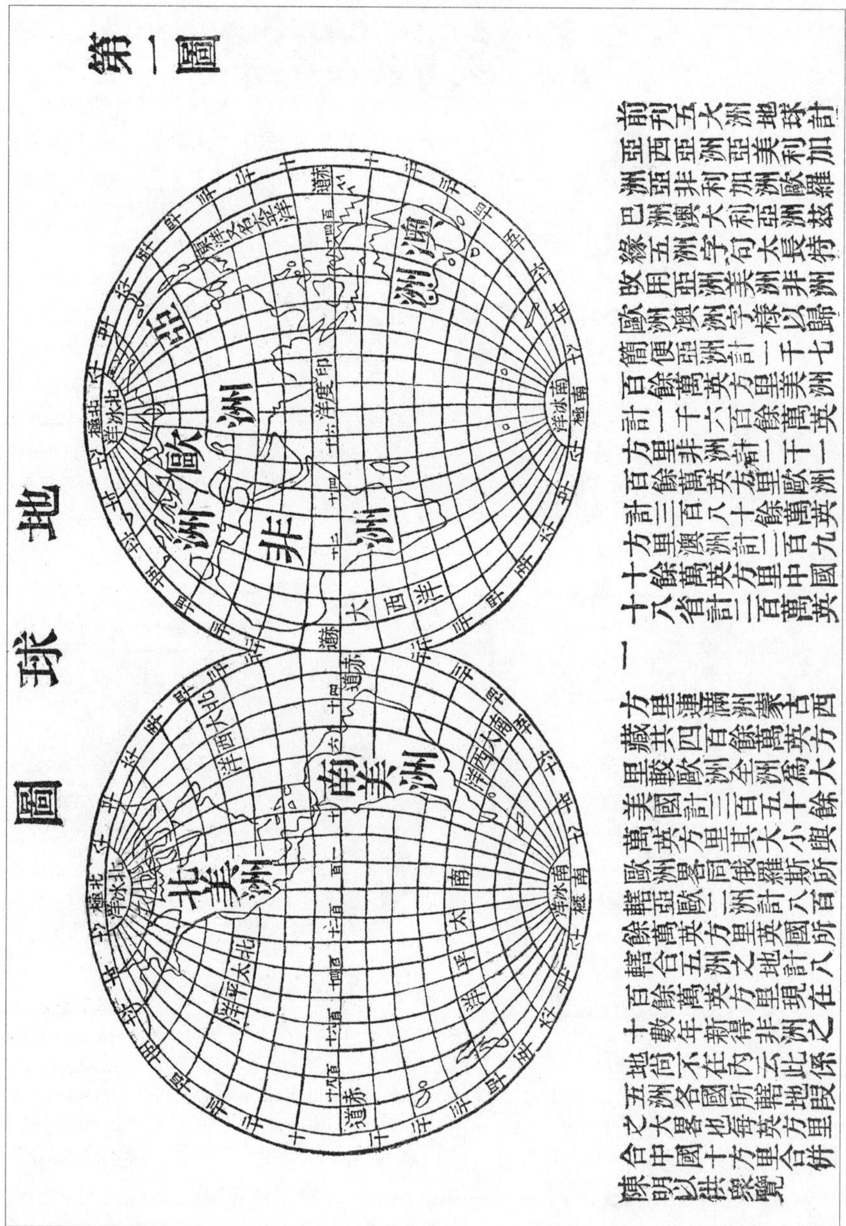

Figure 7. "The Map of the World." Notice on the upper hemisphere the images and characters for "Australia," "Asia," "Europe," and "Africa." Significantly for a Chinese audience in the late Qing dynasty, China is not independently identified.

the right-hand chart of figure 8 as the "teaching that saves the world" *(qiushi jiao)*. It has the most numerous adherents (450 million), and is followed by the three Chinese religions (*Ru Shi Dao*, or "the scholars, the followers of Sakyamuni, and the followers of the Way/Dao") with 400 million, with subsequent references to Hinduism, Islam, and Judaism.[52] There followed charts displaying international statistics for the length of railroads, exports and imports, taxes collected at the national customs offices, the length of telegraph lines, and even the number of warships. When it is realized that this information came into the hands of Chinese citizens after their defeats by allied European and North American forces and when they were about to be humiliated by Japanese naval victories in 1894-95, it is possible to imagine the public shock these comparisons gave to a people used to considering themselves the strongest, most civilized country in the world.

Behind this information blitz was a singular motivation that Richard continued to repeat in both Chinese and English publications: citizens of the Qing dynasty were woefully ignorant of the world around them and therefore suffered the consequences of their ignorance. Among those consequences was their mistreatment of Chinese Christians, who were part of the largest religion in the world (according to the charts Richard produced, carefully citing his source materials under Chinese titles for Chinese readers to follow up). The influence of these basic ideas among reform-minded Chinese in the late 1890s is now well established.[53] Nevertheless, positive recognition of Western civilization and of missionary roles in China was only publicly forthcoming after the extensive massacre of missionaries and Chinese Christians during

52. *Jiao*, translated "teaching" or religion, was later replaced by *zongjiao*, noted by Richard in *A Dictionary of Philosophical Terms Chiefly from the Japanese* (n.p.: Christian Literature Society, 1913), p. 55. It should be noted that the terms he employed for Hinduism, Islam, and Judaism were also older terms. The first is literally "the teachings of India," which is now rendered more commonly as "the religions of India." The second is a particularly sino-centric term, *Huijiao*, "the teachings of the Hui people," since Muslims were believed to be primarily associated in one ethnic group within China. In fact, this was not the case even in the nineteenth century, and though the term is still sometimes employed in contemporary Chinese language, the preferred term by Chinese Muslims is *Yisilan jiao*, or the "teaching of Islam." *Youtai jiao*, or "the teaching of the Jews," has undergone the expected transformation as a "religion" now, but reflects another sentiment that may have been transferred from Europe. The first term, *You*, is written with the "dog" radical, and so suggests an anti-Semitic meaning. Unfortunately, it is still the common reference term for Judaism, though there is some slight move among academics in religious studies to replace the dog radical with one for humans.

53. Wu Huili, "Zhongwen jizai zhong suo jian Weixin yundong qijian Li Timotai de huodong."

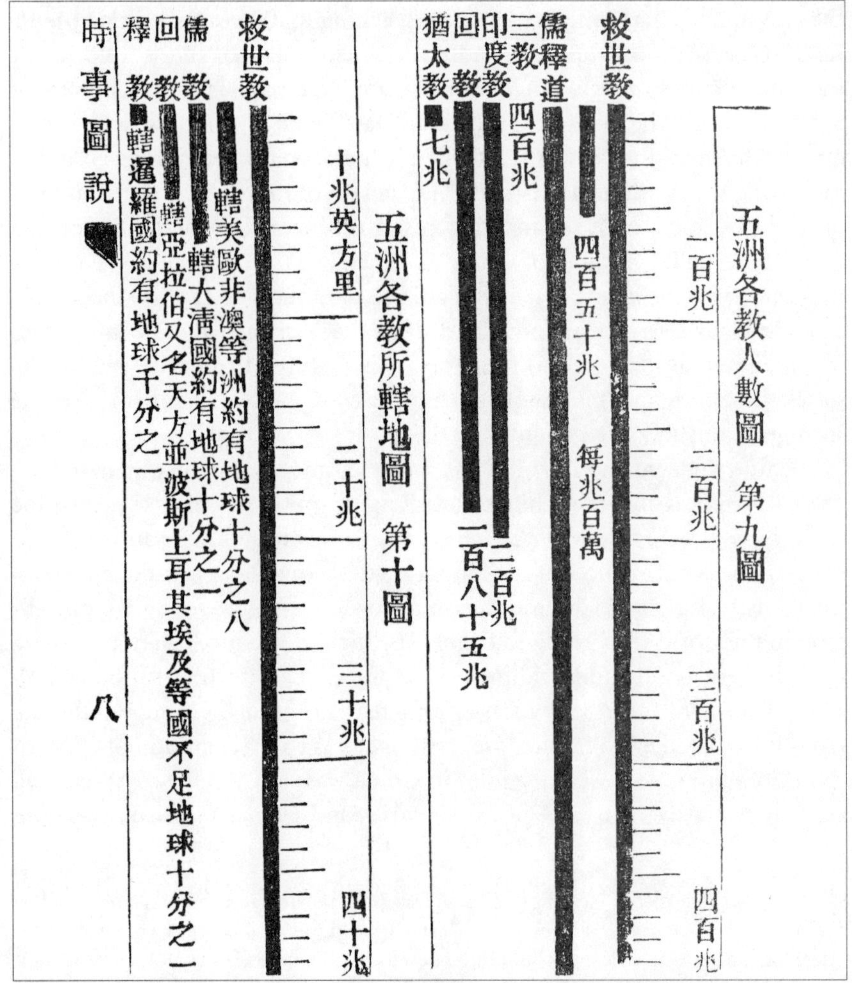

Figure 8. Timothy Richard's charts showing population and territorial extent of the major world religions. The right-hand chart indicates the "Number of People Belonging to Each Religion (literally 'Teaching') in the Five Continents," starting from the right with the "Teaching that Saves the World," followed by the three "Chinese religions" (Ruism ["Confucianism"], Buddhism, Daoism), and then "Hinduism," "Teaching of the Hui People (Islam)," and "Judaism." The chart on the left boasts the landmass covered by each of the religions' adherents within the same five continents, giving the most to the "Teaching that Saves the World" (over 40 million square miles), followed by Ruism ("only" 6 million square miles), Islam (5 million square miles), and Buddhism (less than 2 million square miles).

the so-called Boxer movement of 1900 (known in Chinese as the Society of Righteousness and Harmony, *Yihe tuan*).[54]

Redirecting Chinese Missions: Successes, Justifications, and Unforeseen Complications

It has been argued above that Taylor and Richard were Protestant missionaries of the evangelical stripe, working out correctives to the standard missionary approaches employed in late nineteenth-century China through their own activities and institutions, which became intimately associated with their own names (in Chinese as well as English). Taylor's resistance to institutionalization by insisting on missionary "itinerations" throughout the Qing empire reinvigorated the evangelical vision in numerous missions, so that not only the CIM but many other missions had representatives throughout China by 1900. Richard's practical awareness of the ideological politics behind resistance to missionaries brought him into the limelight as a new "sage from the West," who had come to enlighten Chinese ignorance and aid the empire's entry into the twentieth century as an informed and modernizing member of a still inchoate international "community." Both men's visions successfully reshaped patterns of normal missionary activity well into the first decades of Republican China.

However, we should be careful not to overstate the nature of these adaptations. Although Taylor was a firm advocate of the primacy of itinerant preaching, this strategy developed within a multiform institutional framework that the CIM manifestly supported. Itinerant preaching by missionaries, unsupported by gunboats but trusting in the "faithfulness of God," was Taylor's way of testing the reliability of the Opium War treaty conditions and proving that some of the common people within the Qing empire were open to the Christian message. However, Taylor's premillennial anticipation of the return of Christ to earth did not keep him from planning institutionalized support for the growing number of mission stations under his ultimate supervision. Itinerancy, even for Taylor and the CIM, was only the avant-garde of the missionary enterprise. Once a station was established, other, more standard modes of missionary activity would naturally begin to take place.[55]

54. Documentation of this problem is provided in Paul A. Cohen, *History in Three Keys: The Boxers as Event, Experience, and Myth* (New York, 1997).

55. An American Baptist missionary, Joseph S. Adams, previously a CIM member until 1882, complained that Taylor tried to hand these stations over to "untrained native preachers" much too quickly. He cited Taylor's explicit motive as the "near appearance of

This was demonstrated in 1880 when the CIM initiated its first medical missionaries, and established its famous school for missionary and other children at Zhifu ("the Chefoo School"), while also sending the first women, married and single, into the Chinese hinterland to do their own style of missionary "women's work."[56]

Itinerant missionaries also did more than street preaching, although this may sometimes be overlooked. Taylor himself was a trained medical doctor, and whenever he and others traveled, they carried not only medical supplies but also tracts, books, and gospel posters to sell and use along the way, in both roadside inns and cities where they encountered inquirers and established new stations. Richard himself was one of the first to recognize the distinctive role during the famine relief projects of the late 1870s of CIM missionaries, including Taylor's own wife, Jennie, who helped set up orphanages for needy children. Schools for Chinese children, both boys and girls, were of long-standing interest at CIM stations. Special medical work to relieve addicts of their reliance on opium also became a standard and successful element of the regular CIM activity, sustained principally by the charismatic leadership of Pastor Xi Shengmo. Clearly the CIM was not only an itinerant missionary body; it also supported other creative activities and many more mundane activities under its organizational umbrella.

Similarly, Richard's literary work did not eclipse his abiding interest in the missionary calling to "preach the gospel." In his famous set of essays, *Historical Evidences of Christianity for China,* he included pieces describing the material, intellectual, political, social, moral, spiritual, and present benefits Christianity offered to the Qing empire. Significantly, he wrote his longest pieces on the spiritual and political aspects.[57] Not intending to replace tradi-

---

the LORD" and "His personal reign on earth" (Baptist Missions archives, Archive for the Study of Christianity in China, Hong Kong Baptist University: Adams to Cushing, Rangoon, Burma, 3 December 1882). Nevertheless, this was a period of the greatest adventurous itineration by CIM members into "unreached" areas. However much Taylor emphasized itineration and localization, the greater institutionalization process still become part of the normal strategy following the bolder acts of itinerancy. I must thank my colleague, Roger Callaway, for this information.

56. Broomhall, *HTCOC,* 6:239-40, 250, 294, 316-20.

57. See Richard, "Historical evidences of Christianity for China: the material benefits," *CR* 21, no. 4 (April 1890): 145-50; "The intellectual benefits," *CR* 21, no. 5 (May 1890): 228-32; "The political benefits of Christianity," *CR* 21, no. 10 (October 1890): 435-48; "The social benefits of Christianity," *CR* 21, no. 11 (November 1890): 500-509; "The moral benefits of Christianity," *CR* 22, no. 1 (January 1891): 25-32; "The spiritual benefits of Christianity," *CR* 22, no. 4 (April 1891): 172-77; 22, no. 5 (May 1891): 197-203; 22, no. 6 (June 1891): 245-52; "The historical evidences of Christianity — present benefits," *CR* 22, no. 10 (October

tional missionary activities by literature campaigns, Richard argued forcefully for a mixed and balanced approach taking account of the changing political and social complexities of the Qing empire. The problem in his mind was that the importance of Christian and other general literature about the "true Christian civilization," including the quality and precision of its messages, had been generally underrated. His arguments for "how a few men may make a million converts" manifested his vision for this kind of literature, and his approach was largely vindicated by its effects both before and after the Reform Movement of 1898.[58] One of the very practical results of this literary appeal to true Christian civilization after the Boxer Rebellion was the use of indemnity funds to establish a "Western"-style university in Shanxi for Chinese civil service graduates. Although this visionary educational experiment did not survive the revolution of 1911, it is important to note that its curriculum was to be bicultural, even while most, if not all, of its foreign teachers were British nationals.[59]

The theological justifications utilized by both men nevertheless manifested very different ways of approaching missionary work. These justifications led to important practical differences, which put Taylor and Richard on opposite sides of some very significant issues within Chinese missions. In part, these justifications reflected their individual personalities: Taylor was a reserved man attracted to an ascetic lifestyle and the mystical confirmation of experienced fellowship with Christ; Richard was more practical, driven by detailed plans for the total renovation of the Chinese people under a broad vision of the kingdom of God in Christ. These tendencies received explicit theological justifications in the literature both men published, reflecting what are still contentious problems in the theology of missions to this day.

Shaped by Methodist disciplines and Brethren piety, Taylor appears as a "man of one book." His reading of the Bible was neither narrow nor doctrinaire, but was a reading meditatively absorbed and expressed in terms of "fel-

---

1891): 443-51. These were later collated in a single volume under the main title by Richard, *Historical Evidences of Christianity for China* (Shanghai, 1895), and were also translated into Chinese.

58. Timothy Richard, "How a Few Men May Make a Million Converts," *CR* 32, no. 6 (June 1901): 267-80. His mention in the abstract preceding this article of "this swarming yellow race" shows him using the normal Orientalizations of the day, albeit in this case one that Chinese people used of themselves. Cf. the development of this theme more broadly in *Conversion by the Million*, esp. vol. 1.

59. *Forty-Five Years in China*, pp. 299-310. How much this represented a cultural arm of British imperialistic policy would require a much more detailed study of this institution than we can give here.

lowship with Christ" as the basic form of Christian spiritual life.[60] Persuaded of "the mystical union of Christ and the believer," Taylor made the passages of the Christian Bible take on new spiritual meaning for thousands who heard him speak about the "living Christ," "God's faithfulness," and China's preeminent need.[61] This form of spiritual life had a practical implication for reaching "China's millions." Jesus Christ, the "Incarnate Word of God," joined human beings in their most basic needs, and so the missionary should do this as well. When the apostle Paul sought to extrapolate this truth into missionary activities among the non-Jewish peoples, Taylor emphasized, he only once approached "the learned on their own grounds" (Acts 17, in addressing the Athenian citizens on Mars Hill), but became convinced of "the failure of that method" and so "abandoned it." The "Trinitarian God" would honor the faithful witness of anyone who knew nothing other than "JESUS CHRIST, and Him *crucified*" among the Chinese. When this kind of justification was strengthened by an eschatological anticipation of Christ's early return, mission strategy ended up emphasizing "practice" rather than "theory" or "study."[62] To pursue an intellectual approach was for Taylor a missionary diversion, a tried and failed method manifested for him in both the Delegates' Version of the Chinese Bible (1852-56) with its "intellectual style" and the "Shanxi spirit" he identified with Richard's approach. Ultimately, Taylor's ministerial vision rested with common people uninfluenced by these intellectual trends.[63]

One way to characterize these differences is to identify Taylor's approach as a "minimalist" and Richard's as a "maximalist" missionary strategy.[64] Remaining institutionally and theologically aloof from doctrinaire positions, Taylor took evangelism as the preeminent task of missionaries, understanding that to mean "the presentation of the gospel" without paying special attention to the complications of the Qing cultural contexts in which his CIM representatives moved. For his part, Richard saw the need to address elite members of the Chinese populace with the Christian gospel in its broadest

60. Chauncey Goodrich, "Secrets of Power: A Meditation on the Life of Rev. Hudson Taylor," *CR* 36 (1905): 383.

61. See Griffith John, "In Memoriam. Rev. J. Hudson Taylor, M.R.C.S., F.R.G.S.," *CR* 36 (1905): 392-93, for this assessment of Taylor by a close friend and LMS missionary.

62. See Taylor's theological justifications in three articles published in *China's Millions:* "Lessons from the incarnation," April 1885, pp. 39-40; "Apostolic example," June 1885, pp. 63-64; and "Self-denial versus self-assertion," September 1885, pp. 107-8. Quotations above come from the second article. For a fuller assessment of Taylor's premillennialism, more work is necessary, e.g., on his comments on the Song of Songs in *China's Millions.*

63. Broomhall, *HTCOC,* vol. 2, app. 4, pp. 397-99, for Taylor's misgivings about the Delegates' translation.

64. I am indebted to Professor Andrew Walls for this terminology.

sense, revealing the implications of the creator God as well as a cross-centered theology of salvation. For Richard it was necessary to address questions about comparisons between religions, the significance and impact of scientific knowledge, and the political benefits of reform, because these were maximalist implications drawn from his theological foundation.

Drawn toward a more "practical" theology of missions, Richard translated several practical Christian manuals into Chinese for Chinese Christians and seekers.[65] In addition, he found precedents for his form of missionary activity in Jesus' teachings in the Sermon of the Mount (Matt. 5–7). He saw Jesus as arguing for a "more excellent way," offering something "*surpassing* the past," not by rejecting it or destroying past developments but by fulfilling them. Richard had been deeply influenced by Edward Irving's famous sermon before the LMS of 1824 on similar themes, but he developed the implications of these biblical teachings in his own distinctive manner.[66] Summarizing the practical implications of this point of view for Chinese missionaries, Richard argued as follows:

> My object in writing this is to ascertain who are prepared to say, — "we will guard against the insidious but wicked habit of running down the Chinese, we will give them fair play, we will make ourselves acquainted with all they value highest, and will show them higher knowledge in every branch of education; we are prepared to undergo greater self-sacrifice, we will not expect partial verdicts because we are foreigners; we will exhibit a higher faith and greater devotion. In a word, we shall take the Sermon on the Mount as our text, and for [our] motto, that we have not come to destroy but to fulfil; not to expect to be considered worthy of the kingdom of Heaven except we *exceed* the best in China, endeavouring to be perfect as our Father in Heaven is perfect; looking to the Chinese for support rather than to our over-partial friends at home; and may our blessed Father baptize us with the spirit of fire until we see all the land prostrate before Him.["][67]

65. E.g., Richard translated Jeremy Taylor's *Holy Living*, reflecting his practical concern to provide Chinese believers with specific directions toward a sanctified Christian experience: see Richard, *Tiandao fencheng* (Different lessons about the heavenly way) (Shanghai, ca. 1875).

66. Edward Irving, *Missionaries after the Apostolic School* (London, 1824), based on Matt. 10:11. There Jesus urged his disciples to look out for "worthy" people wherever they went, which Richard interpreted to mean those most educated and religiously involved.

67. Timothy Richard, "Thoughts on Chinese missions: difficulties and tactics," *Chinese Recorder* 11, no. 6 (November-December 1880): 440.

Here was the crux of the matter, which put Taylor and Richard on opposite sides regarding the nature of ancestral rites and, almost certainly, on the tricky question about the appropriate Chinese words for the biblical terms "God," "Spirit/spirit" (divine and human), and "spirits." In the 1890 General Conference of Chinese Missionaries, the American W. A. P. Martin argued that ancestral rites were not outright worship, and so should be treated with leniency, not as unmitigated idolatry. While Richard and another American missionary, Gilbert Reid, who also targeted the Chinese elite, agreed with Martin, the vast majority followed Taylor in opposing this position as theologically incorrect and practically divisive.[68] In his defense Richard drew attention to problems raised by Martin's paper inherent in its use of the term "worship," and pointed to the still greater difficulty that if ancestors were referred to as *shen,* or "spirits" — the term also used by many "low church" missionaries for "God" in the Hebrew Scriptures and New Testament — then to "worship" or "reverence" these *shen* would be tantamount to idolatry.

Richard's and Taylor's handling of this ticklish question illustrates one of the unaddressed problems inherent in their missiological approaches. In his Chinese writings Richard constantly used the Ruist term taken from Ruist canonical literature for "God," that is, *shangdi.* The "Holy Spirit" would then be designated by the words *shengshen,* taking the second term to refer only to spirits and not to God. How Taylor answered this problem is unclear, because we currently know of no Chinese tract or materials he wrote and published. Nevertheless, R. H. Mathews's *Chinese-English Dictionary* (1931), prepared by one of the best CIM missionary-sinologists, distinctly supports readings that prefer the word *shen* as the rendering for "God" and the alternative *shengling* for "the Holy Spirit."[69] If Mathews's usage indicates a general position held by Taylor himself (which may not be the case), it would encourage further doubts as to the wisdom of trying to avoid "intellectual" approaches to Chinese people and others using Chinese language as their basic medium.

68. W. A. P. Martin, "The worship of ancestors — a plea for tolerance," with following debate, in *Report of the Missionary Conference held in Shanghai, May 1890* (Shanghai, 1890), pp. 57-67.

69. Mathews avoids the use of *shangdi* for "God" except in a very few circumstances, generally rendering the term as "the Supreme." The term *shen,* on the other hand, is generally referred to as "god" (not "God") or "spirits," though the phrase *shengling* is rendered "the divine nature, Godhead." The key interpretative point here comes in his choice for the "Holy Spirit," where he does not even employ the term Richard uses *(shengshen)* and only presents the term *shengling* as appropriate. Cf. R. H. Mathews, *Chinese-English Dictionary,* rev. ed. (Cambridge, Mass., 1956), under *ling* (p. 586), *shang* (pp. 779-81), *shen* (pp. 790-92), and *sheng* (p. 800).

If the literature carried by CIM missionaries primarily used *shen* for "God" and *shengling* for the "Holy Spirit," they would regularly have faced the practical problem that their Christian message logically appeared to oppose any form of ritual act of reverence toward another named spirit or *shen*. This is consistent with Taylor's adamant opposition to "ancestral rites" in 1890, and would also explain why Richard, who, much like his predecessor James Legge (1815-97), preferred the Ruist classical term for "God," did not feel that these rites were inherently idolatrous. Although the arguments in 1890 and at other times justifiably dealt with much more than this terminological problem, both usages provided the basis for a particular way of embodying the message of Chinese Christianity. Both terms for "God" are now used in biblical translations among Chinese Protestants, and almost all have followed Taylor in destroying their ancestral plaques on becoming Christians. Whether this also explains the relatively small percentage of Chinese responding to the Christian message during the last two hundred years, notwithstanding rapid growth during the past fifty, is an important practical question with some very significant theological implications.

Nevertheless, Richard's open-ended approach to various religious and political leaders led to anomalous results. As seen above, his interpretative renderings of various Mahayana Buddhist texts have been fundamentally rejected by contemporary Buddhist translators. In addition, the reformer Richard mentioned who personally expressed his belief in the "Fatherhood of God" from reading Richard's Chinese literature, Kang Youwei (1858-1927), was ultimately as liberal in his reading of Christian doctrines as Richard was in rendering Buddhist ideas. Kang was so inconsistent and unaware of certain basic Christian teachings that his commentaries contain many errors. Although Kang himself tended toward a kind of theism late in life, the primary tendency of his thought was shaped by Buddhism, and his most important disciple, Liang Qichao (1873-1929), who worked as personal secretary to Richard in Beijing in 1895, later became a well-known Buddhist advocate.[70] Consequently, it seems that Richard's open approach left other kinds of religious commitments open as well, and so ironically may have been more hindrance than help toward his ultimate goal of Christian witness leading to personal conversion.[71]

70. Lauren Pfister, "Ching Reformers and Christian Religion: The Philosophical Influence and Critique of Christianity in the *Wu Hsu* Reform Movement Leaders — K'ang Yu-Wei, Liang Ch'i Ch'ao and T'an Ssu-T'ung," in *Proceedings of the Eighth International Symposium on Asian Studies* (Hong Kong, 1986), pp. 367-88.

71. But for a counterexample, see Notto R. Thelle, "Karl Ludvig Reichelt, 1877-1952: Christian Pilgrim of Tao Fong Shan," in *Mission Legacies*, pp. 216-24.

In conclusion, the further question remains: How much during their long careers did Taylor and Richard participate in the main trends of British imperial expansion? It is clear that their shared Nonconformist and evangelical theology brought them into conflict with both British and Qing officials, even though Richard was far more successful in winning some Qing officials to his way of viewing China and the modern world. Although neither man could be called an advocate of British imperialist policies, both represented institutions that Chinese officials regularly associated with those policies. Ironically, Taylor's minimalist missionary strategy probably promoted more confrontation between missionaries and Chinese officials because of the missionaries' inadequate sensitivity to Chinese everyday culture and elitist political values, while Richard's more aggressive approach to China's elites earned him the right to explain his view of "true Christian civilization" and predisposed some Qing officials toward a selective acceptance of Christian claims. Both men and the institutions they represented were compromised by the abiding presence of the "unequal treaties," which gave special privileges to missionaries and Christian converts, and both helped create a vision of China and her people that shaped the ways many in the British and Qing empires saw their worlds. The price for these perceived points of complicity with British imperialism was the loss of lives during periods of religious turmoil, notably the Boxer Rebellion in 1900. Both nevertheless lived to see the enlargement of the institutions they established by their own distinctive missionary strategies.

"Who Did They Think They Were?" Some Reflections from a Theologian on Grand Narratives and Identity in the History of Missions

JOHN W. DE GRUCHY

Any reflections by one who has no specialized historical knowledge of the wide range of subjects and issues discussed in this volume must be inevitably less than an informed review and more in the nature of an African praise song, lauding the work that has been done yet slipping in a coded or more direct form of critique. Praise singers are forgiven if they borrow much from others and perhaps exaggerate a little and engage in hyperbole. Their task is to create a polyphony of sounds held together by the cantus firmus of the central melody, which, in this case, is the interplay of representation and experience in late nineteenth- and early twentieth-century British Protestant missionary history.

I

Bernard Lord Manning, that extraordinary Nonconformist don, often made the point that while Dissenters did not usually say the creed Sunday by Sunday, they sang the creed in their hymns. That was the touchstone of good hymnody. It seems appropriate then that this praise song should begin with the praise songs of the missionaries and their supporters. What were they singing when they set sail for distant shores? What hymns were the missionary societies choosing for those services across Britain at which missionaries on furlough told of their endeavors and awoke interest in mission work? And what was the content of the hymns that the missionaries taught their converts and translated into the vernacular? That is an area of research that might shed light on the theme discussed in these essays. For hymnody and liturgy are key indicators of missionary piety, suggesting what they believed and what provided them with spiritual sustenance over the long haul. Hymns shaped their identity and gave it expression. Hymns embodied their theology. Not to understand what they sang is not to understand them at all.

We dare not generalize about all missionaries and all missionary societies, but it is most likely that they sang the hymns of Isaac Watts and Charles Wesley, and the other great and not-so-great hymns of the Evangelical Revival. It is likely also that they sang the hymns that were written as the nineteenth-century missionary movement began to take shape. John Marriott (1780-1825) prayed that God's almighty Word would be heard "where the gospel's day sheds not its glorious ray." Reginald Heber's (1783-1826) "From Greenland's Icy Mountains" included the verse:

> Can we, whose souls are lighted
> With wisdom from on high,
> Can we to men benighted
> The lamp of life deny?
> Salvation! O salvation!
> The joyful sound proclaim,
> Till each remotest nation
> Has learnt Messiah's name.

But a brief look at some verses and hymns written during the period ending in 1914 suggests that they would surely also have been sung on the occasions I have mentioned. While undoubtedly sung together, they sound a different note. These are a few selected verses from among the many more that could have been documented.

> Thy kingdom come! On bended knee . . .
> When knowledge, hand in hand with peace,
> Shall walk the earth abroad:
> The day of perfect righteousness,
> The promised day of God.

(F. D. Hosmer, 1840-1929)

> Thy kingdom come, O God;
> Thy rule, O Christ, begin;
> Break with Thine iron rod
> The tyrannies of sin.

O'er heathen lands afar
Thick darkness broodeth yet;
Arise, O Morning Star,
Arise, and never set.

(Lewis Hensley, 1824-1905)

God of our fathers, known of old,
Lord of our far-flung battle line,
Beneath whose aweful hand we hold
Dominion over palm and pine —
Lord God of hosts, be with us yet,
Lest we forget — lest we forget!

For heathen heart that puts her trust
In reeking tube and iron shard,
All valiant dust that builds on dust,
And guarding, calls not thee to guard,
For frantic boast and foolish word —
Thy mercy on Thy people, Lord!

(Rudyard Kipling, 1865-1936)

There are several points to this excursus in hymnody. One is to remind us that the theology which shaped the missionaries and which they took with them to the farthest corners of the globe was not primarily that of the textbooks, but of the Bible, the prayer book, and the hymnbook. Another is to remind us that much more research needs to be done on our theme using such resources. But the substantive point about an examination of hymnody is that it corroborates much of what has been said in one way or another about the connections between the grand narratives of redemption and God's reign of peace and righteousness throughout the world. While the missionaries and mission boards of our period certainly sang the great songs of evangelical redemption, of salvation from sin, of the cross and its atoning power, at least some of the British and North American ones were also singing about the extension of God's reign over all the earth. They were praying for God's peace in every corner of the world, a peace that would result in freedom from all the tyrannies that oppressed heathendom. They sang as people inspired by a vision of the arrival of the kingdom of God helped along by their own faithfulness in prayer and in dedicated missionary endeavor.

But hymns were also sung mindful of another grand narrative that was shaping people's lives and destiny. The themes of the latter-day hymns correlated with empire! The construction and extension of God's reign somehow found its analogy, and more, in the construction and extension of Victoria's reign; their prayer for universal peace was linked to Pax Britannica; and their vision of the coming kingdom was undoubtedly linked in some way with the birth of a new century. Victoria was not only an example of a righteous ruler, but also an example to all foreign chiefs of one whose reign was blessed because of her belief in Christ. And it was precisely because she, too, rose when the "Hallelujah Chorus" was sung that they gladly aligned their missionary cause with the extension of her benign and righteous rule. It was, after all, her righteous rule that gave legitimacy to the imperial advance, and garnered the support of the missionaries.

Moreover, many of the officials of Her Imperial Majesty were good and faithful churchmen, often closely linked to the missionary societies. A typical case was Lord Milner, a leading imperialist of the time who also served on the board of the Society for the Propagation of the Gospel in Foreign Parts. There were others; for example, those who participated in section VII of the Edinburgh Missionary Conference in 1910. Many such imperial officers believed they also had a divine calling to spread and sustain Victoria's reign, and that doing so was integral to the spreading and sustaining of Christ's reign. Therefore it was inconceivable that the missionaries should be anything but loyal servants — something many British missionaries also believed. They, too, were almost invariably imperialists, representatives of Victoria, even if they were sometimes problematic imperialists who sowed some of the seeds for the empire's demise.

In hindsight, it is clear that the linkage of mission and empire was fatally flawed. But what must not be overlooked is that some missionaries who took that interface seriously were also critical of it — as can be seen from their submissions to the Edinburgh Conference. At the same time, they were also profoundly conscious of the fact that Christian mission could not be separated from its world historical context. Mission was not to be narrowly conceived as evangelism — central as that might be — but as, we might now say, engaging in God's mission in the world. That is always a risky business because it requires a certain brazenness in claiming to know what God wills, and the courage to do what is willed. Historians would not normally want to claim any ability for such discernment, and rightly so, although they can surely show where theologians and missionaries went wrong in the past. Theologians, who more easily go where angels fear to tread, are accustomed to doing so, for their calling is precisely about discerning the signs of the times and what God is calling people to be and do. That is why missiology needs both historians and theologians to lessen the probability of making false moves in the present.

II

Let us move on, then, from the conflation of grand traditions and turn to the identity of the missionaries, their image of themselves, and the way others understood them. The emerging picture is one of multiple identities, often confused and confusing. How did the missionaries image themselves? Who did they think they were representing?

The primary image is undoubtedly that of being those God had called and sent. After all, that is what "missionary" meant. As they understood themselves, they were representatives of the King of Kings and Lord of Lords. They were latter-day Saint Pauls, even if Roland Allen complained that they did not use his methods. They were not representatives of something new in Christianity, but representatives of an ancient tradition that had previously brought the light of the gospel to Europe. They were nineteenth-century links in a chain which bound them to the apostles and was spreading across the earth, shedding light in every dark corner. Would they have gone to Greenland, India, China, and Africa, facing perils unknown, if the King of Kings had not called and sent them? Many only managed to survive because they believed this. Indeed, if their theology changed at this point, if they no longer believed in either God's providence or redemptive purposes for all the world, they had a major crisis of identity, one that forced them to reconsider their vocational options — limited as these usually were.

Undoubtedly the wives of male missionaries shared in this vision (we do not read about husbands of women missionaries!). But what of their children? That is surely an interesting subject for consideration and research, not least because of everything children had to endure for the sake of the missionary cause, many not surviving to tell the tale. What we do know is that children of missionary parents came to have doubts — not unlike those of clergy generally — about their parents' vocation. But not necessarily about the imperial vision and task. Indeed, many missionary children — as well as disillusioned missionaries — became key officials of the empire — educators, governors, doctors, but also entrepreneurs and traders. They often had the necessary languages, the experience of terrain and populace, and of course, contacts necessary for such work. Such a theme suggests the need for further exploration.

III

Yes, indeed, the missionaries believed they were called and sent by God, but they were also undeniably the employees of missionary societies or boards of bishops, and subject to periodic visitations. As such they had to heed directions from their superiors. The mission directors likewise believed the missionaries were in their employ and therefore represented them. Boards and societies did not easily listen to the experience of their representatives. The missionaries, they often thought, were too close to the particular; they did not have the broader picture. Hence the fact that some missionaries, notably the paradigmatic and peripatetic Hudson Taylor, broke away and plowed their own independent furrows.

But there was another dimension to this relationship between mission board and missionary, one that had to do with the broader constituency of the supporting churches. The missionary societies were dependent on the financial support of parishes and congregations, so the missionaries had to represent them, and that implied that they had to respect and represent their religious convictions. They were dependent on those back home for their support and livelihood. But just as some missionaries were problematic imperialists, many were also problematic for their own constituencies back home.

The fact that the late nineteenth century witnessed a growing gap between the piety of the pew and the theology and especially the understanding of the Bible of many a pulpit made all this increasingly problematic and also contributed to the rise of independent missions. That is where the new missionary heroes were to be seen from a popular viewpoint. They were not departing from the Great Commission. But how to represent the missionaries to the mainstream Nonconformist and Anglican constituencies was thus a major concern of the mission boards. But it was not simply a matter of theological differences that separated missionaries from the metropolitan base — this was, after all, not true of all, and probably not true of the majority. The problem had more to do with their changing role. The day of missionary heroes, pioneers, and martyrs saving souls and preaching liberty to the slaves was dying, and the day of missionary administrators, teachers, and doctors had already dawned. Charisma attracts funds; its routinization does not — unless somehow that routinization had to do with the extension of the kingdom of God and its consolidation. Hence the construction of a righteous empire as an essential adjunct of missionary enterprise was a tantalizing option. Just as imperialism might solve some of the problems facing British society itself, it also had the potential for both renewing missionary endeavor and even renewing the home church. Financial support is always a sign of renewal. So maybe more research could be done on the funding of missionary endeavor. Who was giving? What was their motivation? And how was their money being spent?

And then, of course, in some mission fields the missionaries also had to relate to colonial settlers and churches, often finding themselves caught in the cross fire between indigenous rights and aspirations and settler interests. And the settlers still had strong links with their relations back home. So whom did the missionaries represent? "Who do you think you are?" colonists often asked indignantly. This became an even more difficult question to answer once the missionaries themselves began to imbibe views about race and Anglo-Saxon superiority that were in conflict with the Scriptures but in tune with science. Were they representatives of modernity? In one sense undoubtedly so. Missionaries were often the first to introduce people to the benefits of modernity. But were they also to pass on worldviews that conflicted with the Bible, or to represent the piety of those back home? Ironically, some of the "findings" of science on matters of race reinforced the racism of the colonists, often drawing the missionaries into alliance with them rather than with their own converts and mission communities. The fact was, the missionaries were also European and white. They were the blood brothers and sisters of the colonists. Hence the confusion of identities at times of social tension and crisis, times when missionaries were forced to choose sides between empire and reign of God, between colonial interests and those of their converts.

IV

Many missionaries were individualists, and not a few were a little eccentric. Indispensable qualities at times, but how difficult this makes generalization even before one turns to matters of denominational tradition, strategy, and goals — each with its own variants. The missionaries' identity as Protestant or Anglican (at least those on whom this volume has focused) was undoubtedly strong. But neither Protestantism nor Anglicanism was monochrome. Certainly there was not a great deal in common between certain groups, not only in theological conviction and confession, but sometimes also in social class, background, and education. "Who do you think you are?" was a question that might well have been put by some upper-class High Church clergy to some Nonconformist missionaries who, if they were back home, would surely know their place. And they would probably have asked the same question in return. The tussle between Nonconformists and Anglicans in South Africa can be well documented. Many exceptions notwithstanding, there were Nonconformist missionaries who relished a situation in which they were more equal than they would have been back home, a situation in which they were often regarded and acted as unordained bishops living in appropriate style, and were able to demonstrate that their loyalty to the queen was equal to that of any priest for whom she was supreme governor of the church.

But when we do consider confessional differences, we begin to see how difficult it really is to talk about "the missionaries" — no easier than to speak about "the natives." Nonconformist evangelicals, Scottish Presbyterians, Anglican Evangelicals, Anglican Tractarians, Norwegian pietists, Holiness groups, Plymouth Brethren, Irish Jesuits — each represented a different theological tradition. But the same was often true within each denominational group. Congregationalists, Baptists, and Methodists did not all share the same views either amongst themselves or within their respective circles. Scottish Presbyterians, many of them deeply influenced by the Scottish Enlightenment with its strong commonsense realism, were not exactly Methodist in outlook. They were also wary of English bishops in a way that echoed centuries of church history north of the English border — especially but not only Tractarian bishops who were more dangerous than the Roman variety because at least with the latter you knew where you were.

This provides a reminder of the historic problem of church and state in Britain and Europe generally, and how this impacted the relationship between missions and empire. Clearly the inherited models did not quite fit on the mission fields and often proved quite unserviceable. The Lutheran doctrine of the two kingdoms, the Erastianism of the Anglicans, and the voluntaryism of the Nonconformists made sense in those times and places where they were hard fought and won convictions. But how did one fit them into the peculiar circumstances of British colonies? Experience demanded new models, but new models could not be designed by theologians back home and then put into effect on foreign shores. They, too, could only come about through decades of uncertainty, struggle, and messy politicking, and hard-nosed theological debate. To what extent, then, did imperialism affect the theology of church and state of the missions and their sending churches and the traditions in which they stood? One example will make the point. The Anglican Church in South Africa is a Free Church — it must be if it is not the established church! What does this do to its identity? Who does it represent now? And how does this impact the worldwide Anglican communion, which is itself a product of British imperialism at least to a significant extent?

Being British (and sometimes specifically being Scottish) was also part of missionary identity in a way that related not only to being representative of empire, but concomitantly being different from (inherently superior to?) the missionaries of other countries, especially those not Anglo-Saxon. Those who felt this most were, of course, the missionaries who were not British in origin, even if Protestant. How were they to relate to British imperialism if they were living within its ambit? This problem was exacerbated if the nations to which they themselves belonged were also among those joining the imperial scramble for territory — whether Protestant Germany or Catholic Spain. We should consider not only how the Norwegians related to the British colonial authorities in Natal, but how Irish Catholic missionaries adjusted to similar contexts given the situation back in their homeland. Norwegians may have regarded the British with a certain amount of admiration; Irish Catholics certainly did not. The role of non-British missions under the Union Jack must therefore be expanded to include the role of missionaries, especially Roman Catholic missionaries, from those countries where Britain was seen as an oppressive enemy. If Protestant missionaries feared Catholic advance because of its unbiblical doctrine of justification by works, consider how Catholics feared Protestant control given that outside the Catholic Church there was no salvation. The Catholics knew whom they represented. Clearly the place of Roman Catholic missions has to be part of our research program, something missing from the discussion in this volume though always somewhere in the background. And what about the Eastern Orthodox, the Copts, and others who, even though usually only on the periphery of the empire, were invariably affected by it? In any case, Protestantism was on the move — it was the century of pan-Protestantism. Or was it? Is that not a Protestant view of things? While it is necessary to establish and respect the manageable limits of any scholarly project, it is also important to be on one's guard against being too Protestant, even too Anglican, in focus.

V

There were missionaries other than those mentioned thus far, but usually not placed under this rubric. There were the wives of missionaries and the growing numbers of single women both in religious orders and outside. They had clearly defined roles back in the sending country, whatever their social class, but these roles were now becoming confused. One reason for this was that many of them had greater intelligence and skills than their male missionary superiors. A related fact was that despite this, they had little institutional authority. What authority they had was usually derived from who they were and who their husbands were — it was not part of their job description. Whom did they represent? Their experience was varied, often tragic, sometimes far more positive, but usually mundane, demanding, out of the limelight. As in the First World War, they "manned" the factories but were not allowed to fire the guns; they knitted the socks but did not wear the boots. Yet it was on the mission field, at least to a significant degree, that the role of women in the

Western church was being reshaped by experience. The ordination of women in North America was certainly connected to this experience, and so too, though much later, it was in the colonies that women were first ordained to the Anglican priesthood.

The role of women in mission was problematic for male missionaries because it was another complicating factor in determining their own identity, much as the ordination of women to the Anglican priesthood proved to be a problem to many priests. Issues of gender and power relations had to be faced, and often in a way that had not yet been faced or dealt with satisfactorily back home. The arrival of women missionaries also created problems in indigenous communities, more so in patriarchal societies than in matriarchal, but also there too. Changes in the social status and role of women in Britain and America might not always be appreciated within an African or Asian community. To what extent where these changes part of the liberating power of the gospel, and to what extent where they the playing out of a home agenda on foreign soil? Much research is needed on such and related themes if we are going to understand the ways in which cultures interact with each other through the medium of Christianity.

VI

White, Anglo-Saxon, Protestant missionaries, called and sent by God, responsible to mission boards and to home constituencies, were faced with another challenge to identity once their converts began to exercise their own ministry. For if women were often the backbone of missionary endeavor, what of those missionaries who really bore the brunt once the heroic age was past — the indigenous converts? Without these missionaries, many of them also women, the missionary advance would have been stopped at first base. They were usually far more successful missionary evangelists than the expatriates were, and they often found themselves in conflict with each other. Power relations on mission stations became a major problem and often led to the formation of indigenous churches free of missionary control. "Who did they think they were?" "Whom did they represent?" "To whom were they responsible?" were questions the missionaries asked. They certainly did not represent their chiefs, nor did they represent the mission boards, the missionaries, or Her Imperial Majesty. In their own minds they represented Christ. First-generation converts had a zeal for the gospel that second- and third-generation missionaries — the grandchildren of the Evangelical and later revivals — did not normally have.

But they, too, and especially their children were soon sucked into the imperial cause with serious consequences for their self-identity. Mark, for instance, the way African Christians in South Africa pledged their loyalty to Britain, some even in the final conflicts that brought down the power of the chiefs. Certainly during the Anglo-Boer War and the First World War they were ardent loyalists — despite the fact that they received in return from the British Colonial Office a slap in the face. Indeed, British colonialism not only helped destroy African power. At times it also hid its own efforts at expansion behind expressions of concern to liberate the African from the unrighteous control of the Boers! As a condition of making peace with the Boers in 1902, and in order to avoid offending the sensitivities of other white South Africans, the future of Africans was handed to the Boers on the proverbial plate. After all this, there had to be something in the imperial myth for it to exert such an attraction that that loyalty continued through the Second World War, and finally helped draw the new South Africa back into the Commonwealth in the 1990s. For African converts the question of representation became as complex, then, as for the missionaries — and sometimes far more dangerous. Where did their loyalties lie? But the worldwide church owes it to them for helping to rescue Christianity from being perceived as nothing more than a European religion of imperialism tied to modernity, and at least for making another image possible. The process of the Africanization of Christianity is, I believe, the central theme for missionary studies in Africa today. But what precisely does it mean?

VII

Let us return to our original image of the missionary as an expatriate male called and sent, and consider how this identity was formed and shaped. What precisely were such missionaries taught? What did the mission societies require in their theological education curriculum? Were they educated in a way which really prepared them for what lay ahead, not least the challenges of empire and the challenges to their own self-image? Few if any had anything like the kind of training for mission that subsequently became available. Here is another theme that awaits further exploration.

So a great deal depended on experience. How did experience shape their identity and determine their role? Like any new ordinand thrust into his or her first parish, the going is usually heavy (as the horse race commentators say), or, to change the metaphor, the honeymoon period soon ends. Then everything learned in one's early studies of systematic theology is either ditched or, hopefully, reworked in the light of experience. And it is in this process that, again hopefully, theology comes alive, becomes relevant and sustaining. This was certainly true of the missionaries. The likes of Robert Moffat were well equipped for laying out the gardens at Kuruman, but not for learning Sechuana and translating the Bible. That, he and many others had to learn by hard experience, and what they achieved is nothing short of miraculous. What, then, about their helpers? Those who educated them in indigenous languages and were indispensable to the success of all their other projects?

But let us return to the training of the expatriate missionaries. Many questions come to mind, but we cannot explore or even mention them here. Nevertheless, for example, we might ask about the hermeneutical tools and skills they were equipped with, or not. To what extent were they influenced in their training by the Enlightenment, and if they were, how had they managed to incorporate it into their scheme of things? Were they in any sense trained to understand other religions and cultures? Given the fact, as I suspect, that they were not trained in such matters at all or not very well, it is remarkable how some, though perhaps not too many, sometimes managed to overcome such deficiencies. A further question may be asked in terms of this volume's theme: How many missionaries were trained in the wiles of what we now refer to as ideological suspicion — able to detect the subtle and not so subtle abuse of religion in imperial plans and projects? Probably none. They had to become as wise as serpents on the job. The wonder is that some were able to see through European pretense and put up some resistance. But generally they were not versed in critical theological reflection, and if they were, as Bishop Colenso was, they soon found the going very heavy indeed. But did they always learn from their experience? Were they trained to listen or only to speak? To teach and not to learn? What did the missionaries say about what they learned from their converts — if anything? Did they admit their mistakes, and if so, how did they articulate them? There is a whole set of questions that need to be asked in reading their diaries that have maybe not yet been given sufficient thought.

A two-way traffic in ideas was obviously beginning to take place during this period, even if the dominant trend was from Europe to places elsewhere. So it is understandable that European theologies, ideologies, and anthropologies, bundles of concepts such as "social Darwinism," were all lifted out of their context and transplanted to the ends of the earth by missionaries without much critical thought about the process and its implications. That they seldom fitted reality soon became clear to some, however; that they were sometimes ditched is equally true. But often they were adopted and adapted, and even turned around by converts in such a way that they became swords in the struggle against imperialism and ecclesiastical domination. Sometimes they seeded and fertilized the growth of indigenous churches and nationalist movements, which ultimately undermined the imperial adventure itself and sent the missionaries home. And sometimes the churches and societies back home began to understand themselves better as a result. Racism in Europe would not have been seen for what it is if it had not been identified as a crime against God and humanity in places like South Africa.

The ultimate irony in all this came, however, when the converts and their descendants themselves became missionaries sent to reevangelize Britain and the Continent. That, of course, is another story that cannot detain us here. But it may be worth considering the need to engage in comparative research on these latter-day missionaries in relation to their predecessors who have been at the center of the inquiry represented in these essays. For one thing, they do not need, nor do they have any chance of being aided by forms of, imperialism. But who these missionaries represent and what their experience is, is a matter for another discussion.

VIII

Historians and theologians need each other. Historians seek to establish the way things were and why; theologians are concerned to go beyond the "what" to how things should be. In their different ways both should therefore address the fundamental question, "So what?" If they do not, then the danger of theologians trying to count the number of angels able to dance on a pinhead is likely to be equaled by that of historians trying to recover information about their names. My credentials are not primarily those of an historian, but I am convinced that theologians must endeavor to be good historians in order to do theology. The reverse may often also be true. For those of us with a contemporary concern for the mission of the church, and therefore who regard missiology as a focal point in doing theology, the need for historians and theologians to be engaged in critical dialogue becomes essential. We need to be rooted in the concreteness of history, both past and contemporary, yet exploring the horizons of what should and might yet be. For theologians, therefore, the success of this volume is not to be judged only by the standard of the essays it contains, the discussion they provide, or even the fresh research they generate, but ultimately by the way they inform contemporary attitudes and actions. A project such as this, whatever its other benefits, is invaluable in furthering such a cause.

Bibliography

Ajayi, J. F. A. *Christian Missions in Nigeria, 1841-1891.* London, 1965.

Anderson, G. H., ed. *Biographical Dictionary of Christian Missions.* New York, 1998.

Anderson, Olive. "The Growth of Christian Militarism in Mid-Victorian Britain." *English Historical Review* 86 (1971): 46-72.

Annett, Edward A. *William Carey, Pioneer Missionary in India.* London, n.d.

Anstey, Roger. *The Atlantic Slave Trade and British Abolition, 1760-1810.* London, 1975.

Arnold, David. *The Congress in Tamilnad.* New Delhi, 1977.

———. *Imperial Medicine and Indigenous Societies.* Manchester, 1988.

Arnot, Frederick Stanley. *Missionary Travels in Central Africa.* Glasgow, 1914.

———. *Garenganze or Mission Work in Central Africa.* London, n.d.

Ayandele, E. A. *The Missionary Impact on Modern Nigeria, 1842-1914.* London, 1966.

Bagal, Shri Jogesh Chandra, ed. *Bankim Rachanavali.* Calcutta, 1969.

Balfour, Lady Frances. *A Memoir of Lord Balfour of Burleigh K.T.* London, n.d.

Barry, Alfred. *The Ecclesiastical Expansion of England in the Growth of the Anglican Communion: The Hulsean Lectures for 1894-95.* London, 1895.

Bean, Lucy, and Elizabeth Van Heyningen, eds. *The Letters of Jane Elizabeth Waterston, 1866-1905.* Cape Town, 1983.

Beaver, Robert P. *All Loves Excelling: American Protestant Women in World Mission.* Grand Rapids, 1968.

Bebbington, D. W. *The Nonconformist Conscience: Chapel and Politics, 1870-1914.* London, 1982.

———. "Evangelicals and Reform." *Third Way,* May 1983, pp. 10-13.

———. "The Persecution of George Jackson: A British Fundamentalist Controversy." In *Persecution and Toleration,* edited by W. J. Sheils. Studies in Church History 21. Oxford, 1984.

Bell, G. K. A. *Randall Davidson: Archbishop of Canterbury.* 2 vols. London, 1935; 2nd ed., 1938.

Bentley, James. *Ritualism and Politics in Victorian Britain: The Attempt to Legislate for Belief.* Oxford, 1978.

Besant, Annie. "Hinduism and Nationality." *New India,* 9 January 1915, p. 7.

Best, G. F. A. "Popular Protestantism in Victorian Britain." In *Ideas and Institutions of Victorian Britain,* edited by Robert Robson. London, 1967.

Boegner, M. "Missions et gouvernements: de l'acte de Berlin au traité de Versailles." *Le Monde Non-Chrétien* 1 (1931): 59-78.

Bohr, Paul Richard. *Famine in China and the Missionary: Timothy Richard as Relief Administrator and Advocate of National Reform, 1876-1884.* Cambridge, Mass., 1972.

Bolt, Christine. *Victorian Attitudes to Race.* London, 1971.

Bonk, Jonathan J. *The Theory and Practice of Missionary Identification, 1860-1920.* Lewiston, 1989.

Bourdillon, J. A. "Opportunity of the Unrest in India." *Church Missionary Review,* August 1909, pp. 449-57.

Bowker, J. M. *Speeches, Letters, and Selections from Important Papers of John Mitford Bowker.* Grahamstown, 1864. Reprint, Cape Town, 1962.

Broomhall, A. J. *Hudson Taylor and China's Open Century.* 7 vols. London, 1981-89.

Byrne, Lavinia. *The Hidden Journey: Missionary Heroines in Many Lands.* London, 1993.

Cain, P. J., and A. G. Hopkins. *British Imperialism: Innovation and Expansion, 1688-1914.* London, 1993.

Cairns, H. A. C. *Prelude to Imperialism: British Reactions to Central African Society, 1840-1890.* London, 1965.

Cameron, N. M. de S., ed. *Dictionary of Scottish Church History and Theology.* Edinburgh, 1993.

Chadwick, Owen. *The Victorian Church.* 2nd ed. 2 vols. London, 1970-71.

———. *The Secularization of the European Mind in the Nineteenth Century.* Cambridge, 1975.

Chamberlain, M. E. *The New Imperialism.* London, 1970.

Chamberlin, David, ed. *Some Letters from Livingstone.* London, 1940.

Chatterjee, Partha. *The Nation and Its Fragments.* New Delhi, 1993.

Chowdhury-Sengupta, Indira. "Reconstructing Spiritual Heroism: The Evolution of the Swadeshi Sannyasi in Bengal." In *Myth and Mythmaking,* edited by Julia Leslie. Richmond, 1996.

Christensen, Torben, and William R. Hutchison, eds. *Missionary Ideologies in the Imperialist Era: 1880-1920.* Aarhus, 1982.

Christofersen, A. F. *Adventuring with God: The Story of the American Board Mission in Africa.* Edited by R. Sales. Durban, [1967].

Clements, Keith. *Faith on the Frontier: A Life of J. H. Oldham.* Edinburgh and Geneva, 1999.

Clifford, John. *Typical Christian Leaders.* London, 1898.

———. *God's Greater Britain.* London, 1899.

Cnattingius, Hans. *Bishops and Societies: A Study of Anglican Colonial and Missionary Expansion, 1698-1850.* London, 1952.

Cohen, Paul A. "Missionary Approaches: Hudson Taylor and Timothy Richard." In *Papers on China: Volume 11.* Cambridge, Mass., 1957.

———. *China and Christianity: The Missionary Movement and the Growth of Chinese Antiforeignism, 1860-1870.* Cambridge, Mass., 1963.

———. *History in Three Keys: The Boxers as Event, Experience, and Myth.* New York, 1997.

Cooke Yarborough, J., ed. *The Diary of a Working Man (William Bellingham) in Central Africa.* London, n.d.

Cookey, S. J. S. *Britain and the Congo Question, 1885-1913.* London, 1968.

Cousins, H. T. *From Kafir Kraal to Pulpit: The Story of Tiyo Soga.* London, 1899.

Cox, Jeffrey. "Audience and Exclusion at the Margins of Imperial History." *Women's History Review* 3, no. 4 (1994): 501-14.

———. "George Alfred Lefroy 1854-1919: A Bishop in Search of a Church." In *After the Victorians: Private Conscience and Public Duty in Modern Britain: Essays in Memory of John Clive,* edited by Susan Pedersen and Peter Mandler. London and New York, 1994.

Cracknell, K. *Justice, Courtesy, and Love: Theologians and Missionaries Encountering World Religions, 1846-1914.* London, 1995.

Crook, Paul. "Historical Monkey Business: The Myth of a Darwinized British Imperial Discourse." *History* 84, no. 276 (1999): 633-57.

Curtin, Philip D. "'Scientific' Racism and the British Theory of Empire." *Journal of the Historical Society of Nigeria* 2, no. 1 (1960): 40-51.

———. *The Image of Africa: British Ideas and Action, 1780-1850.* London, 1965.

Dachs, A. J. "Missionary Imperialism: The Case of Bechuanaland." *Journal of African History* 13 (1972): 647-58.

Davis, D. B. "The Emergence of Immediatism in British and American Antislavery Thought." *Mississippi Valley Historical Review* 48 (1962): 209-30.

Dawson, E. C. *James Hannington, First Bishop of Eastern Equatorial Africa, 1847-85.* London, 1887.

Dennis, James S. *Centennial Survey of Foreign Missions.* Edinburgh and London, 1902.

Desheng, Dai [James Hudson Taylor]. *Xianshen Zhonghua* (Sacrificing life for China). Edmonton, 1986.

Dickins, Shirley J. *Grenfell of the Congo: Pioneer Missionary and Explorer.* London, n.d.

Dickson, Mora. *Beloved Partner: Mary Moffat of Kuruman.* London, 1974.

Donaldson, Margaret E. "The Invisible Factor — Nineteenth Century Feminist Evangelical Concern for Human Rights." In *Women Hold Up Half the Sky: Women in the Church in Southern Africa,* edited by Denise Ackermann, Jonathan A. Draper, and Emma Mashinini. Pietermaritzburg, 1991.

Drummond, Henry. *Tropical Africa.* London, 1888.

"Education and Mass Movements in India: Report and Resolutions Adopted by the General Committee of March 12, 1912." *Church Missionary Review,* April 1912, pp. 247-49.

Eliot, Sir Charles. *The East Africa Protectorate.* London, 1905.

Ellison, John, and G. H. S. Walpole, eds. *Church and Empire: A Series of Essays on the Responsibilities of Empire.* London, 1907.

Elmslie, W. A. *Among the Wild Ngoni.* Edinburgh, 1899.

Etherington, Norman. "Gender Issues in South-East African Missions, 1835-85." In *Missions and Christianity in South African History,* edited by Henry Bredekamp and Robert Ross. Johannesburg, 1995.

———. "Missions and Empire." In *The Oxford History of the British Empire.* Vol. 5, *Historiography,* edited by Robin Winks. Oxford, 1999.

Evangelical Free Church Catechism, An. London, [1899].

Fitzgerald, Rosemary. "A 'Peculiar and Exceptional Measure': The Call for Women Medical Missionaries for India in the Later Nineteenth Century." In *Missionary Encounters: Sources and Issues,* edited by Robert A. Bickers and Rosemary Seton. Richmond, 1996.

———. "Piety and Physic: Women Medical Missionaries in India, 1860-1914." CWC Position Paper. Unpublished.

Foskett, Reginald, ed. *The Zambesi Journal and Letters of Dr John Kirk, 1858-63.* Edinburgh, 1965.

Foster, I. T. "Anglican Evangelicalism and Politics, 1895-1906." Ph.D. diss., University of Cambridge, 1994.

Francis-Dehqani, Guli. "CMS Women Missionaries in Persia: Perceptions of Muslim Women and Islam, 1884-1934." In *The Church Mission Society and World Christianity, 1799-1999,* edited by Kevin Ward and Brian Stanley. Grand Rapids and Richmond, Surrey, 2000.

Fraser, Donald. *The Future of Africa.* London, 1911.

———. *Winning a Primitive People: Ngoni, Senga, Tumbuka.* London, 1914.

———. *African Idylls: Portraits and Impressions of Life on a Central African Mission Station.* London, 1925.

———. *The Autobiography of an African, Daniel Mtusu.* London, 1925.

Friend, Elizabeth. "Professional Women and the British Empire 1880-1939." Ph.D. diss., University of Lancaster, 1998.

Frykenberg, Robert E. "On Roads and Riots in Tinnevelly: Radical Change and Ideology in Madras Presidency during the Nineteenth Century." *South Asia,* n.s., 4, no. 2 (December 1981): 34-52.

———. "The Emergence of Modern Hinduism as a Concept and as an Institution." In *Hinduism Reconsidered,* edited by Gunther D. Sontheimer and Hermann Kulke. New Delhi, 1989.

Gairdner, W. H. T. *"Edinburgh 1910": An Account and Interpretation of the World Missionary Conference.* Edinburgh and London, 1910.

Gaitskell, Deborah. "Upward All and Play the Game: The Girl Wayfarers' Association in the Transvaal 1925-1975." In *Apartheid and Education: The Education of Black South Africans,* edited by Peter Kallaway. Johannesburg, 1984.

———. "'Getting Close to the Hearts of Mothers': Medical Missionaries among African Women and Children in Johannesburg between the Wars." In *Women and*

Children First: International Maternal and Infant Welfare, 1870-1945, edited by Valerie Fildes, Lara Marks, and Hilary Marland. London, 1992.

———. "At Home with Hegemony? Coercion and Consent in the Education of African Girls for Domesticity in South Africa before 1910." In *Contesting Colonial Hegemony: State and Society in Africa and India*, edited by Dagmar Engels and Shula Marks. London, 1994.

———. "'Praying and Preaching': The Distinctive Spirituality of African Women's Church Organizations." In *Missions and Christianity in South African History*, edited by Henry Bredekamp and Robert Ross. Johannesburg, 1995.

Geetha, V., and S. V. Rajadurai. "One Hundred Years of Brahminitude: Arrival of Annie Besant." *Economic and Political Weekly* 30, no. 28 (15 July 1995): 1768-73.

Gill, Sean. *Women and the Church of England from the Eighteenth Century to the Present*. London, 1994.

Girouard, Mark. *The Return to Camelot: Chivalry and the English Gentleman*. New Haven, 1981.

Glover, W. B. *Evangelical Nonconformists and Higher Criticism in the Nineteenth Century*. London, 1954.

Gollock, Minna C. "The Share of Women in the Administration of Missions." *International Review of Missions* 1, no. 4 (1912): 674-87.

Goodrich, Chauncey. "Secrets of Power: A Meditation on the Life of Rev. Hudson Taylor." *Chinese Recorder* 36 (1905): 379-86.

Gossett, T. F. *Race: The History of an Idea in America*. New York, 1996.

Gracey, Mrs. J. T. *Eminent Missionary Women*. New York, 1898.

Graham, R. H. Carson. *Under Seven Congo Kings*. London, n.d.

Greenfeld, Liah. *Nationalism: Five Roads to Modernity*. Cambridge, 1992.

Grove, Richard H. *Ecology, Climate, and Empire: Colonialism and Global Environmental History, 1400-1940*. Cambridge, 1997.

Gründer, H. *Christliche Mission und deutscher Imperialismus 1884-1914*. Paderborn, 1982.

Gu, Changsheng. *Chuanjiaoshi yu jindai Zhongguo* (Missionaries and modern China). Shanghai, 1981.

Guha, Ranajit. *A Disciplinary Aspect of Indian Nationalism*. Santa Cruz, Calif., 1989.

Gurney, T. A. "Modern Imperialism and Missions." *Church Missionary Intelligencer*, n.s., 27 (July 1902): 485-86.

Haggis, Jane. "White Women and Colonialism: Towards a Non-recuperative History." In *Gender and Imperialism*, edited by Clare Midgley. Manchester, 1998.

Hakeda, Yoshito S., trans. and comm. *The Awakening of Faith Attributed to Asvaghosha*. New York, 1967.

Hamer, D. A. *The Politics of Electoral Pressure: A Study in the History of Victorian Reform Agitations*. Hassocks, Sussex, 1977.

Hance, G. R. *The Zulu Yesterday and To-day*. New York, 1916.

Hansen, Karen T., ed. *African Encounters with Domesticity*. New Brunswick, N.J., 1992.

Harcourt, Freda. "Disraeli's Imperialism, 1866-1868: A Question of Timing." *Historical Journal* 23 (1980): 87-109.

Harrison, Mark. *Public Health in British India: Anglo-Indian Preventive Medicine, 1859-1914*. Cambridge, 1994.

Hastings, Adrian. "Were Women a Special Case?" In *Women and Missions: Past and Present: Anthropological and Historical Perceptions,* edited by Fiona Bowie, Deborah Kirkwood, and Shirley Ardener. Oxford, 1993.

———. *The Church in Africa, 1450-1950*. Oxford, 1994.

Heeney, Brian. *The Women's Movement in the Church of England: 1850-1930*. Oxford, 1988.

Helmstadter, R. J. "The Nonconformist Conscience." In *The Conscience of the Victorian State,* edited by Peter Marsh. Hassocks, Sussex, 1979. Reprinted in Gerald Parsons, ed., *Religion in Victorian Britain,* vol. 4, *Interpretations* (Manchester, 1988).

Heredia, Rudolph. "Education and Mission: School as Agent of Evangelization." *Economic and Political Weekly,* 16 September 1995, pp. 2332-40.

Hertslet, E., comp. *A Complete Collection of the Treaties and Conventions . . . between Great Britain and Foreign Powers.* Vol. XIX. London, 1895.

Hilton, Boyd. *The Age of Atonement: The Influence of Evangelicalism on Social and Economic Thought, 1785-1865*. Oxford, 1988.

Hiney, Tom. *On the Missionary Trail: The Classic Georgian Adventure of Two Englishmen, Sent on a Journey around the World, 1821-29*. London, 2000.

Ho, Ping-ti. "In Defense of Sinicization: A Rebuttal of Evelyn Rawski's 'Reenvisioning the Qing.'" *Journal of Asian Studies* 57 (1998): 123-55.

Hobhouse, Walter. *The Church and the World in Idea and History: The Bampton Lectures for 1909*. London, 1910.

Hogg, W. R. *Ecumenical Foundations: A History of the International Missionary Council and Its Nineteenth-Century Background.* New York, 1952.

Holmes, Timothy. *Journey to Livingstone: Exploration of an Imperial Myth.* Edinburgh, 1994.

Holt, Basil. *Greatheart of the Border.* Kingwilliamstown, 1976.

Hudson, Dennis. "Arumuga Navalar and the Hindu Renaissance among Tamils." In *Religious Controversy in British India,* edited by Kenneth Jones. Albany, N.Y., 1992.

Hughes, H. P. *The Philanthropy of God.* London, 1890.

Hughes, H. P., and Henry S. Lunn. *Summary Statement of the Facts and Arguments upon which the "New Missionary Policy" is Based.* N.p.: Wesleyan Methodist Missionary Society, 1890.

Hughes, Heather. "'A Lighthouse for African Womanhood': Inanda Seminary, 1869-1945." In *Women and Gender in Southern Africa to 1945,* edited by Cheryl Walker. Cape Town and London, 1990.

Hunt, Nancy R. "Colonial Fairy-Tales and the Knife and Fork Doctrine in the Heart of Africa." In *African Encounters with Domesticity,* edited by Karen T. Hansen. New Brunswick, N.J., 1992.

Hyam, Ronald. *Britain's Imperial Century, 1815-1914*. 2nd ed. London, 1993.

Ingham, E. G. "Why Should There Be a 'Pause'?" *Church Missionary Review* 60 (May 1909): 257-64.

———. *From Japan to Jerusalem.* London, 1911.

Irschick, Eugene. *Politics and Social Conflict in South India.* Berkeley, 1969.

Irving, Edward. *Missionaries after the Apostolic School.* London, 1824.

"Is the Moral Supremacy of Christendom in Danger?" *Theosophist* 26, no. 5 (February 1906): 393.

Isherwood, John S. "An Analysis of the Role of Single Women in the Work of the Church Missionary Society, 1804-1904, in West Africa, India and China." Master's thesis, Manchester University, 1979.

Jeal, Tim. *Livingstone.* London, 1974.

John, Griffith. "In Memoriam. Rev. J. Hudson Taylor, M.R.C.S., F.R.G.S." *Chinese Recorder* 36 (1905): 392-93.

Johnson, Gordon. "Partition, Agitation and Congress: Bengal, 1904 to 1908." In *Locality, Province, and Nation,* edited by Gallagher, Johnson, and Seal. Cambridge, 1973.

Johnson, James, ed. *Report of the Centenary Conference on the Protestant Missions of the World held in Exeter Hall.* 2 vols. London, 1888.

Johnson, Rita Therese. "Timothy Richard's Theory of Christian Missions to the Non-Christian World." Ph.D. diss., St. John's University, 1966.

Johnson, Ven. William Percival. *My African Reminiscences, 1875-1895.* London, n.d.

Johnston, W. Ross. *Sovereignty and Protection: A Study of British Jurisdictional Imperialism in the Late Nineteenth Century.* Durham, N.C., 1973.

Kane, J. Herbert. "J. Hudson Taylor, 1832-1905: Founder of the China Inland Mission." In *Mission Legacies: Biographical Studies of Leaders of the Modern Missionary Movement,* edited by Gerald Anderson et al. Maryknoll, N.Y., 1994.

Keith, A. B. *The Belgian Congo and the Berlin Act.* Oxford, 1919.

Kennedy, Dane. "Imperial History and Post-Colonial Theory." *Journal of Imperial and Commonwealth History* 24 (1996): 345-63.

Kent, J. H. S. "Hugh Price Hughes and the Nonconformist Conscience." In *Essays in Modern English Church History in Memory of Norman Sykes,* edited by G. V. Bennett and J. D. Walsh. London, 1966.

Kirkwood, Deborah. "Protestant Missionary Women: Wives and Spinsters." In *Women and Missions: Past and Present: Anthropological and Historical Perceptions,* edited by Fiona Bowie, Deborah Kirkwood, and Shirley Ardener. Oxford, 1993.

Knorr, Klaus E. *British Colonial Theories, 1570-1850.* 1944. Reprint, London, 1963.

Knox, Robert. *The Races of Men: A Philosophical Enquiry.* London and Philadelphia, 1850.

Koebner, Richard, and H. D. Schmidt. *Imperialism: The Story and Significance of a Political Word, 1840-1960.* Cambridge, 1964.

Kopf, David. *British Orientalism and the Bengal Renaissance.* Berkeley, 1969.

Koskinen, A. A. *Missionary Influence as a Political Factor in the Pacific Islands.* Helsinki, 1953.

Koss, Stephen. "Wesleyanism and Empire." *Historical Journal* 18 (1975): 105-18.

Kruger, Bernhard. *The Pear Tree Blossoms: A History of the Moravian Mission Stations in South Africa, 1737-1869*. Genadendal, 1966.

Kumaradoss, Y. Vincent. "The Attitude of Protestant Missionaries in South India towards Indian Nationalism with Special Reference to Tamil Nadu, 1900-1907." *Indo-British Review* 15, no. 1 (1988): 133-46.

Lang, Cosmo Gordon. "The Empire and the Church." In *The Empire and the Century*, edited by Charles Sydney Goldman. London, 1905.

Laws, Robert. *Reminiscences of Livingstonia*. Edinburgh, 1934.

Lefroy, G. A. "Our Indian Empire." In *Church and Empire: A Series of Essays on the Responsibilities of Empire*, edited by John Ellison and G. H. S. Walpole. London, 1907.

Legge, James. *Confucianism in Relation to Christianity*. London, 1877.

Leslie, R. N., Jr. "Christianity and the Evangelist for Sea Power: The Religion of A. T. Mahan." In *The Influence of History on Mahan: The Proceedings of a Conference Marking the Centenary of Alfred Thayer Mahan's "The Influence of Sea Power upon History, 1660-1783,"* edited by J. B. Hattendorf. Newport, R.I., 1991.

Livingstone, David. *Dr. Livingstone's Cambridge Lectures together with a prefatory letter by the Reverend Professor Sedgwick*. Edited with an introduction, life of Dr. Livingstone, notes, and appendix by the Reverend William Monk. London and Cambridge, 1858.

———. *Missionary Travels and Researches in South Africa*. London, 1857.

Livingstone, David, and Charles Livingstone. *Narrative of an Expedition to the Zambezi and its Tributaries and of the Discovery of Lakes Shirwa and Nyassa, 1858-1864*. London, 1865.

Livingstone, David N. *Darwin's Forgotten Defenders: The Encounter between Evangelical Theology and Evolutionary Thought*. Grand Rapids, 1987.

Livingstone, W. P. *Mary Slessor of Calabar*. London, 1916.

———. *Christina Forsyth of Fingoland: The Story of the Loneliest Woman in Africa*. London, 1919.

———. *The Hero of the Lake: A Life of Dr. Robert Laws for Boys*. London, 1933.

———. *Laws of Livingstonia: A Narrative of Missionary Adventure and Achievement*. London, n.d.

———. *A Prince of Missionaries, the Rev. Alexander Hetherwick*. London, n.d.

Lloyd, Roger. *The Church of England, 1900-1965*. London, 1966.

Lodwick, Kathleen L. *The Chinese Recorder Index: A Guide to Christian Missions in Asia, 1867-1941*. 2 vols. Wilmington, Del., 1986.

Long, Una, ed. *The Journals of Elizabeth Lees Price*. 1956.

Lorimer, Douglas A. *Colour, Class, and the Victorians: English Attitudes to the Negro in the Mid-Nineteenth Century*. Leicester, 1978.

Louis, W. R., and Jean Stengers, eds. *E. D. Morel's History of the Congo Reform Movement*. Oxford, 1968.

Low, B. R. C. *Seth Low*. New York and London, 1925.

Machin, G. I. T. *Politics and the Churches in Great Britain, 1832 to 1868*. Oxford, 1977.

A. M. Mackay, Pioneer Missionary of the Church Missionary Society to Uganda, by his sister. London, 1893.

Mackenzie, Anne, ed. *Missionary Life among the Zulu-Kafirs. Memorials of Henrietta Robertson wife of the Rev. R. Robertson. Compiled chiefly from letters and journals written to the Late Bishop Mackenzie and his sisters.* Cambridge and London, 1866.

MacKenzie, John M. *Propaganda and Empire: The Manipulation of British Public Opinion, 1880-1960.* Manchester, 1984.

———. "David Livingstone: The Construction of a Myth." In *Sermons and Battle Hymns: Protestant Popular Culture in Modern Scotland,* edited by Graham Walker and Tom Gallagher. Edinburgh, 1990.

———. "Empire and Metropolitan Cultures." In *The Oxford History of the British Empire.* Vol. 3, *The Nineteenth Century,* edited by Andrew Porter. Oxford, 1999.

———. "The Iconography of the Exemplary Life: The Case of David Livingstone." In *Heroic Reputations and Exemplary Lives,* edited by Geoff Cubitt and Allen Warren. Manchester, 2000, pp. 84-104.

———, ed. *Imperialism and Popular Culture.* Manchester, 1986.

———, ed. *David Livingstone and the Victorian Encounter with Africa.* London, 1996.

Mackintosh, C. W. *Coillard of the Zambezi: The Lives of François and Christine Coillard of the Paris Missionary Society in South and Central Africa.* London, 1907.

Macnair, James I. *The Story of the Scottish National Memorial.* Blantyre, 1929.

Macpherson, Robert. *The Presbyterian Church in Kenya: An Account of the Origins and Growth of the Presbyterian Church of East Africa.* N.p., n.d.

Mahan, A. T. *The Harvest Within: Thoughts on the Life of the Christian.* Boston, 1909.

Malik, Kenan. *The Meaning of Race.* London, 1996.

Marks, S. *Divided Sisterhood: Race, Class, and Gender in the South African Nursing Profession.* London, 1994.

Martin, Roger H. *Evangelicals United: Ecumenical Stirrings in Pre-Victorian Britain, 1795-1830.* Metuchen, N.J., and London, 1983.

Martin, W. A. P. "The worship of ancestors — a plea for tolerance." In *Report of the Missionary Conference held in Shanghai, May 1890,* 57-67. Shanghai, 1890.

Mathew, A. *Christian Missions, Education, and Nationalism: From Dominance to Compromise, 1870-1930.* New Delhi, 1988.

Maughan, Steven. "'Regions Beyond' and the National Church: Domestic Support for the Foreign Missions of the Church of England in the High Imperial Age, 1870-1914." Ph.D. diss., Harvard University, 1995.

———. "'Mighty England Do Good': The Major English Denominations and Organisation for the Support of Foreign Missions in the Nineteenth Century." In *Missionary Encounters: Sources and Issues,* edited by Robert A. Bickers and Rosemary Seton. Richmond, 1996.

McCracken, K. J. *Politics and Christianity in Malawi, 1875-1940.* Cambridge, 1977.

McLeod, Hugh. *Religion and Society in England, 1850-1914.* New York, 1996.

Meintjes, Sheila. "Family and Gender in the Christian Community at Edendale, Natal, in Colonial Times." In *Women and Gender in Southern Africa to 1945*, edited by Cherryl Walker. Cape Town and London, 1990.

Mensendick, C. William. "The Protestant Missionary Understanding of the Chinese Situation and the Christian Task from 1890 to 1911." Ph.D. diss., Columbia University, 1958.

Midgley, Clare, ed. *Gender and Imperialism.* Manchester, 1998.

Minutes of Several Conversations of the People called Methodists. London, 1891.

"Miracles after Missions: An Interview with Kim-Kwong Chan, The." *Christian History* 15, no. 4, issue 52 (1996): 42-44.

Moffat, Robert. *Missionary Labours and Scenes in Southern Africa.* London, 1846.

Monroe, James. "The Teaching of the Higher Criticism Incompatible with Missionary Work." *East and the West* 1 (October 1903): 413-20.

Montgomery, H. H. *Foreign Missions.* London, 1902.

———. *Service Abroad: Lectures Delivered to the Divinity School of the University of Cambridge.* London, 1910.

———. *The S.P.G.: Its Principles and Ideals.* London, 1915.

———, ed. *Mankind and the Church, Being an Attempt to Estimate the Contribution of Great Races to the Fullness of the Church of God.* London, 1907.

Montgomery, Helen B. *Western Women in Eastern Lands.* New York, 1911.

Montgomery, Maud. *Bishop Montgomery: A Memoir.* London, 1933.

Mother Cecile in South Africa, 1883-1906: Foundress of the Community of the Resurrection of Our Lord, compiled by a sister of the Community. London, 1930.

Mott, John R. *Addresses and Papers of John R. Mott.* 6 vols. New York, 1946-47.

Mowat, R. C. "From Liberalism to Imperialism: The Case of Egypt, 1875-1887." *Historical Journal* 16 (1973): 109-24.

Murray, Jocelyn. "Gender Attitudes and the Contribution of Women to Evangelism and the Ministry in the Nineteenth Century." In *Evangelical Faith and Public Zeal: Evangelicals and Society in Britain, 1780-1980*, edited by John Wolffe. London, 1995.

———. "The Role of Women in the Church Missionary Society, 1799-1917." In *The Church Mission Society and World Christianity, 1799-1999*, edited by Kevin Ward and Brian Stanley. Grand Rapids and Richmond, Surrey, 2000.

Neill, Stephen. *A History of Christian Missions.* Harmondsworth, 1964.

Newbigin, Lesslie. *Foolishness to the Greeks: The Gospel and Western Culture.* London, 1991.

Nicholls, Brenda M. "Harriette Colenso and the Issues of Religion and Politics in Colonial Natal." In *Missions and Christianity in South African History,* edited by Henry Bredekamp and Robert Ross. Johannesburg, 1995.

Nockles, Peter Benedict. *The Oxford Movement in Context: Anglican High Churchmanship, 1760-1857.* Cambridge, 1994.

O'Connor, Daniel. *Gospel, Raj, and Swaraj: The Missionary Years of C. F. Andrews, 1904-14.* Frankfurt am Main, 1990.

Oddie, Geoffrey. "Indian Christians and the National Congress, 1885-1910." *Indian Church History Review* 2, no. 1 (June 1968): 45-54.

———. "Anti-missionary Feeling and Hindu Revivalism in Madras: The Hindu Preaching and Tract Societies, 1886-1891." In *Images of Man: Religious and Historical Process in South Asia,* edited by Fred W. Clothey. Madras, 1982.

Ogilvie, James N. *Our Empire's Debt to Missions.* London, 1924.

O'Hanlon, Rosalind. *Caste, Conflict, and Ideology: Mahatma Jotirao Phule and Low Caste Protest in Nineteenth-Century Western India.* Cambridge, 1985.

Oldham, J. H. *Christianity and the Race Problem.* London, 1926.

Oliver, Roland. *The Missionary Factor in East Africa.* London, 1952 and 1965.

One Hundredth Report of the Wesleyan Methodist Missionary Society, The. London, 1914.

Pal, Bipin Chandra. *Mrs. Annie Besant: A Psychological Study.* Madras, 1917.

Pascoe, C. F. *Two Hundred Years of the S.P.G.: An Historical Account of the Society for the Propagation of the Gospel in Foreign Parts, 1701-1900.* 2 vols. London, 1901.

Pfister, Lauren. "Ching Reformers and Christian Religion: The Philosophical Influence and Critique of Christianity in the *Wu Hsu* Reform Movement Leaders — K'ang Yu-Wei, Liang Ch'i Ch'ao and T'an Ssu-T'ung." In *Proceedings of the Eighth International Symposium on Asian Studies.* Hong Kong, 1986.

Philip, John. *Researches in South Africa.* 2 vols. London, 1828.

Piggin, Stuart. "Sectarianism vs. Ecumenism: The Impact on British Churches of the Missionary Movement to India, c. 1800-1860." *Journal of Ecclesiastical History* 27 (1976): 387-402.

Porter, Andrew. "Cambridge, Keswick and Late Nineteenth Century Attitudes to Africa." *Journal of Imperial and Commonwealth History* 5, no. 1 (October 1976): 5-34.

———. "Evangelical Enthusiasm, Missionary Motivation, and West Africa in the Late Nineteenth Century: The Career of G. W. Brooke." *Journal of Imperial and Commonwealth History* 6, no. 1 (October 1977): 23-46.

———. "Religion and Empire: British Expansion in the Long Nineteenth Century, 1780-1914." *Journal of Imperial and Commonwealth History* 20 (1992): 370-90.

———. *European Imperialism, 1860-1914.* London, 1994.

———. "'Cultural Imperialism' and Protestant Missionary Enterprise, 1780-1914." *Journal of Imperial and Commonwealth History* 25, no. 3 (1997): 367-91.

———. "Religion, Missionary Enthusiasm, and Empire." In *The Oxford History of the British Empire.* Vol. 3, *The Nineteenth Century,* edited by Andrew Porter. Oxford, 1999.

———. "Language, 'Native Agency' and Missionary Control: Rufus Anderson's Journey to India 1854-55." In *Missions and Missionaries: Studies in Church History: Subsidia 13,* edited by Pieter N. Holtrop and Hugh McLeod. Woodbridge, Suffolk, 2000.

Porter, Bernard. *The Lion's Share.* 3rd ed. London, 1996.

Potter, Sarah C. "The Social Origins and Recruitment of English Protestant Missionaries in the Nineteenth Century." Ph.D. diss., University of London, 1975.

Potts, E. D. *British Baptist Missionaries in India, 1793-1837: The History of Serampore and Its Missions.* Cambridge, 1967.

Price Evans, E. W. *Timothy Richard: A Narrative of Christian Enterprise and Statesmanship in China.* London, 1945.

Prins, Gwyn. *The Hidden Hippopotamus.* Cambridge, 1980.

Ranger, Terence. "Taking Hold of the Land: Holy Places and Pilgrimages in Twentieth-Century Zimbabwe." *Past and Present* 17 (1987): 158-94.

Rawski, Evelyn S. "Reenvisioning the Qing: The Significance of the Qing Period in Chinese History." *Journal of Asian Studies* 55 (1996): 829-50.

Raychauduri, Tapan. *Europe Reconsidered.* New Delhi, 1988.

Rees, Wyn, ed. *Colenso Letters from Natal.* Pietermaritzburg, 1959.

"Religion and Sectarianism." *Theosophist* 27, no. 1 (October 1905): 27-36.

Report of the Third Decennial Missionary Conference held at Bombay, 1892-3. Bombay, 1893.

Report of the Women's Auxiliary of the Wesleyan Methodist Missionary Society for the Year Ending December 31st, 1914. London, 1915.

"Restless India." *Harvest Field,* September 1896, pp. 327-37.

Rich, P. B. "Albert Luthuli and the American Board Mission in South Africa." In *Missions and Christianity in South African History,* edited by H. Bredekamp and R. Ross. Johannesburg, 1995.

Richard, Timothy. *Tiandao fencheng* (Different lessons about the heavenly way). Shanghai, 1875.

———. "Thoughts on Chinese missions: difficulties and tactics." *Chinese Recorder* 11, no. 6 (November-December 1880): 430-41.

———. "Christian persecutions in China — their nature, causes, remedies." *Chinese Recorder* 15 (1884): 237-48.

———. *Shishi xinlun* (New essays on the affairs of these days). 3 vols. Shanghai, 1894.

———. *Historical Evidences of Christianity for China.* Shanghai, 1895.

———. "How a Few Men May Make a Million Converts." *Chinese Recorder* 32, no. 6 (June 1901): 267-80.

———. *Conversion by the Million in China.* 2 vols. Shanghai, 1907.

———. *The New Testament of Higher Buddhism.* Edinburgh, 1910.

———. *A Dictionary of Philosophical Terms Chiefly from the Japanese.* N.p.: Christian Literature Society, 1913.

———. *An Epistle to All Buddhists throughout the World.* With Chinese translation by Min Houshao. N.p., 1916.

———. *Forty-Five Years in China: Reminiscences by Timothy Richard.* New York, 1916.

———, ed. *The Awakening of Faith in the Mahayana Doctrine — the New Buddhism.* Shanghai, 1907.

———, trans. *Guide to Buddhahood, Being a Standard Manual of Chinese Buddhism.* Shanghai, 1907.

Robbins, Keith. "The Spiritual Pilgrimage of the Rev. R. J. Campbell." *Journal of Ecclesiastical History* 30 (1979): 261-76.

Robert, Dana. *American Women in Mission: A Social History of Their Thought and Practice.* Macon, Ga., 1996.

Robertson, W. A. Scott. *British Contributions to Foreign Missions.* London, 1872.

Ross, Andrew. *John Philip (1775-1851): Missions, Race, and Politics in South Africa.* Aberdeen, 1986.

———. *Blantyre Mission and the Making of Modern Malawi.* Bonn, 1996.

———. "Livingstone: The Man behind the Mask." In *The London Missionary Society in Southern Africa,* edited by John de Gruchy. Cape Town, 1999.

Row, G. Venkataranga. "A Christian View of Hinduism." *Indian Review,* January 1913, pp. 19-23.

Rowbotham, Judith. "'This Is No Romantic Story': Reporting the Work of British Female Missionaries, c. 1850-1910." *North Atlantic Missiology Project* Position Paper 4. Cambridge, 1996.

Sadasivan, D. *The Growth of Public Opinion in the Madras Presidency.* Madras, 1974.

Said, Edward. *Orientalism.* New York, 1979.

Sarkar, Sumit. *The Swadeshi Movement in Bengal: 1903-1908.* New Delhi, 1973.

———. "Indian Nationalism and the Politics of Hindutva." In *Making India Hindu: Religion, Community, and the Politics of Democracy in India,* edited by David Ludden. New Delhi, 1996.

Savage, David. "Evangelical Educational Policy in Britain and India, 1857-60." *Journal of Imperial and Commonwealth History* 22 (1994): 423-61.

Seager, R., II. *Alfred Thayer Mahan: The Man and His Letters.* Annapolis, Md., 1977.

Seager, R., II, and D. D. Maguire, eds. *Letters and Papers of Alfred Thayer Mahan.* Vol. 3, *1902-1914.* Annapolis, Md., 1975.

Searle, G. R. *The Quest for National Efficiency: A Study in British Politics and Political Thought, 1899-1914.* London, 1971.

Sell, Alan P. F. *Defending and Declaring the Faith: Some Scottish Examples, 1860-1920.* Exeter, 1987.

Selous, Frederick Courteney. *Sunshine and Storm in Rhodesia.* London, 1896.

Semmel, Bernard. *Imperialism and Social Reform: English Social-Imperial Thought, 1895-1914.* Cambridge, Mass., 1960.

Semple, Rhonda. "Women, Gender and Changing Roles in the Missionary Project: The London Missionary Society and the China Inland Mission, 1885-1910." *North Atlantic Missiology Project* Position Paper 39. Cambridge, 1997.

Sen, Priyaranjan. *Western Influence in Bengali Literature.* Calcutta, 1966.

Seton, Rosemary. "'Open Doors for Female Labourers': Women Candidates of the London Missionary Society, 1875-1914." In *Missionary Encounters: Sources and Issues,* edited by Robert A. Bickers and Rosemary Seton. Richmond, 1996.

Sharpe, Eric J. *Not to Destroy but to Fulfil.* Uppsala, 1965.

———. *The Theology of A. G. Hogg.* Madras, 1971.

Shenk, William. *Henry Venn — Missionary Statesman.* Maryknoll, N.Y., 1983.

Shepherd, A. P. *Tucker of Uganda: Artist and Apostle, 1849-1914.* London, n.d.

Simpson, P. Carnegie. *Christus Crucifixus.* London, 1909.

Smiles, Samuel. *Self-Help.* Centennial edition. London, 1959.

Smith, Edwin W. *The Mabilles of Basutoland.* London, 1939.

———. *The Life and Times of Daniel Lindley (1801-80).* London, 1949.

Smith, Herbert Maynard. *Frank, Bishop of Zanzibar: Life of Frank Weston, D.D. 1871-1924*. London, [1926].

Smith, Samuel. *My Life Work*. London, 1902.

Society for the Propagation of the Gospel in Foreign Parts. *Two Hundred Fourteenth Annual Report of the Society for the Propagation of the Gospel in Foreign Parts for the Year 1914*. London, 1915.

Stanley, Brian. *The Bible and the Flag: Protestant Missions and British Imperialism in the Nineteenth and Twentieth Centuries*. Leicester, 1990.

———. *The History of the Baptist Missionary Society, 1792-1992*. Edinburgh, 1992.

———. "Manliness and Mission: Frank Lenwood and the London Missionary Society." *Journal of the United Reformed Church History Society* 5 (1996): 465-69.

Stead, W. T. *The Best or the Worst of Empires: Which?* London, 1906.

Stephen, George. *Anti-slavery Recollections in a Series of Letters Addressed to Mrs Beecher Stowe*. [1854]. London, 1971.

Stephens, Geoffrey. *H. H. Montgomery — the Mutton Bird Bishop*. University of Tasmania Occasional Paper 39. Hobart, 1985.

Stock, Eugene. *The History of the Church Missionary Society: Its Environment, Its Men, and Its Work*. 4 vols. London, 1899 and 1916.

———. "The Position of the Society." *Church Missionary Intelligencer*, n.s., 28 (December 1903): 881-88.

———. "Concerning Some Misconceptions." *Church Missionary Intelligencer*, n.s., 29 (January 1904): 31-37.

———. *My Recollections*. London, 1909.

Studdert-Kennedy, Gerald. *British Missions, Indian Nationalists, and the Raj*. New Delhi, 1991.

———. *Providence and the Raj: Imperial Mission and Missionary Imperialism*. New Delhi and London, 1998.

Sundkler, Bengt. *The Christian Ministry in Africa*. London, 1960.

Swaisland, Cecillie. "Wanted — Earnest, Self-Sacrificing Women for Service in South Africa: Nineteenth-Century Recruitment of Single Women to Protestant Missions." In *Women and Missions: Past and Present: Anthropological and Historical Perceptions*, edited by Fiona Bowie, Deborah Kirkwood, and Shirley Ardener. Oxford, 1993.

Tatlow, Tissington. *The Story of the Student Christian Movement of Great Britain and Ireland*. London, 1933.

Taylor, Mrs. Howard. *Pastor Hsi: Confucian Scholar and Christian*. London, 1900.

Taylor, J. Hudson. "Lessons from the incarnation." *China's Millions*, April 1885, pp. 39-40.

———. "Apostolic example." *China's Millions*, June 1885, pp. 63-64.

———. "Self-denial versus self-assertion." *China's Millions*, September 1885, pp. 107-8.

Taylor, J. V. *The Growth of the Church in Buganda*. London, 1958.

Thelle, Notto R. "Karl Ludvig Reichelt, 1877-1952: Christian Pilgrim of Tao Fong

Shan." In *Mission Legacies: Biographical Studies of Leaders of the Modern Missionary Movement,* edited by Gerald Anderson et al. Maryknoll, N.Y., 1994.

Thomas, G. *Christian Indians and Indian Nationalism, 1885-1910: An Interpretation in Historical and Theological Perspectives.* Frankfurt, 1979.

Thomas, J. V. "The Role of the Medical Missionary in British East Africa, 1874-1904." D.Phil. thesis, University of Oxford, 1982.

Thomas, S. V. "The Hindu Tract Society." *Madras Christian College Magazine,* April 1889.

Thompson, E. W. "Movements of Hinduism in South India." In *Fourth Decennial Missionary Conference Held at Madras, 1902.* London, 1902.

Thompson, H. P. *Into All Lands: The History of the Society for the Propagation of the Gospel in Foreign Parts, 1701-1950.* London, 1951.

Thompson, John. *China and Its People in Early Photographs.* New York, 1982.

Torrance, David E. *The Strange Death of the Liberal Empire: Lord Selborne in South Africa.* Liverpool, 1996.

Tucker, Henry W. *The English Church in Other Lands; or the Spiritual Expansion of England.* London, 1886 and 1901.

"Two Catechisms." *Harvest Field* 13, no. 7 (July 1902): 250-51.

Urban-Mead, Wendy. "The 'Civilizing' Mission of Elizabeth Lees Price: Domesticity, Christianity, and Imperialism in Southern Africa, 1854-1883." Master's thesis, State University of New York at Albany, 1995.

Viswanathan, Gauri. *Outside the Fold: Conversion, Modernity, and Belief.* Princeton, N.J., 1998.

Walls, Andrew F. "British Missions." In *Missionary Ideologies in the Imperialist Era: 1880-1920,* edited by Torben Christensen and William R. Hutchison. Aarhus, 1982.

Wann, A. B. *The Message of Christ to India: With a Memoir and Appreciations of the Author.* Edited by J. Morrison. Edinburgh and London, 1925.

W[ard], G[ertrude]. *The Life of Charles Alan Smythies.* Edited by Edward Francis Russell. London, 1899.

Webb, Allan B. *Sisterhood Life and Woman's Work in the Mission Field of the Church.* London, 1883.

Wells, James. *Stewart of Lovedale: The Life of James Stewart.* London, 1909.

Welter, B. "The Feminization of American Religion: 1800-1860." In *Clio's Consciousness Raised: New Perspectives on the History of Women,* edited by M. S. Hartman and L. Banner. New York, 1974.

Wesley, John. *Thoughts on Slavery.* London, 1774.

Westwood, Peter J. *David Livingstone: His Life and Work as Told through the Media of Postage Stamps and Allied Material.* Blantyre, 1986.

[Wilkinson, Mrs.]. *A Lady's Life and Travels in Zululand and the Transvaal during Cetewayo's reign, being the African letters and journals of the late Mrs Wilkinson.* London, 1882. Reprint, Pretoria, 1975.

Williams, C. Peter. "The Recruitment and Training of Overseas Missionaries in England between 1850 and 1900." M.Litt. thesis, University of Bristol, 1976.

———. *The Ideal of the Self-Governing Church: A Study in Victorian Missionary Strategy.* Leiden, 1990.

———. "'The Missing Link': The Recruitment of Women Missionaries in Some English Evangelical Missionary Societies in the Nineteenth Century." In *Women and Missions: Past and Present: Anthropological and Historical Perceptions,* edited by Fiona Bowie, Deborah Kirkwood, and Shirley Ardener. Oxford, 1993.

Willis, Justin. "The Nature of a Mission Community: The UMCA in Bonde." *Past and Present* 140 (1993): 127-54.

Wilson, George Herbert. *The History of the Universities' Mission to Central Africa.* London, 1936.

Wilson, M., and L. M. Thompson, eds. *The Oxford History of South Africa.* 2 vols. London, 1970.

Wolffe, John. *God and Greater Britain: Religion and National Life in Britain and Ireland, 1843-1945.* London and New York, 1994.

Women's Auxiliary of Wesleyan Methodist Missionary Society. *The Story of the Women's Auxiliary, 1858-1922.* London, 1923.

World Missionary Conference, 1910. *Report of Commission I: Carrying the Gospel to All the Non-Christian World.* Edinburgh and London, n.d.

———. *Report of Commission VII: Missions and Governments.* Edinburgh and London, n.d.

———. *Vol. IX: The History and Records of the Conference.* Edinburgh and London, n.d.

Wright, M. *German Missions in Tanganyika, 1891-1941.* Oxford, 1971.

Wu, Huili. "Zhongwen jizai zhong suo jian Weixin yundong qijian Li Timotai de huodong" (Timothy Richard in Chinese literature, 1895-1898). M.Phil. thesis, Chinese University of Hong Kong, 1974.

Wynne, G. Robert. *The Church in Greater Britain.* London, 1901.

Yates, T. E. *Venn and Victorian Bishops Abroad.* Studia Missionalia Uppsaliensia 33. Uppsala and London, 1978.

Young, Richard Fox, and S. Jabanesan. *The Bible Trembled.* Vienna, 1995.

Yuan, Weishi. *Wan Qing dabianju zhong de sichao yu renwu* (Ideological trends and people during the great changes within the last years of the Qing dynasty). Shenzen, 1992.

Index